THE WG&L HANDBOOK OF

INTERNATIONAL FINANCE

EDITOR

DENNIS E. LOGUE

AMOS TUCK SCHOOL OF BUSINESS ADMINISTRATION
DARTMOUTH COLLEGE

WARREN, GORHAM & LAMONT

COLLEGE DIVISION South-Western Publishing Co.

Cincinnati Ohio

Acquisitions Editor: Christopher Will
Production Editors: Sharon Smith and Sue Ellen Brown
Marketing Manager: Denise Carlson
Cover Designer: Lotus Wittkopf

FV60AA

Library of Congress Cataloging-in-Publication Data

The WG&L handbook of international finance / editor, Dennis E. Logue.
    p. cm.
  Includes bibliographical references and index.
  ISBN 0-538-84253-9
  1. International finance. 2. Foreign exchange market.
3. Securities. 4. Banks and banking, International. 5. Accounting—
Standards. 6. International business enterprises—Finance.
I. Logue, Dennis E.
HG3881.W45 1995
332'.042—dc20   94-20613
                                      CIP

 I(T)P
International Thomson Publishing

South-Western College Publishing is an ITP Company. The ITP trademark is used under license.

 This book is printed on acid-free paper that meets Environmental Protection Agency standards for recycled paper.

Preface

As the editor for the W, G, & L *Handbook of Modern Finance, Third Edition,* I am happy to note that South-Western Publishing Company is publishing this series of five "break-out" readings books for use in your classroom:

The W, G, & L *Handbook of International Finance*
The W, G, & L *Handbook of Financial Markets*
The W, G, & L *Handbook of Securities and Investment Management*
The W, G, & L *Handbook of Financial Policy*
The W, G, & L *Handbook of Short-Term and Long-Term Financial Management.*

These readers make a unique contribution to the classroom in that they are written primarily from the practitioner's point of view; showing students how the principles they are learning in class can be applied to real-world financial problems.

Thus they are ideally suited to supplement courses in Corporate Finance, Investments, Capital Markets, Financial Institutions, and International Finance both at the undergraduate and MBA level. They are also ideally suited for use in an executive education program.

These readers cover virtually every major technical, analytical, and theoretical financial question likely to be raised by active, inquisitive corporate financial and business executives, strategic planners, accountants (public and private), attorneys, security analysts, and bankers. They provide your students with insights for solving day-to-day business problems as well as provide guidance in long-term planning. Institutional arrangements are explained; relevant economic and financial theory and its application are presented and described. In addition, sophisticated quantitative analyses are presented in the context of real-world examples, numerous figures illustrate textual explanations, and end-of-chapter readings direct interested readers to additional technical literature in the field. The intent has been to produce a series of readings books that will help students understand the practical applications of the theory presented in their textbooks, thus helping them become better-prepared business professionals.

The W, G, & L *Handbook of International Finance* discusses and describes concepts and techniques relevant to international financial decision making. Contributors include:

Robert Z. Aliber
Professor of International Economics and Finance, Graduate School of Business, University of Chicago

Gunter Dufey
Professor of International Business and Finance, School of Business Administration, University of Michigan

Mark R. Eaker
Professor of Finance, Colgate Darden School, University of Virginia

Robert Grosse
Director, International Business and Banking Institute, University of Miami

Lee H. Radebaugh
Professor of Accounting and International Business, Brigham Young University

Anant Sundaram
Professor, Amos Tuck School of Business Administration, Dartmouth College

Anant Sundaram
Professor, Amos Tuck School of Business Administration, Dartmouth College

Sivakumar Venkatarmany
Center for International Business Education and Research, University of Miami

The editor wants to thank all of the authors who have worked so hard to produce highly focused chapters with a strong managerial slant. All are to be thanked and congratulated.

In addition to the authors, thanks must also go to Audrey Hanlon, who helped organize the work done by Tuck; Beverly Salbin of Warren Gorman Lamont, who brought so much to the party that she deserves much more recognition than this; and to Leora Harris and Vibert Gale, also of WGL, whose skills contributed so much to the final product.

Finally, I want to thank South-Western Publishing Company for bringing these readers to the college market.

DENNIS E. LOGUE

Hanover, New Hampshire
November 1993

Contents

Preface   iii

1. The International Monetary System   1
   Robert Z. Aliber

Introduction   2
International Payments Before World War I   3
International Payments from World War I to World War II   6
Postwar Economic Planning and the Bretton Woods System   10
U.S. Payments Deficits in the 1960s   12
Breakdown of the Bretton Woods System   13
Post-Bretton Woods System   15
Future of the International Monetary System   19
Suggested Reading   19

2. Foreign Exchange Markets and Currency Risk   21
   Gunter Dufey

Introduction   22
Foreign Exchange Market   22
Assessing Corporate Foreign Exchange Risk   40
Management of Economic Exposure: Management and Hedging   49
Corporate Practice and the Relevance of Currency Hedging   56
Suggested Reading   58

3. International Financial Markets   63
   Anant Sundaram

Introduction   64
Regular and Direct Securites   64
Derivative Securities   72
Future Market Evolution and Potential Regulation   83
Suggested Reading   85

4. International Banking   87
   Robert Grosse and Siwakumar Venkataramany

Introduction   89
Historical Perspectives   92
Current Perspectives   93
International Banking Activity in Selected Countries   95
Foreign Exchange Markets   104

Euromarkets   111
Trade Financing   119
Cross-Border Credit Extension   128
Cross-Border Liabilities   134
Other International Banking Services   137
Managerial Issues   140
Other International Banking Structures   149
Future of International Banking   150
Suggested Reading   150

5. International Accounting   153
Lee H. Radebaugh

International Dimensions of Accounting   154
Differences in Accounting Standards and Disclosure Practices   154
Accounting for Foreign Currency Transactions and Translations of
   Foreign Currency Financial Statements   167
International Tax Issues   182
Performance Evaluation and Control   185
Conclusion   188
Suggested Reading   189

6. Investment and Financing Decisions for Multinational Corporations   191
Mark R. Eaker

Introduction   192
Motives for International Investment   192
Assessment of Foreign Cash Flows   194
Capital Budgeting Techniques   205
Political and Operating Risk   209
Financing Foreign Subsidiaries   215
Managing Foreign Exchange Risks   219
Suggested Reading   223

Index   225

Chapter 1

The International Monetary System

ROBERT Z. ALIBER

1.01 Introduction 2

1.02 International Payments Before World War I 3
[1] U.S. Gold Standard 3
[2] Bills of Exchange 4
[3] Inflation and Dollar Inconvertibility 4
[4] Cable Transfers 5

1.03 International Payments From World War I to World War II 6
[1] World War I Gold Embargo 6
[2] Shaky Return to Gold Parities in the Postwar Period 7
[3] Nationalization of U.S. Gold Holdings 9

[4] Beggar-Thy-Neighbor Policies 10

1.04 Postwar Economic Planning and the Bretton Woods System 10

1.05 U.S. Payments Deficits in the 1960s . . . 12

1.06 Breakdown of the Bretton Woods System 13

1.07 Post–Bretton Woods System 15
[1] Floating Exchange Rates 15
[2] Nongold International Reserve Assets 16
[3] Alternative Exchange Rate Arrangements 17

1.08 Future of the International Monetary System 19

Suggested Reading 19

1.01 INTRODUCTION

The primary task of an international monetary system is to facilitate trade, investment, and other transactions across national borders so that their costs are not significantly higher than those for domestic transactions. One party to every international transaction must buy or sell a foreign currency; for example, a U.S. importer may be obliged to pay a German seller in deutsche marks, and so the importer first must buy the deutsche marks. If the German exporter instead receives payment in U.S. dollars, the exporter must sell the dollars to buy the deutsche marks.

International transactions differ from domestic transactions in several important ways: (1) Transactions costs are higher; (2) future exchange rates are unknown; and (3) exchange controls may delay or prohibit payments abroad. The lower the costs and risks of foreign exchange transactions, the smaller the excess of the costs of international transactions over domestic transactions. The costs and risks of international transactions differ with the type of international arrangements.

The central or key elements in reducing the costs and risks of foreign exchange transactions are to reduce the uncertainty about exchange rates and to minimize the costs to the domestic economy of the lower level of uncertainty about exchange rates. Within the United States, a dollar is a dollar now and forever; similarly, in the United Kingdom, a pound is a pound. While the U.S. dollar price of the U.K. pound is known with certainty for today's transactions, the U.S. dollar price of the U.K. pound for various future dates is not known. Hence, there is considerable uncertainty.

International payments arrangements can be viewed as a three-tiered structure. At the retail level, traders and investors buy and sell demand deposits denominated in different currencies. At the wholesale level, the payments arrangements center on the transactions among major commercial banks, which buy and sell foreign exchange with each other. The third tier in the structure of payments arrangements involves the national central banks or monetary authorities, which buy and sell their own currencies in the foreign exchange market, primarily to limit changes in exchange rates. These monetary authorities also set the institutional framework for the organization of foreign exchange trading.

An international financial arrangement describes the prevailing set of treaties, laws, commitments, conventions, and practices that affect the costs and risks of payments among countries. An international monetary system is the legal subset of these arrangements and primarily involves commitments that national governments have made to each other about the institutional aspects of their intervention in the foreign exchange market. The gold standard of the late nineteenth century was based on legislation in each country that the national currency, such as the U.S. dollar, the U.K. pound, and the French franc, could be converted into gold at a fixed price or parity, plus or minus a small handling charge. Whenever traders or investors wished to buy gold, banks in each country were obliged to sell gold and buy their note and deposit liabilities on demand. In contrast, the Bretton Woods system of the 1950s and 1960s was based on an international treaty, the Articles of Agreement of the International Monetary Fund (IMF), and the counterpart legislation in each IMF member country. This treaty spelled out the obligation of each member country to buy and sell its own currency within a stipulated range of prices in the foreign exchange market, the procedures that each member country would follow when it wished to change the foreign exchange value of its currency, the circumstances when a country might apply nonprice controls on the foreign payments and receipts of its residents, and the rights of the member country to borrow foreign currencies from the IMF. Under the Articles of Agreement of the

IMF, the United States was obliged to prevent the foreign exchange value of the U.S. dollar from deviating significantly from the U.S. gold parity of $35 an ounce. Similarly, Japan was committed to preventing the price of the U.S. dollar in terms of yen from deviating significantly from its parity of 360 yen to the U.S. dollar.

Some monetary systems involve the term "standard," as in the gold standard or the bimetallic standard. This term is used in the sense of measures and connotes that the value of the standard unit of the national money, such as the U.S. dollar or the U.K. pound, is expressed or measured in terms of a given weight of gold or silver or some other commodity of stipulated purity. For example, the United States used the gold standard in the latter part of the nineteenth century because the U.S. legislation required that the $10 coin (the Eagle) contain 232.2 grains of gold. The term "arrangement" is the most comprehensive or inclusive term for the variety of payments practices extant at any moment; the term "system" involves the legal-based set of payments arrangements; and the term "standard" applies to those systems that involve commodity moneys, such as gold or silver.

Payments arrangements have evolved over the centuries as traders and investors have sought to reduce the costs and risks of international payments. Changes in technology have facilitated the reduction in these costs, and while sometimes changes in national monetary policies have reduced these costs, at other times, they have led to significant cost increases.

This chapter examines the changes in the foreign exchange value of the U.S. dollar from a historical perspective. For many of the last 200 years, the dollar was pegged to gold and the foreign exchange value of the dollar was set by its relation to the price of gold compared with the price of gold in terms of other national moneys, such as the U.K. pound, the French franc, and the deutsche mark. At the time of the Civil War, the link between the dollar and gold was broken, resulting in a floating price for the dollar in the foreign exchange market; in 1879, the dollar was again pegged to gold at its prewar parity. During World War I, many countries broke the link between their currencies and gold, and so the value of their currencies in the foreign exchange market was determined by market forces, although various central banks bought and sold their currencies in the foreign exchange market to limit changes in exchange rates. Some countries adopted controls on international payments in the 1930s. A system of pegged exchange rates was not restored until the 1940s. In the early 1970s, industrial countries again stopped pegging their currencies in the foreign exchange market.

1.02 INTERNATIONAL PAYMENTS BEFORE WORLD WAR I

[1] U.S. Gold Standard

From 1792 to 1973, the foreign exchange value of the U.S. dollar in terms of the currencies of most other major countries was based on the relationship between the dollar and commodity gold. The U.S. Coinage Act of 1792, one of the first laws passed by the U.S. Congress, provided for the establishment of a mint and stipulated that the principal U.S. coin would be the $10 Eagle, which weighed 270 grains, standard for coin containing $^{11}/_{12}$ gold or 247.5 grains of fine or pure gold. (There are 480 grains of gold in a troy ounce.) Gold was legal tender for all payments; payment in gold was adequate to satisfy debts. At that time, the weight of the U.K. sovereign was 123.274 grains of gold 916⅔ thousands fine. Since both the dollar and the sovereign had values expressed in terms of gold, the price of the dollar in terms of the sovereign could be inferred from the ratio of the price of each coin in terms of gold; thus, the dollar price of one sovereign was $4.86 once an adjustment was made for the difference in the fineness or gold content of the two coins.

In 1834, the U.S. Congress reduced the gold content of the Eagle to 258 grains standard or 232 grains of pure gold. Legislation in 1837 fixed the gold content of U.S. coins at the ratio of 9:10, which meant that the U.S. gold parity, the dollar price of gold, was $20.67; the U.S. gold parity remained until 1933. Legislation in 1849 provided for a double eagle ($20), a quarter eagle ($5), and a gold dollar ($1).

As long as the dollar price of an ounce of gold was fixed at $20.67, the United States was on the gold standard. Gold was an important component but not the largest component of the U.S. money supply, since the use of gold in payments was less convenient and more costly than the use of bank notes or U.S. Treasury notes.

[2] Bills of Exchange

The use of gold in international payments between the United States and Great Britain and the United States and other foreign countries was modest during the gold standard period. Most international payments involved transactions in bills of exchange, which were comparable to postdated checks. U.S. firms with payments to make in London in 30 or 60 days would buy sterling-denominated bills of exchange denominated in the U.K. pound that U.S. exporters were selling in New York and Philadelphia and other U.S. port cities. The U.S. exporters had received these bills from British importers and had shipped them to the United States to sell for U.S. dollars. U.S. importers with payments to make in London compared the dollar price of making these payments with bills of exchange with the dollar price of making the same payments by shipping gold. Using bills of exchange for international payments was almost always less costly than using gold, since the shipping costs were lower and the bills of exchange could be replaced if lost (and hence they were less expensive to insure). Moreover, the bills earned interest while en route, while gold did not.

[3] Inflation and Dollar Inconvertibility

Payments in gold in the United States were suspended in December 1861, eight months after the beginning of the Civil War. The cessation of gold payments reflected the fact that wartime finance was leading to a significant increase in the U.S. money supply and, as a result, in the U.S. price level. The U.S. authorities could not maintain the fixed dollar price of gold at a time when most other U.S. prices were increasing; from 1861 to 1864, the U.S. price level more than doubled. Since the United Kingdom continued on the gold standard and the price of gold remained unchanged in terms of the U.K. pound, changes in the dollar price of the pound were reflected in changes in the dollar price of gold, which doubled from 1860 to 1864.

The similarity in the increase in the dollar price of the pound and the increase in the U.S. domestic price level focuses on the concept of the real exchange rate, which is the nominal or market exchange rate adjusted to reflect the differences in the U.S. and foreign price levels. From the point of view of the competitive position of producers in the United States and various foreign countries, stability of the real exchange rate is more important than stability of the nominal exchange rate. Both the nominal

FIGURE 1-1

The U.S. Dollar Price of the U.K. Pound

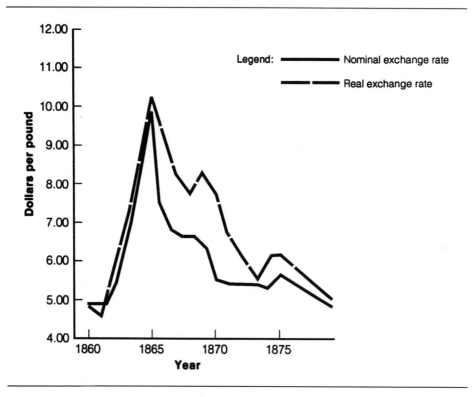

measure and real exchange rates for the period 1860–1878 are shown in Figure 1-1. The depreciation of the dollar after the Civil War appears to be lower than might be inferred from the increase in the U.S. price level relative to increase in the U.K. price level.

In January 1879, the U.S. Congress passed legislation making the dollar convertible into gold at the pre–Civil War price of $20.67 per ounce. The return to gold convertibility for the dollar at parity was possible because the U.S. price level had fallen relative to the U.K. price level; at the same time, the dollar had appreciated and the dollar price of gold declined. The gold parities of the major countries and the foreign exchange value of the dollar in terms of other countries are shown in Figure 1-2.

[4] Cable Transfers

In the 1870s, two changes in technology reduced the costs of international payments. One was the change to steam from sail as the power for ocean transport, with the result being that the time and costs of shipping both gold and bills of exchange across the Atlantic Ocean declined. The second was the development of the Trans-Atlantic

FIGURE 1-2

Parities of Major Currencies Under the Gold Standard

Source: M.L. Muhleman, Monetary Systems of the World *(New York: Charles H. Nicoll, 1894), as adapted in Thomas Mayer, James S. Dusenberg, and Robert Z. Aliber,* Money, Banking and the Economy *(New York: W.W. Norton, 1987)*

Country	Unit	Weight[a]	Fineness[b]	Value of One Pure Ounce	Dollar Parity
United States (1897)	Dollar	1.672	0.900	$20.67	—
United Kingdom (1816)	Pound	7.988	0.917	3/17/10½	$4.860
France (1878)	Franc	0.3226	0.900	fr107.1	0.193
Germany (1871)	Deutsche mark	0.398	0.900	DM86.8	0.238
Italy (1878)	Lira	0.3226	9.900	L107.1	0.193
Netherlands (1875)	Florin	0.672	0.900	F51.4	0.402

[a] Weight of standard coin in grams.
[b] Fineness of standard coin equals the proportion of pure gold.

Cable, which introduced a new way to make immediate payments between New York and London and between New York and other European financial centers. Cable transfers could be used to change the ownership of bank deposits in London and these other foreign centers. Thus, a U.S. importer with a payment to make in London could buy a U.K. pound deposit from a bank in New York; the New York bank could cable the London bank to transfer ownership of this deposit to the party designated by the U.S. importer. The introduction of the cable meant that international payments could be made within one or two days, whereas payments made by shipping bills of exchange usually required a two-week lead time.

1.03 INTERNATIONAL PAYMENTS FROM WORLD WAR I TO WORLD WAR II

[1] World War I Gold Embargo

Soon after World War I began, belligerent countries in Europe seeking to hoard gold for military and security reasons lifted the requirement that their currencies be convertible into gold, much as the United States had at the beginning of the Civil War. At the same time, they embargoed gold exports. Once these national currencies were no longer convertible into gold, they were no longer effectively pegged to each other. The combination of extensive intervention by various national monetary authorities in Europe in the foreign exchange market and exchange controls to restrict payments abroad by their residents (which were intended to conserve holdings of gold and foreign exchange for the war effort) limited the depreciation of these currencies to a modest range below their prewar values in terms of the U.S. dollar.

Because of the war, the imports of European countries increased sharply relative to their exports, with the excess of imports over exports financed by selling assets and by borrowing abroad, especially in New York. The U.K. government, for example, requisitioned the foreign securities owned by U.K. residents. Before the war, trade between the United States and the United Kingdom was denominated in the U.K. pound, which meant that U.S. exporters and importers acquired the exchange risk, since they received and made payments in pounds. Once the war began, trade and payments were regulated on a centralized basis; U.K. importers needed government approval before they could buy foreign goods. U.K. holdings of U.S. dollars became concentrated in the hands of the U.K. monetary authorities. U.S. exporters sold their goods to U.K. importers for dollars, and U.S. importers paid in dollars; U.K. importers and exporters acquired the exchange risk.

[2] Shaky Return to Gold Parities in the Postwar Period

At the end of World War I, there was widespread sentiment in favor of a return to the gold standard and the parities for gold for individual countries that had prevailed before the war. The ability of countries to peg their currencies to gold at their prewar parities was constrained by the large differences in national inflation rates during the war. Either the price levels in Western Europe would have to decline or the U.S. price level would have to increase so that the prewar gold parities would once again be appropriate and sustainable. In real or price-level adjusted terms, the currencies of the European countries had appreciated greatly during the war because of the extensive reliance on exchange controls. Without this required change in the relationship among national price levels, the currencies of the Western European countries would have been overvalued and these countries would have incurred payments deficits.

Moreover, there was concern that the return to the gold standard would be jeopardized by a shortage of gold. The rationale for this concern was that the world price level after the war was significantly higher than before the war, which meant that gold mining costs would be higher and the volume of gold production would diminish. Moreover, the commodity demand for gold would increase, because the prices of silver and other metals had increased with the general price level.

Several League of Nations conferences in the early 1920s developed recommendations to facilitate the return to the gold standard. In an effort to reduce the use of gold both by private and by national central banks, the conferences recommended that some central banks, especially the newer ones in the countries established in Central Europe from the breakup of the Austro-Hungarian Empire, should hold their international reserve assets in the form of foreign exchange (i.e., liquid assets such as bank deposits, Treasury bills, or banker's acceptances denominated in the U.K. pound or in the U.S. dollar). This became known as the gold exchange standard. A second recommendation was that the use of gold for private payments be reduced.

The period between World War I and World War II was one of great disorder in international monetary arrangements. Soon after World War I, U.K. authorities ceased supporting the pound in the foreign exchange market, and the currency depreciated by more than 20 percent. In the early 1920s, a number of defeated countries, including Austria and Germany, were subject to hyperinflation and adopted new currencies. Both the United Kingdom and France sought to return to the gold standard at their prewar parities. Large fluctuations occurred in the foreign exchange value of the pound and the franc in terms of the dollar, as shown in Figure 1-3.

The United Kingdom pegged the pound to gold at its prewar parity in May 1925, but there was general belief that the pound was overvalued, so the maintenance of the prewar parity required high interest rates in London, driving unemployment in the United Kingdom above 10 percent. France, in contrast, eventually stabilized the for-

FIGURE 1-3

Price Levels and Exchange Rates (1913–1930)

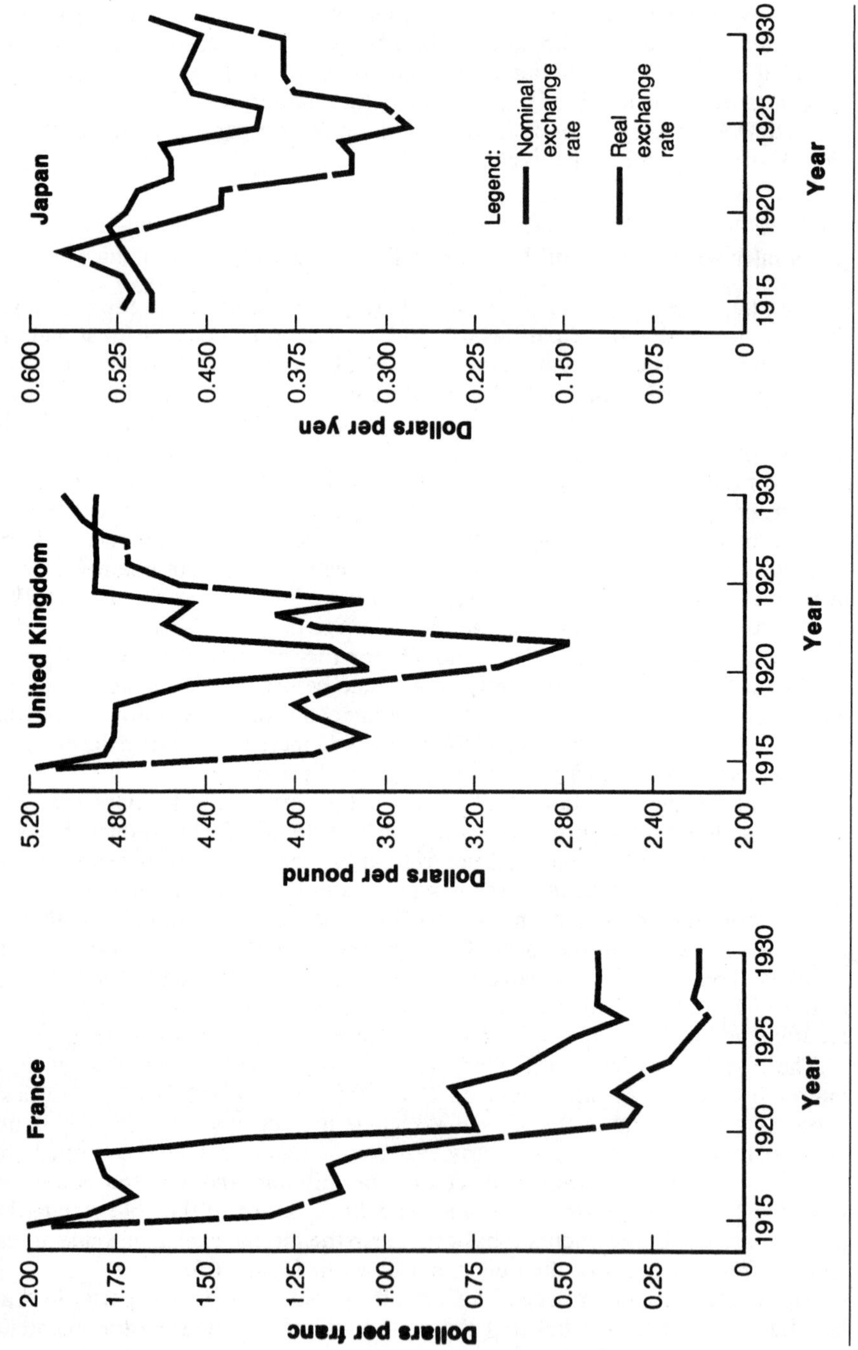

eign exchange value of the French franc at one sixth of its prewar price in terms of gold and the U.S. dollar.

Once the French franc was again pegged to gold, a system of pegged exchange rates was established. However, this structure created considerable tension because of the belief that the pound was overvalued and the franc undervalued. To avoid attracting funds from London, the French pursued a low-interest rate policy. Moreover, U.S. authorities provided modest loans to the Bank of England, and French authorities agreed that the Bank of France would hold part of its reserve assets in the form of deposits in the Bank of England.

The system of pegged exchange rates reestablished in the mid-1920s began to unravel in the early 1930s. In the spring of 1931, the Austrian schilling was subject to a speculative attack by investors concerned by the closing of the Credit Anstalt, the leading bank in Austria. Banks in Germany previously had made substantial loans to the Austrians. As the likelihood declined that the Austrian banks would be able to pay interest on these loans, some investors withdrew funds from banks in Germany. Germany responded by tightening exchange controls. Speculative pressure was deflected to the United Kingdom and to the foreign exchange value of the pound. In September 1931, the United Kingdom ceased supporting the pound because the economic costs of unemployment associated with high-interest-rate monetary policies were deemed too high. When the pound was no longer pegged, it depreciated, and the competitive position of U.K. firms in world markets inevitably improved while that of its trading partners worsened. Speculative pressure then was diverted to the United States and to other countries whose currencies remained pegged to gold. U.S. exports declined and U.S. imports increased in response to the improved competitive position of U.K. producers in world markets. The United States was subject to an outflow of gold by investors that anticipated that the U.S. authorities would follow the U.K. example and stop selling gold at the established U.S. parity.

[3] Nationalization of U.S. Gold Holdings

Immediately upon taking office in March 1933, President Franklin Roosevelt closed the banks to forestall further runs. U.S. gold holdings were nationalized; all U.S. citizens were required to sell gold to the U.S. Treasury at the established parity. The U.S. dollar was then floating in the foreign exchange market, much as it had during the Civil War, and the U.S. dollar depreciated modestly. In the late summer of 1933, U.S. authorities sought to increase the dollar price of gold as a way to raise the U.S. price level, promote the U.S. economic recovery, and thus cause an increase in employment and a decline in business failures. To raise the dollar price of gold, a subsidiary of the U.S. government's Reconstruction Finance Corporation began to buy gold. As the dollar price of gold increased, the foreign exchange value of the dollar declined in terms both of the currencies that were still pegged to gold (e.g., the French franc) and the floating currencies.

In January 1934, U.S. authorities decided to peg the price of the dollar at $35 per ounce of gold. The speculative pressure became diverted to the French franc and to other currencies that remained pegged to gold; these countries—France, the Netherlands, and Belgium—comprised the Gold Bloc. In September 1936, they abandoned their gold parities.

[4] Beggar-Thy-Neighbor Policies

The successive changes in exchange parities in the 1931–1936 period became known as beggar-thy-neighbor policies; the implication was that individual countries devalued their currencies as a way to increase their exports and employment at the expense of the exports and employment in their trading partners. Most countries, however, devalued only after their currencies were subject to speculative attack.

One response to the decline of competitive power when trading partners depreciated currencies was increased reliance on tariffs and exchange controls to limit payment deficits. Controls on international payments were increasing; the international economy was fragmenting or disintegrating behind higher tariffs, tariff preferences, exchange controls, and uncertainty about future exchange rates.

At the end of the 1930s, the price of the U.S. dollar in terms of the currencies of most other countries was not very different from the price that had prevailed a decade earlier, before the Great Depression began. The dollar price of the U.K. pound was \$4.8662 in 1928 and \$4.8894 in 1938. The French franc price of the dollar had been 25.50 francs in the late 1920s; by the late 1930s, the price was 35.90 francs.

By the beginning of World War II, the United States had become the dominant international financial power. The dollar was strong; the United States had a large payments surplus. U.S. official holdings of monetary gold were nearly 60 percent of total worldwide official holdings and much higher than those of the next-largest 10 countries combined. The price of gold in terms of the dollar and most other currencies was 75 percent higher than it had been in the previous decade. If there had been a gold shortage in the 1920s, there was a gold glut in the late 1930s, as evidenced by the sharp increase in U.S. gold holdings from \$3.9 billion at the end of 1929 to \$16 billion at the end of the 1930s. In some ways, the increase in the value of gold holdings effected in the 1930s through the sequence of exchange rates changes could be viewed as an unplanned response to the gold shortage in the period immediately after World War I.

1.04 POSTWAR ECONOMIC PLANNING AND THE BRETTON WOODS SYSTEM

During the early 1940s, the economic dislocations of the interwar period and the combination of high unemployment, substantial variability in exchange rates, and the growth in trade barriers and exchange controls were held to be some of the causes for World War II. The planners for the postwar period in the United States, the United Kingdom, and their wartime allies recommended the establishment of three multinational institutions: the IMF, to deal with exchange rates and international payments; the International Bank for Reconstruction and Development (World Bank) to finance postwar reconstruction; and the International Trade Organization, which led to the General Agreement on Tariffs and Trade (GATT) to provide a framework for negotiating reductions in tariffs and other trade barriers and negotiating trade disputes and other commercial policy arrangements.

The Bretton Woods system, established by the Articles of Agreement of the IMF in 1944, followed the U.S. proposal that a multinational institution manage a pool of national currencies from which a member country might borrow to help finance its payments deficits. The rationale was that the more readily a country might borrow foreign currencies, the less likely this country would follow the beggar-thy-neighbor exchange rate policies associated with the 1930s. The Articles of Agreement provided that each member country would state a value or a parity for its currency in terms either of gold or the U.S. dollar and then would undertake to prevent the foreign exchange value of its currency from deviating from this parity by more than one quarter of one percent in spot foreign exchange transactions within its territory. Each member would change the foreign exchange value of its currency only in accord with stipulated procedures and usually with the approval of the IMF. (Eventually, the view developed that the member country had to be in fundamental disequilibrium before it might change the parity for its currency.) Each member country agreed not to apply exchange controls on international payments by its residents after an initial postwar transitional period.

Each country was obliged to subscribe to the capital of the IMF on becoming a member. The amount of its capital subscription was determined on the basis of a formula that included a country's share of world trade and its share of world monetary gold holdings. Each member country paid one fourth of its capital subscription in gold and the remaining three fourths in its own currency, in the form of a non-interest-bearing demand note. Each member country could borrow currencies owned by the IMF in proportion to its own quota. In deciding whether to approve the request for a loan, the IMF was not supposed to be concerned with the member's domestic economic or social policies. Each member was obliged to sell its currency to the IMF in exchange for gold, and the IMF could borrow currencies from its members over and above the amounts available through the capital subscription.

Under the Bretton Woods system, international payments between traders and investors in different countries involved transfer of ownership of demand deposits in banks located in different countries and denominated in different currencies. A U.K. importer with a payment to make in the United States would buy a dollar demand deposit with a demand deposit denominated in the pound through a transaction with the commercial banks. The commercial banks might have acquired the dollar deposits from an exporter in London with receipts from sales in the United States, from another bank, or, in a few cases, from the Bank of England. The Bank of England would have sold dollars to limit the decrease in the foreign exchange value of the pound to a level significantly below its parity. Similarly, a Japanese importer with a dollar payment to make would buy a dollar deposit from a commercial bank in Tokyo, which might have obtained these dollars from a Japanese exporter, another bank in Tokyo, or the Bank of Japan, which would have sold dollars to prevent the yen from depreciating significantly below its parity.

Each member country could hold its international reserve assets in the form of gold or liquid securities such as demand and time deposits and banker's acceptances, denominated in the dollar, the pound, or some other currency. There were no limits on the volume of international reserve assets a country could acquire. In addition, there was no mechanism to supply countries as a group with an increase in the international reserve assets in response to the increase in the demand for these assets comparable to the central banks within each country that supplied an increase in money to match the increase in the demand for money.

The 1950s and the 1960s were decades of rapid growth in world trade and national incomes, as trade barriers and payments controls were reduced. West Germany and Japan, which had been occupied after World War II, became fully integrated into the international economy. The world price level was reasonably stable. After 1949, changes in exchange parities were infrequent (most countries had devalued their currencies in September 1949 to compensate for the more rapid increase in price levels in Western Europe than in the United States). Thus, the U.K. pound was devalued in 1967 and the French franc was devalued twice, once in 1959 and again in 1969. The deutsche mark was revalued twice, once in 1961 by 5 percent and again in 1969 by about 10 percent. The foreign exchange values of the Swiss franc, the yen, and the Italian lira were not changed for more than 20 years. Only a few countries permitted their currencies to float, and then usually only for a brief period, pending the adoption of a new parity. (Canada was an exception; the Canadian dollar floated from 1950 to 1962.) Because most changes in exchange rates involved devaluations relative to the U.S. dollar, the foreign exchange value of the dollar was modestly higher in 1970 than in 1950.

The prosperity of the world economy during these several decades was sometimes attributed to the stabilizing features of the Bretton Woods system, which was seen as a modern-day counterpart to the gold standard, which facilitated the rapid growth of the world economy in the 30 years prior to World War I. An alternative interpretation was that the rapid economic growth facilitated adherence to a system of pegged exchange rates by the monetary authorities in various countries.

These stable economic arrangements, however, were subject to two different types of pressures in the late 1960s, each of which centered on the United States. One was a growing shortage of international reserve assets, especially gold (much like the gold shortage anticipated after World War I). Because of the absence of any mechanism that could produce increases in the supply of international reserve assets in response to increases in the demand, other countries could add to their holdings of gold and foreign exchange only if the United States incurred payments deficits. U.S. gold holdings declined from $23 billion in 1950 to $11 billion at the end of 1970. Over the same period, foreign holdings of liquid dollar assets increased from $9 billion to $68 billion.

The combination of the decline in U.S. gold holdings and the increase in U.S. dollar holdings of foreign central banks and foreign private parties was a consequence of the devaluations of the currencies of the countries in 1949, which greatly improved the competitiveness of foreign goods in the world markets and especially in the U.S. market. Foreign monetary authorities set the values of their currencies in the foreign exchange market to achieve payments surpluses, leaving the United States with corresponding payments deficits.

1.05 U.S. PAYMENTS DEFICITS IN THE 1960s

In 1959, the United States began to adopt measures to limit U.S. payments abroad and to reduce U.S. gold sales. Through the 1960s, increasingly restrictive measures were adopted to achieve the same objectives. Initially, procurement under various U.S. foreign aid programs was tied to U.S. sources of supply. U.S. military forces abroad bought more goods in the United States than in the countries in which they were stationed. West Germany and other U.S. allies were encouraged to buy more military equipment in the United States to offset U.S. military expenditures in their countries. In 1963, the U.S. authorities applied a tax on U.S. imports of foreign securities. In 1965, voluntary controls were applied to capital outflows of U.S. firms. In 1968, mandatory controls were applied to the foreign investments of U.S. banks, firms, and residents.

One result of these measures was that the market in U.S. dollar deposits and other financial instruments denominated in the dollar began to develop rapidly in London and other foreign financial centers, primarily because the banks that produced these deposits did not encounter some of the costs incurred for dollar-denominated deposits in the United States. Foreign firms and governments found that they could borrow dollars in London and other offshore centers at lower interest rates than in the United States. Foreign investors could obtain higher interest rates on dollar deposits in London and in Luxembourg than on comparable dollar deposits in the United States. Thus, the offshore market in dollar deposits and other types of dollar securities increased.

The U.S. payments deficits persisted despite the wide range of measures taken to reduce U.S. payments abroad and to increase foreign payments to the United States. Eventually, the view developed that the U.S. payments deficits would decline only if a mechanism was established that would enable other countries to satisfy their demand for international reserve assets without forcing the United States to incur the corresponding payments deficits.

The establishment of Special Drawing Rights (SDRs) as a new reserve asset within the framework of the IMF was the response to the perceived shortage of reserves. SDRs could be a store of value for national central banks, comparable to securities denominated in the U.S. dollar or some other national currency. Ten billion dollars of SDRs were produced over a three-year period beginning in 1969 and was then distributed to IMF members in proportion to their quotas in the IMF. An SDR was a unit of account, with its value determined as the weighted average of the foreign exchange values of the currencies of the major industrial countries. SDRs would be transferred among countries in the settlement of payments imbalances; thus, the Bank of England could sell SDRs to the U.S. Treasury to obtain dollars, which it then might use to buy the pound in the foreign exchange market.

One of the ironies is that just as the SDR arrangement was being implemented to reduce the likelihood that U.S. payments deficits could be attributed to the demand for reserve assets, the U.S. inflation rate began to increase significantly above the inflation rates in the major U.S. trading partners. The U.S. demand for imports surged, as did the U.S. payments deficit, but the surge in the deficit could no longer be explained in terms of the demand for reserve assets.

1.06 BREAKDOWN OF THE BRETTON WOODS SYSTEM

Shortly after the devaluation of the U.K. pound in November 1967, the private demand for gold increased sharply because of the belief that the monetary price of gold was too low. In the 30 years since the U.S. gold parity had been set at $35 in 1934, the U.S. consumer price level had increased by 150 percent. For the first time in the postwar period, the private demand for gold exceeded new gold production; as a result, official institutions were obliged to sell gold from their reserves to maintain a market price close to the U.S. parity of $35. Throughout the 1950s and until 1965, the private demand for gold was less than new production, so official gold holdings were increasing, although at a declining annual rate. When the private demand for gold at $35 exceeded new production, U.S. authorities, reluctant to sell gold to maintain the $35 parity, took the lead in developing a two-tier gold price system. The U.S. gold parity of $35 would be retained for transactions between official institutions, while private parties were obliged to buy and sell gold at the free market price. Central banks would no longer arbitrage gold from their official reserves to the private market to prevent the free market price from rising above $35. In the late 1960s, the free market price varied between $35 and $43. With a free market price higher than the official parity, monetary authorities were reluctant to sell gold to finance their payments deficits.

Another pressure leading to a breakdown in the Bretton Woods system was that in the late 1960s, the U.S. price level began to increase more rapidly than the price levels in other major industrial countries. A change in the price of the dollar in terms of the currencies of most other industrial countries would be necessary; either the dollar price of gold would have to be increased while the price of gold stayed more or less constant in terms of the currencies of other industrial countries, or the currencies of the other industrial countries would have to be revalued in terms of gold. U.S. authorities were reluctant to raise the dollar price of gold. They believed that just as other countries had devalued their currencies relative to the dollar when their currencies had become overvalued, so they should revalue their currencies relative to the dollar when their currencies had become undervalued. The monetary authorities in some other industrial countries took the view that the dollar price of gold should be increased, on the rationale that they had been obliged to devalue their currencies when their price levels increased more rapidly than those of their trading partners and the United States should follow the same course. This impasse over whether the United States or its major trading partners should take the initiative in changing the alignment of the exchange rates lasted from 1968 through mid-1971. During this period, the cumulative U.S. payments deficits totaled $40 billion, with the consequence that foreign holdings of U.S. dollar securities increased rapidly.

Under the Bretton Woods system, countries subject to persistent payments deficits eventually were obliged to devalue their currencies when they could no longer finance their payments deficits. Countries with persistent payments surpluses were under far less pressure to revalue their currencies, although a few were concerned that large payments surpluses might lead to a too-rapid rate of growth of domestic money. The United States was in an exceptional position, for it might incur payments deficits without limit as long as the countries with payments surpluses were willing to acquire dollar assets. In April 1970, Canada permitted its dollar to float. More than a year later, Germany and the Netherlands also permitted their currencies to float.

In August 1971, the U.S. government adopted a package of measures designed to break the impasse over the rigidity in the exchange rate structure. The U.S. Treasury closed its gold window and indicated that it would no longer sell gold to foreign official institutions at the $35 parity. Moreover, the U.S. government applied a 10 percent tariff surcharge to dutiable imports, with the implication that this tariff would be withdrawn after the other industrial countries revalued their currencies. The European countries and Japan ceased pegging their currencies in the foreign exchange market, and their currencies appreciated. The U.S. government adopted controls to limit increases in prices and wages, so that the improvement in the U.S. international competitive position resulting from the change in the foreign exchange value of the U.S. dollar would not be offset by a resurgence in the U.S. inflation rate.

In late 1971, U.S. authorities and their counterparts in other industrial countries agreed to a new set of currency parities; effectively, the other currencies were revalued by 12 percent or the U.S. dollar was devalued by 12 percent. U.S. authorities raised the dollar price of gold by 8.6 percent to $38, although the U.S. Treasury's gold window remained closed. Finally, there was agreement on the need for a new international monetary system, one that could cope with crises much more readily than the Bretton Woods system had.

The new set of pegged exchange rates negotiated in late 1971 lasted about one year

FIGURE 1-4

Nominal and Real Exchange Rate Indexes (1983–1992, Selected Years)

Year	United States Nominal	United States Real	United Kingdom Nominal	United Kingdom Real	Japan Nominal	Japan Real	France Nominal	France Real	Germany Nominal	Germany Real
1983	114.2	112.7	91.6	92.0	107.8	100.1	87.3	96.1	107.6	99.3
1985	127.1	121.7	88.2	92.8	115.8	99.0	85.4	100.6	107.7	96.8
1988	88.0	85.9	83.8	94.3	181.6	135.5	85.7	102.8	121.8	106.3
1990	86.5	87.9	79.3	94.6	156.8	105.7	88.1	103.3	124.9	106.7
1991	85.5	87.3	80.0	98.1	170.0	112.6	86.8	101.7	124.2	104.6
1992	84.5	86.4	76.9	95.2	178.7	115.0	89.4	105.1	127.3	106.6

Note: Measured against 15 industrial country currencies.
Source: J.P. Morgan, World Financial Markets *(various years)*

and broke down when investors shifted funds from U.S. dollars to deutsche marks in response to a sharp increase in interest rates on securities denominated in deutsche marks. Early in 1973, the West German authorities ceased pegging their currency because the domestic costs of attempting to maintain a system of pegged exchange rates was judged too high. Other industrial countries followed immediately. The plan for a new monetary system, commissioned under the Smithsonian Agreement in 1972, was almost obsolete at its release, because it was based on a system of pegged exchange rates. Such a system was not likely to be feasible at a time when the inflation rate in the United States was approaching 10 percent and when other countries were committed to a lower inflation rate.

1.07 POST–BRETTON WOODS SYSTEM

[1] Floating Exchange Rates

The dominant feature of the period since the move toward floating exchange rates in the first quarter of 1973 has been the volatility of the movement in the foreign exchange value of the U.S. dollar. (See Figure 1-4.) From 1979 to 1985, the dollar appreciated by 60 percent. From 1985 to 1988, the dollar depreciated by 60 percent. The range of movement in the foreign exchange value of the dollar has been similar to the range of movements in the foreign exchange value of national currencies during the 1920s. However, the antecedents to the decisions to permit currencies to float during these two periods differ significantly. The movement to floating exchange rates after World War I reflected sharp differences among countries' inflation rates during the war. The differences among countries' inflation rates in the 1960s were much more modest; for example, the largest difference in any one year between the inflation rates in the United States and West Germany was 8 percent. The annual difference in inflation rates averaged about 3 percent, while the average annual change in the deutsche mark price of the dollar was 10 percent. Moreover, U.S. inflation rates in the 1970s and 1980s ranged from 2 to 15 percent, whereas (except for the period immediately after World

War I) the U.S. price level was reasonably stable in the 1920s. In the 1970s, two oil price shocks had a modest impact on the world price level, perhaps increasing the world inflation rate by two to three percentage points in 1974 and again in 1980; however, the United States and most of its major trading partners were experiencing double-digit inflation rates before the first oil price shock.

One other significant feature of the post–Bretton Woods period has been the sharp variability of the market price of gold. Private investors bid up the price of gold from $43 at the end of 1971 to $200 in 1973 and 1974. When the anticipated inflation rate declined, the market price of gold declined almost $100. In 1976, the market price of gold again began to increase as the worldwide inflation rate began to increase. The gold price peaked at $970 an ounce in January 1980. Then, with the decline in the inflation rate, the price of gold began to fall. The price of gold in the 1983–1992 period has ranged from $300 to $450 an ounce.

As a result of the surge in the level of the gold price, the value of gold reserves of national central banks increased. Although few central banks traded gold, many began to calculate the value of their gold holdings on the basis of gold's market price, with the consequence that the gold component of international reserves was more than 10 times larger than in the 1960s.

The oil price increases of the 1970s meant that the oil-exporting countries realized large payments surpluses, which led to a surge in their holdings of international reserve assets. Initially, there was concern that the oil-exporting countries would acquire such a large share of the system's reserve assets that the international reserve holdings of other countries would be depleted; however, their oil export earnings could be used to finance either the increase in their commodity imports or the increase in their imports of securities, including deposits in the major international commercial banks. Cumulatively, the oil-exporting countries had payments surpluses that approached $200 billion in the 1974–1982 period. The surge in their holdings of international reserve assets led to a sharp increase in their deposit holdings in the major international banks, which facilitated an increase in the loans by these banks to many of the developing countries.

Commercial bank loan finance or "liability management" replaced the use of owned reserves in the financing of payments deficits. Thus, many developing countries were able to finance the increase in their oil import bills with bank loans; the external debt of these countries increased from $120 billion in 1972 to $850 billion in 1982. When the commercial banks realized that the external debt of these countries was large relative to their export earnings or their income, they attempted to stop lending to these countries. In the absence of funds from new bank loans, the developing countries were unable to pay the interest on the outstanding loans. If the oil price increase and the Organization of Petroleum Exporting Countries (OPEC) surpluses were the dominant concern of the 1970s, the external debts of the developing countries were the dominant concern of the 1980s.

[2] Nongold International Reserve Assets

A third significant aspect of the 1970s and the 1980s was the surge in the nongold component of international reserves. In the 1960s, one means proposed to correct the shortage of international reserve assets was for the major countries to permit their currencies to float. Their central banks would then no longer need to support their currencies in the foreign exchange market, and the demand for these assets would decline. The irony is that the period of floating exchange rates has been associated with a sharp increase in the value of international reserve assets. A modest component

FIGURE 1-5

Value of International Reserve Assets

Source: International Monetary Fund, International Financial Statistics *(Washington, D.C.: International Monetary Fund)*

	1960	1965	1970	1975	1980	1985	1992
Gold	$37.9	$41.8	$37.0	$ 41.8	$ 42.5	$ 36.5	$ 31.3
Foreign exchange	18.5	24.0	45.5	162.4	378.4	382.5	910.2
Reserve position in IMF	3.6	5.4	7.7	14.8	21.4	42.5	46.6
SDRs	—	—	3.1	10.2	15.0	20.0	17.7

Note: U.S. dollars in billions at the end of the year.

of the increase in the value of international reserve assets resulted from the OPEC payments surpluses. A larger component resulted from purchases of U.S. dollar securities by central banks that wanted to limit the appreciation of their currencies. Most of the increase in the international reserve assets was denominated in the dollar, although there was continued growth in the volume of reserves denominated in a few other currencies.

Within a decade, the urgency of the reserve shortage that led to the establishment of SDR had disappeared. Individual countries still had problems financing their payments deficits, but the concern that there would be a reserve shortage diminished. Indeed, the probability was high that the unplanned growth in international reserve assets had led to a reserve glut, even though few countries appeared to have excessive reserves. Over the postwar period, IMF quotas had increased about as rapidly as world trade. Because of the surge in the price of gold and increases in dollars and other currencies of various central banks, however, the share of reserves provided by the IMF in the total worldwide reserves declined. (See Figure 1-5.)

[3] Alternative Exchange Rate Arrangements

In the 1960s, the major countries of Western Europe joined in an economic community and made great strides in reducing the barriers that segmented their economies; tariffs on intra-European trade were reduced or eliminated, as were many other nontariff barriers. There was a communitywide tariff on imports from other countries, a Common Agricultural Policy, and steps toward fiscal harmonization (for example, each country adopted the value-added tax as a form of indirect taxation). Also an initiative toward a common monetary policy took the form of a joint float; some members of the community pegged their currencies to each other to reduce the uncertainty associated with financing intra-European trade and investment transactions. (See Figure 1-6.)

Once it became evident that the industrial countries would permit their currencies to float for an indefinite period, member countries of the IMF no longer adhered to their IMF commitments. To legitimize the current practices in the foreign exchange market, a new amendment (the so-called Second Amendment, the First Amendment being the establishment of the SDR) to the Bretton Woods system was adopted. Member countries were allowed to pursue any type of exchange rate system, and many

FIGURE 1-6

Exchange Rate Arrangements (as of March 31)

Classification Status	1982	1985	1988	1992
Currency pegged to				
U.S. dollar	38	32	38	24
French franc	13	14	14	14
Russian ruble	0	0	0	6
Other currency	5	4	5	6
SDRs	15	12	7	5
Other currency composite	23	31	31	29
Flexibility limited vis-à-vis a single currency	10	7	4	4
Cooperative arrangements	8	8	8	9
Exchange rate adjusted according to a set of indicators	5	6	5	3
Managed floating	20	19	21	23
Independently floating	8	14	17	44
Total	145	147	150	167

Source: International Monetary Fund, Exchange Arrangements and Exchange Restrictions *(various issues)*

countries continued to peg their currencies. Although the major industrial countries permit their currencies to float, more than 100 countries (mostly the smaller ones) continue to peg their currencies to reduce the uncertainty that their traders and investors incur in the foreign exchange market. Some of these countries peg their currencies to the U.S. dollar, some to the French franc, and some to the SDR or to an alternative market basket of currencies. The choice of the currency to peg to is largely determined by trade patterns; countries tend to peg their currencies to that of their largest trading partner. There was concern that countries might attempt to manipulate the foreign exchange value of their currencies to achieve their objectives in a style reminiscent of the beggar-thy-neighbor policies of the 1930s. Therefore, the IMF was charged with multilateral surveillance of the exchange market practices of its members.

With the move to floating exchange rates, however, the IMF needs to police and maintain a system of pegged exchange rates. The role of the IMF is increasingly oriented to the exchange rate problems and the monetary and fiscal policies of the developing countries.

One counterpart to the volatility of the movement in exchange rates was the growth in the volume of protectionist import measures. The increase in the demand for protection reflected the fact that when a country's currency appreciated sharply in real terms, the competitive position of firms producing in that country declined. Foreign producers could increase their share of the domestic market because changes in the exchange rate gave them a price advantage of as much as 25 percent or 30 percent. To forestall the decline in market share (or even the downward pressure on domestic prices, wages, and profits), producers sought tariff protection.

In recent years, the movements in exchange rates have been abrupt and large. National authorities and analysts have been puzzled by changes in exchange rates that are considerably larger than would have been predicted or inferred from the differences in the changes in national price levels. There is little evidence that the large swings in exchange rates are a consequence of official intervention by central banks and the various national monetary authorities; rather, the intervention of these authorities was undertaken to limit such swings. Despite the movements in exchange rates, world trade has grown more than world income. Nevertheless, the costs and risks incurred by those involved in international trade and investment have increased rapidly, and it seems plausible that world trade and payments would have grown even more rapidly if the variations in exchange rates had been smaller.

1.08 FUTURE OF THE INTERNATIONAL MONETARY SYSTEM

One of the lessons of the 1980s is that a system of pegged exchange rates is difficult to maintain during a period of inflation, especially when inflation rates are significantly different among major countries. As inflation rates become more nearly similar, the range of movement in the exchange rates is likely to decline. The costs of pegging national currencies also are likely to diminish; thus, monetary authorities may again seek to peg their currencies. Within the European Community, the exchange rate–pegging activities already have been extensive in the European Monetary System, as the Europeans sought to reduce the costs and the risks involved in their intra-European transactions. In December 1991, the Europeans committed themselves to a common currency by the late 1990s under the Maastricht Agreement. In August 1993, the entire currency agreement was set aside, thereby delaying indefinitely the move to a common currency.

The next step in the return toward greater exchange rate stability will involve developing arrangements so that the yen and the currencies of the Western European countries are again pegged to the U.S. dollar, but this is unlikely until there is greater harmonization of inflation rates.

Suggested Reading

Aliber, Robert Z. *The International Money Game*. New York: Basic Books, 1987.

Bank for International Settlements. *Annual Report* (various years). Basel, Switzerland: Bank for International Settlements.

De Vries, Margaret G. *The IMF in a Changing World: 1945–1985*. Washington, D.C.: International Monetary Fund, 1986.

International Monetary Fund. *Annual Report* (various issues). Washington, D.C.: International Monetary Fund.

———. *Exchange Arrangements and Exchange Restrictions* (various issues). Washington, D.C.: International Monetary Fund.

———. *International Financial Statistics* (various issues). Washington, D.C.: International Monetary Fund.

Jack, D.T. *The Restoration of European Currencies*. London: P.S. King & Son Ltd., 1927.

Mayer, Thomas, James S. Dusenberry, and Robert Z. Aliber. *Money, Banking and the Economy*. New York: W.W. Norton, 1987.

Solomon, Robert. *The International Monetary System 1945–1981*. New York: Harper & Row, 1982, 1989.

Chapter 2

Foreign Exchange Markets and Currency Risk

GUNTER DUFEY

2.01 **Introduction** 22

2.02 **Foreign Exchange Market** 22

[1] Basic Function of the Foreign Exchange Market 22

[2] Foreign Exchange: Spot and Forward Rates 24

[3] Controlling Risk 24

[4] Trading Practices and Rate Quotations 27

[5] Black Markets and Multiple Exchange Rates 29

[6] Theory: Interest Rates, Exchange Rates, and Prices and Output 30

[7] Forecasting Exchange Rates and Managerial Implications 36

[8] Political Risk 37

[9] Exchange Risk 38

2.03 **Assessing Corporate Foreign Exchange Risk** 40

[1] Accounting Exposure 40

[2] Alternative Accounting Methods 41

[3] Statement of Financial Accounting Standards No. 52 42

[4] Economic or Cash Flow Exposure ... 44

[5] Contractual Versus Noncontractual Returns 45

[a] Currency Denomination 45

[b] Time Dimension 46

[6] Implementation of Economic Exposure Analysis 47

[7] Critique of the Traditional View 47

[8] Corporate Exchange Risk in a Theoretical Perspective 49

2.04 **Management of Economic Exposure: Management and Hedging** 49

[1] Forecasting for Risk Control 50

[2] Financial Versus Operating Strategies 51

[3] Debt Denomination: Strategy Versus Tactics 51

[4] Foreign Currency Options and Exchange Risk Management 53

2.05 **Corporate Practice and the Relevance of Currency Hedging** 56

[1] Corporate Exchange Risk Management Practice 56

[2] Relevance of Managing Corporate Exchange Exposure 57

Suggested Reading 58

2.01 INTRODUCTION

Business firms have internationalized their activities considerably. This trend has manifested itself not only in increased involvement in international trade and foreign operations but also in the fact that even firms without explicit international transactions have become subject to the direct and indirect effects of foreign competition to a much larger extent than in the past.

The impact of exchange rate changes on business operations tends to be pervasive, and concern is not limited to specific financial functions such as corporate treasury.[1] For the purposes of analysis, it is useful to consider foreign exchange (forex) rate changes as a source of risk distinct and separate from other risks, such as shifts in technology, consumer preferences, labor relations, and government policies. The impact of exchange rate changes on the firm must not, however, be viewed in a simplistic, mechanical fashion. It is necessary to take account of all effects on the firm for which a causal link with exchange rate changes can be identified. For example, exchange rate changes are often directly linked to exchange controls or drastic shifts in macroeconomic policy. By the same token, forex rate changes may cause adjustments in consumer behavior or may alter the future path of labor costs in a systematic fashion.[2]

2.02 FOREIGN EXCHANGE MARKET

[1] Basic Function of the Foreign Exchange Market

The world economy is composed of nation-states. A fundamental economic characteristic of modern nation-states is the exercise of monetary sovereignty. Technically, this involves two distinct aspects:

1. *The government.* Usually through its agency, the central bank, the government maintains a monopoly on supplying the means of payments. The issuing of coin and paper currency, together with the institutional arrangements regulating the volume of bank demand (current) liabilities used to transfer funds among private and public entities in the economy, represent the essential aspects of the supply of moneys in a national economy.

2. *Legal tender laws.* In order to assure the use of the national currency in good times and bad, these laws stipulate that debts to both private and public parties be legally discharged with the transfer of an appropriate amount of the national money. In other words, creditors cannot refuse payment in local currency.

All of this means that money is very much a national phenomenon, useful only within the political boundaries of a country. By the same token, money never leaves the country, casual observation notwithstanding.[3]

---

[1] Waters (1979).

[2] Oxelheim and Wihlborg (1987).

[3] Merchants may accept currency from another country as a service, but they will bring it quickly to the local bank, where it is counted, packed, and shipped back to its country of issue. Also, when people lose trust in the future value of local money, they may attempt to use another country's means of payment, but this is exactly what legal tender laws are designed to curtail.

What is usually referred to as an outflow of money in the context of international transactions is in reality merely the transfer of the ownership of means of payments, usually demand deposits in the national banking system, from domestic to foreign residents. Technically, demand deposits never leave the national payments circuit.

Thus, in order to make payments abroad, it is necessary ultimately to obtain forex or, in other words, ownership of the means of payment (currency or demand deposits) in the country of the recipient of the funds. The recipient may accept foreign means of payment but usually sells the foreign money immediately in order to obtain the domestic money needed to pay expenses. Therefore, international payments involve exchanges in ownership of national means of payment. This exchange occurs in the forex market, where buyers and sellers of currencies interact (that is, one country's means of payment is bought in return for another country's means of payment, which is then sold.)

The major participants in this market are financial institutions that borrow or lend abroad and that undertake financial transactions with their foreign affiliates. Parties to international transactions, such as exporters and importers, usually do not participate directly; instead, their banks act for them. Also, central banks may and often do participate in the forex market, attempting either to influence the value of their respective currencies in pursuit of national economic goals or to make international payments related to "autonomous" purposes, such as servicing debt, importing merchandise, increasing ownership of foreign liabilities, and giving foreign aid.

Anyone whose consumption, saving, or investment behavior leads to international payments is directly or indirectly involved in the forex market. Cross-border payments arise in conjunction with almost all international transactions, i.e., gifts, exports, imports, service transactions, and investments (lending or borrowing). The notable exceptions among international transactions not involving the forex market are private or public donations of real goods and certain intergovernmental transactions, including those with international agencies such as the World Bank or the International Monetary Fund.

All transactions by the participants in the forex market affect the demand or the supply of foreign means of payment, which are called forex or foreign currencies. The interaction of supply and demand in the forex market determines the exchange rate at any given point in time. It is defined as the price of one unit of currency in terms of another currency. Therefore, transactions in the forex market can be expressed in terms of supply and demand of national currencies. Specifically, transactions classified as credits in the balance of payments—exports of merchandise, services, and claims (capital imports)—are sources of forex and result in an increased supply of forex relative to the supply of domestic currency. The increased supply of forex and the increased demand for the domestic means of payment caused by payments made by nonresidents for domestic exports will result in the domestic currency's appreciation (i.e., an increase in the domestic currency's value relative to foreign currencies).

Transactions classified as debits in the balance of payments—imports of merchandise, services, and claims (capital exports)—are uses of forex and result in increased demand for forex relative to the demand for the domestic currency. The increased demand for forex and the concomitant increased supply of the domestic currency result in the domestic currency's depreciation (i.e., a decrease in value relative to foreign currencies). Because of the reciprocal nature of the forex market, in which the demand for one currency equals the supply of the other and vice versa, each transaction affects the exchange rate through its effect on supply and demand.

[2] Foreign Exchange: Spot and Forward Rates

So far, it has been assumed that there is no difference between the time buyers and sellers agree on a price (rate) and the time the "merchandise" (ownership of demand deposits) is actually delivered. However, as in many other markets, agreement on a rate (price) and actual delivery (payment, settlement, or clearing) usually happen at two different times.

Conventions in the forex markets call for delivery on the second business day after a rate has been agreed on for so-called spot transactions.[4] Trades that call for delivery on the third day or later are known as forward transactions. Typically, forward transactions are done for "even dates" (i.e., one week, a month (30 days), or multiples thereof.)[5] However, banks accommodate corporate customers for "odd" dates at a small price in the form of a less advantageous rate.

The general purpose of a forward transaction is to fix the exchange rate for the respective maturity, instead of waiting for the (uncertain) spot rate that will prevail just prior to that time.

[3] Controlling Risk

Why would anyone want to fix the exchange rate contractually for a future period? One reason is the anticipated receipt of foreign currency funds in the future or an obligation to make a payment at a future point in time. The classic illustration is a U.S. importer who orders merchandise from abroad, knowing that he must pay, e.g., $100,000 (Canadian) 90 days later. By purchasing $100,000 (Canadian) 90 days forward for $85,000 (U.S.), he knows exactly the U.S. dollar price of the merchandise, on the basis of which he has made his decision. In other words, through the forward market he has "locked in" the U.S. dollar price; the explicit cost is unaffected by the vagaries of the spot rate between the time he commits to the purchase and the time he has to deliver the funds.

To put it differently, the transaction is covered (hedged);[6] should the future spot rate of the Canadian dollar rise above the contractually agreed-on forward rate of $0.85 (U.S.), e.g., to $0.86 (U.S.), the importer incurs a loss on his payable (liability), because $100,000 (Canadian) now costs $86,000 (U.S.) (i.e., $1,000 [(U.S.)] more). On the other hand, he has gained on his forward contract, which obliges the other party (usually a bank) to deliver $100,000 (Canadian) for $85,000 (U.S.). Relative to the then-prevailing spot rate of $0.86 (U.S.), he has gained $1,000 (U.S.) on the forward contract (an asset) that guarantees he will receive $100,000 (Canadian) for only $85,000 (U.S.). Thus, the loss on the liability was exactly offset by the gain on the asset.

---

[4] A holiday in either country simply moves the settlement day for both currencies one day further. U.S. dollars against Canadian dollars and Mexican pesos are typically traded for next-day value. Modern communications technology sometimes permits dealing in European currencies for next-day value ("Tom next"), or even same-day settlement (cash), but the rate quoted to the party that requests these special terms will be slightly different from the spot rate.

[5] In order to find the settlement date for, e.g., 3-month (90-day forward) rates, one finds the value date for the spot transaction and checks whether the same date 3 months hence is a business day, as long as the business day is within that same month. If the value date would fall into the next month, the last (common) business day that occurs in the settlement months is used.

[6] Within the narrow context of the forex market, the terms "hedging" and "covering" are used synonymously; in the context of international investment, finer distinctions must be drawn.

Of course, should the spot rate move in the other direction, e.g., to $0.84 (U.S.), his potential gain on his payable is offset by the loss on the forward contract. But such is the nature of hedging; one gives up the opportunity for both gains and losses, focusing instead on the profitability of the underlying transaction that will give rise to the future receipt or payment of foreign funds: exports, imports, investments, and borrowings.

There is a second reason for fixing the exchange rate for some future date. If one feels strongly that the future spot rate, say 90 days hence, will be lower than the 90-day forward rate available now, one might want to engage in a little speculation: entering into a forward contract to exchange, e.g., $100,000 (Canadian) for $85,000 (U.S.) 90 days from now will yield $1,000 (U.S.) if the expectation comes true and one is able to purchase Canadian dollars at the then-prevailing rate of $0.84 (U.S.). Indeed, money can be made at any future spot rate that is lower than the forward rate of $0.85 (U.S.), but one would lose money if the spot rate happens to be above $0.85 (U.S.).

Because of the profit potential, many people are constantly attempting to predict the future spot rates and enter into forward commitments. All of these transactions will not be without effect on the forward rate relative to the current spot rate. To illustrate, say that today's spot rate for Canadian dollars is $0.84 (U.S.), but market participants as a group think the Canadian dollar is going to depreciate (weaken), that is, the spot rate is likely to drop within the next 3 months. In that case, the 90-day forward rate will be lower than today's spot rate, e.g., $0.83 (U.S.). Thus, the difference of $0.01 (U.S.) reflects market expectations; it represents the market's forecast of the future spot rate 90 days from now.

But the difference between the present spot rate and the present forward rate has additional economic content. Note in the case of the U.S. importer's problem with the Canadian dollar payable that the use of the forward market is not the only way to remove uncertainty stemming from future spot rates. The importer could simply borrow an appropriate amount of U.S. dollars when he enters into the commitment to pay $100,000 (Canadian) 90 days hence;[7] he would then exchange them at the prevailing spot rate, invest them in Canada for 90 days, and use the funds at maturity of this Canadian dollar asset to pay off the Canadian dollar liability. (This transaction is known as a money market hedge.)

When comparing the two alternatives, the importer will look at (1) the difference between the interest rate for the U.S. dollar loan less the interest on his Canadian dollar investment and (2) the difference between the spot rate and the forward rate. Thus, if the spot rate is $0.84 (U.S.) and the forward rate for 90 days is $0.83 (U.S.), the difference would amount to $1,000 (U.S.) on a purchase of $100,000 (Canadian) forward. If the amount of interest received on the Canadian dollar investment exceeds the interest cost on the U.S. dollar loan by more than $1,000 (U.S.), the importer will protect himself through the money market (borrowing and investing) transactions; if the interest difference is less than $1,000 (U.S.), he will find it advantageous to cover through the forward market, i.e., purchase Canadian dollars forward (sell U.S. dollars forward).

These illustrations show that the difference between the spot rate and the forward rate not only reflects market expectations but is analogous to interest.

---

[7] The appropriate amount of U.S. dollars is equal to that required to purchase $100,000 (Canadian) less the amount of interest earned in Canada for 90 days.

A well-known approximation formula allows us to convert an exchange rate differential into a per annum rate:

$$\frac{\text{Forward rate} - \text{spot rate}}{\text{spot rate}} \left(\frac{360}{\text{days in forward contract}} \right) (100)$$
$$= \pm \text{ premium or discount per annum}$$

For the above illustration:

$$\frac{\$0.83 - \$0.84}{\$0.84} \left(\frac{360}{90} \right) (100) = -4.76 \text{ per annum}$$

Thus, the 90-day forward Canadian dollar trades at a 4.76 percent per annum discount to the spot Canadian dollar relative to the U.S. dollar.[8]

Once the interest equivalence of the forward premium or discount is understood, a new way of making money opens up: international interest arbitrage. Arbitrage is defined as the simultaneous buying and selling in two or more markets to profit from price discrepancies for assets of the same riskiness. If the interest rate differential between, e.g., the United States and Canada is not equal to the forward differential, one can undertake international borrowing and lending (investing) and cover the exchange risk with a forward transaction. To illustrate, if interest rates on 90-day U.S. dollar loans are 10 percent per year and Canadian money market rates are 16 percent, one can move funds to Canada by exchanging them at the spot rate of $0.84 (U.S.), "cover" the investment with a forward contract at $0.83 (U.S.), and earn 1.2 percent $(16 - 10 - 4.8)$ without exchange risk.

The simultaneous purchase or sale of one currency (in this case, Canadian dollars in the spot market) for one value date and the offsetting sale or purchase of the same currency for another (here Canadian dollars 90 days forward) is called a foreign currency swap. Hence, the per annum forward premium or discount is known as the swap rate.

Because many people are attracted by the opportunity to earn returns without exchange risk, such opportunities disappear rapidly; the activities of international interest arbitragers (if unrestricted by governmental controls) affect spot and forward rates as well as interest rates (for instruments of equal riskiness) in the respective currencies until interest rate parity is established, as shown by

$$\frac{\text{FWD}}{\text{SPOT}} = \frac{(1 + i_A)}{(1 + i_B)}$$

---

[8] From a Canadian perspective, one would say that the U.S. dollar trades at 4.76 percent per annum premium, since

$$\frac{1}{0.83} = 1.2048$$

$$\frac{1}{0.84} = 1.1905$$

$$\frac{1.2048 - 1.1905}{1.1905} \left(\frac{360}{90} \right) (100) = 4.76\% \text{ per annum}$$

It is pertinent that the U.S. dollar is the reference currency in all forex transactions. Hence, all forex calculations are done from a U.S. dollar perspective. Exceptions to this are the U.K. pound, Australian dollar, and New Zealand dollar.

where i_A and i_B refer to the representative interest rates in countries A and B, respectively, and FWD and SPOT refer to the price of a unit of currency B expressed in terms of currency A.

For many currencies, viable forward markets do not exist. Invariably, this is because of the existence of (or fear of impending) exchange and credit market controls. Even for the small number of major currencies for which relatively unregulated, active markets for medium-term and long-term credits at fixed interest rates exist, forward facilities beyond 12 to 18 months used to be quite rare. One explanation is that longer-term forward contracts would require bank traders to create offsetting asset or liability positions that are regarded as risky and impinge on established capital adequacy norms. With the growth of active offshore markets for fixed-rate notes and bonds in various currencies and refined hedging techniques, markets for long-dated forwards have improved considerably.

[4] Trading Practices and Rate Quotations

Changes in net forex positions arise continuously as banks deal with their corporate clients. In order to accommodate those customers effectively without holding large inventories, banks rely on the interbank market. Indeed, interbank trading for most major banks accounts for 90 percent and more of total transaction volume. This phenomenon can be explained by liquidity and information requirements. Only a bank that is active in the interbank market can buy and sell forex in substantial amounts, i.e., adjust its positions quickly by having ready access to many counterparties. Furthermore, profitable forex trading requires the acquisition of timely and relevant information. While traders are provided with expensive monitoring equipment, relevant information about the state of the market and the actions of the various players can be obtained in the final analysis only from the continuous, active participation. It is only the access to detailed information and the traders' skill in interpreting it that allows them to take profitable positions over time.

Obviously, banks attempt to control the inherent risks. They do so by limiting the size of positions that traders can take. The allocation of these limits is influenced mainly by the bank's strategic objectives with respect to forex trading, currencies, the creditworthiness of counterparties, and each dealer's track record.

The trader's intent to buy or sell is expressed through his or her quotes (although traders make sure that their intent is not too obvious in order to deprive the counterparties of useful information). For example, the senior traders in any dealing room get a feel for the market by reviewing the relevant news on their terminals. If markets are volatile, they may begin work earlier in order to contact colleagues in dealing rooms of the bank that are several time zones ahead to discuss market activity. After quick discussions with management inside and contacts outside the bank, and after checking markets for gold and various financial instruments, traders would arrive at their own quotes on the basis of the desired position in the currency (or currencies) for which they have primary responsibility.

Traders usually give two numbers when quoting forex rates. For example, in a deutsche mark–per-dollar quote by a European bank of 2.006/2.007, the deal would indicate the commitment to buy dollars at DM2.0060 per U.S. dollar and sell dollars at DM2.0070, following the classic trader's principle to buy low and sell high. A quote of 2.0060/70 by a U.S. dealer signals his or her interest in buying deutsche marks at

2.0070 per dollar and selling them for 2.0060. To compound the confusion, 2.0060 is still referred to as the bid rate and 2.0070 as the offer rate.

Obviously, as the dealer must obtain more deutsche marks per dollar than he or she sells to avoid going broke. Unfortunately, this quotation practice causes difficulties for students of forex markets in the United States. Confusing matters further is an exception: U.K. pounds are quoted in "direct" terms, i.e., $1.42 (U.S.) per pound.

Modern telecommunications advances enable dealers to obtain rate information through the foreign currency page of one of the data transmittal services, such as Reuters and Telerate. Typical screen information is as follows:

			SPOT	*1 Month*	*3 Months*	*6 Months*	*12 Months*
1113	DM	182	40/50	39/37	107/105	202/198	290/282
1114	SFC[a]	153	60/75	32/29	96/93	197/191	372/352
1112	FFL[b]	607	10/20	113/121	346/365	675/700	1,265/1,340
1115	DFL[c]	206	10/30	38/37	105/102	199/195	281/271
1118	BFC[d]	38	18/38				
1120	LIT[e]		1,295/1,297				
1116	YEN	153	08/18	27/25	85/82	172/168	280/270
1110	CAN[f]	133	22/25	11/13	25/28	86/92	180/200
1111	£[g]	154	15/25	57/56	162/160	293/289	589/590
1117	ECU[h]	113	22/32				

[a] Swiss franc.

[b] French franc.

[c] Dutch florin.

[d] Belgian franc.

[e] Italian lira.

[f] Canadian dollar.

[g] U.K. pound.

[h] European currency unit.

Because time is money, traders also use shorthand to quote rates. Typically, a trader will say: "Deutsche marks are 40/50, 39/37, 107/105, 202/198, 290/282." This means that the spot rate is 18.240/50 and the 1-month, 3-month, 6-month, and 12-month forward rates for the U.S. dollar, from a German bank's perspective, are DM1.8201 bid, 1.8213 offer; 1.8133 bid, 1.8145 offer; and these rates are obtained by subtracting the "points" 39/37, 107/105, and so forth from the bid-ask prices for spot U.S. dollar. A descending order of the points means subtraction from the spot rate, or a discount on forward U.S. dollars. If the U.S. dollar had traded at a premium, traders would quote first the lower adjustment points, signaling that these must be added to spot bid-ask rates. In order to remember these rules, one might make use of the fact that bid-ask spreads tend to become wider for longer maturities. This fact will prove helpful in double-checking forward rate quotations.

Traders do not quote the full rate on the telephone but simply the last two decimal points, e.g., "60 and 75," as their counterparts are aware of the preceding numbers at any moment in time. Suppose, in response to a Swiss franc–per-dollar quote of 1.5360/75, a bank sells the trader in Zurich $1 million. Before filling out the purchase voucher,[9] the trader says loudly to his or her colleagues, "We get 1 million U.S. at

---

[9] Also referred to as "ticket," this procedure is becoming more and more automated as the use of minicomputers spreads in trading rooms.

60,'' upon which the chief trader might adjust the rates to, perhaps, 55/70 if he or she wants to avoid further purchases of dollars. Quotes between traders of major banks are good for up to $5 million or the equivalent if it is a major currency. Otherwise, traders specify the amount. If a trader is unwilling to commit himself or herself, he or she add "for indication only."

The difference between the buy and sell rates is the spread for the trader. If the trader is not interested in dealing, quotes with a very wide spread between bid and ask will be given. If the trader wishes to purchase a currency, the bid price will be raised, and, likewise, if the trader is interested only in selling, the sell (or ask) price will be lowered. If the trader is interested in volume, dealing on both sides of the market, he or she would naturally quote in such a way as to show very narrow spreads between the bid and ask price. Still, the extent to which traders will reduce their spreads is limited, because the spread is one source of trading profit.

[5] Black Markets and Multiple Exchange Rates

So far, it has been assumed that governments will not interfere with the acquisition or sale of foreign money. However, in many countries restrictions on foreign payments are a fact of life. And while forex control systems vary a great deal, not only do they invariably affect the level of the exchange rate, but they tend to bring forth parallel markets, with the result that there are two or more exchange rates for the same currency.

Assume that a given country has a comprehensive system of exchange controls; residents are not permitted to purchase forex without explicit permission from the exchange control authorities. Further, residents who receive foreign moneys, for whatever reason, must surrender these funds to the authorities in return for domestic money at an official rate. The law includes rules prohibiting the unauthorized export of domestic currency and other negotiable securities.[10] Without fail, black markets spring up, both inside and outside of the country, where bank notes and other negotiable instruments are exchanged for foreign currencies. In addition, the rate at which domestic currency is bought and sold is higher than the rate at which the authorities make foreign currency available; more of the domestic currency must be delivered for each unit of the foreign currency.

The premium of the black market rate over the official rate depends on a combination of three factors: (1) the allocation policy of the forex authorities; (2) the level of the official rate relative to demand; and (3) the penalties and efficiency of enforcement policies.

Apart from this differential over the official rate, there is also a substantial spread between buy and sell rates, reflecting the risk of making illegal exchanges within the country and/or the danger involved in bringing domestic bank notes outside or inside the country in contravention to laws and regulations.[11]

Because of the high administrative cost of comprehensive exchange controls, where

---

[10] Such laws are often supplemented by rules that limit the importation of domestic currency to catch funds that have found their way abroad illegally. A good survey of exchange controls in various countries can be found in the annual report *Exchange Restrictions* published by the International Monetary Fund.

[11] The extreme spreads for some countries' bank notes are caused not so much by the low volume but rather by the existence of exchange controls that makes arbitrage risky and expensive.

literally every international transaction has to be approved, less ambitious countries have resorted to an approach based on segregating international transactions, forcing each through a distinct segment of the forex market.

A good example is provided by the United Kingdom. For many years prior to 1978, U.K. investors were allowed to purchase securities outside of the sterling area (the group of countries pegged to sterling) only with forex funds that became available through the sale of foreign securities by other U.K. residents. The demand for such funds regularly exceeded the supply at the prevailing exchange rate, particularly since a portion of the foreign currency proceeds was required to be surrendered to the Bank of England by the seller in return for domestic sterling funds.

The resulting difference between the official exchange rate for current and investment transactions and the rate applicable to foreign investments became known as the London investment dollar premium, expressed as a percentage over the official spot rate. Over the years, this premium had fluctuated widely, largely in response to expectations regarding the relative merits of investments outside of the United Kingdom versus those in the U.K. securities market.

Many other countries have used similar devices. Belgium, France, and Italy, for example, have at times split the forex market into two sections: one for current account transactions, and one for capital, or financial transactions. The central banks intervened primarily in the market for current account transactions, while the financial rates have typically fluctuated without intervention.

At times, South American countries have pushed such schemes to extremes, with rates not only for current and financial transactions but also for various exports and imports, depending on the particular category. From a forex market perspective, trading in these currencies becomes very difficult, with the result that markets become thin and the spreads between bid and ask become very wide, which is only one of the costs associated with such policies.

[6] Theory: Interest Rates, Exchange Rates, and Prices and Output

The equivalence of exchange rate changes and interest rates was discussed previously in the context of hedging a Canadian dollar payable arising from an export transaction. Note that this principle applies to all financial assets and claims, not just to payables, which include all kinds of securities with contractually set returns (i.e., not equities). This interest rate parity is what is known as an after-the-fact or ex post relationship, where currently available interest rates for equivalent instruments denominated in two different currencies and the difference between spot and forward rates are examined. Since a sufficient difference leads to (riskless) opportunity, it is the basis for foreign exchange swaps and related arbitrage transactions.

Another way of expressing this relationship between exchange rates and interest rates is to specify what is actually exchanged in forex and securities markets. In the forex markets, current and future units of foreign money are traded for domestic money; similarly, on the domestic (foreign) securities market, current units of domestic (foreign) money are exchanged for future funds. The schematic presentation in Figure 2-1 shows the markets and the relevant rates.[12] Knowing how these markets are interre-

---

[12] This view has been suggested by Deardorff (1979).

FIGURE 2-1

Interrelationship Between Forex and International Credit Markets

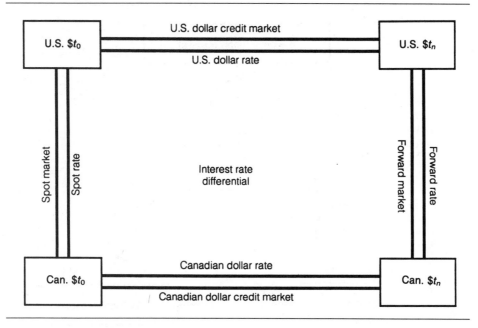

lated, however, does not help in forecasting what rates will be in the future, i.e., the before-the-fact or ex ante relationship.

Traditional market theory explains the determination of prices (rates) of financial assets by supply and demand. This can easily be reconciled with the modern view of markets by stressing the role of expectations. What really matters are the expectations of market participants about future demand and supply and all of their determinants. It follows that in markets where prices are established in such a manner, current prices incorporate the expectations of market participants about future prices, such as exchange rates and interest rates. What Figure 2-1 shows is that interest rates and exchange rates are simultaneously determined by the same set of expectations. But, if one assumes that market participants act rationally, expectations must be formed on some basis. Which factors determine the relevant expectations?

The determination of the level of interest rates in an economy is a complex process, and a number of competing explanations describe the processes by which interest rates are determined.[13] In an international context, the primary concern is, of course, with relative changes in interest rates. The monetarist framework focuses on the excess supply of money. Differences in the rates of growth of excess money among countries cause (relative) price-level changes. This relationship is shown, in a one-country con-

---

[13] This section relies on a synthesis by Giddy (1976). Theories of interest rate determination are associated with the works of Wicksell, Keynes, Hicks, and Fisher. Any good introductory book on money and banking will bring the reader up to date.

FIGURE 2-2

International Equilibrium Framework

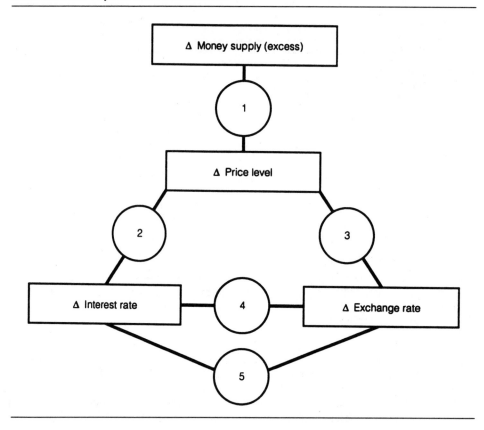

text, in Link 1 of Figure 2-2. More profoundly, the rate of change in the general price level (inflation) in a country is determined by the difference between the rate of growth in real output and the growth in the effective supply of money.

The underlying idea is that when the rate of change in the money supply differs from the need for additional liquidity resulting from changes in real output, the general level of prices in the economy will change. The real need for money changes because of changes in the level of output of goods; if more goods are produced, more money is needed to trade them at the existing price levels. If the money supply changes by an amount larger than the increase in output of goods, it can only be absorbed by an increase in prices such that the new output at new, higher prices requires the new, greater amount of money supply. As a consequence, an excessive increase in the money supply causes prices to rise.

The second link identifies the relationship between changes in interest rates and changes in price levels. In a theory generally attributed to Fisher,[14] interest rates have

---

[14] Fisher (1980).

two components: a real return plus an adjustment for price-level changes. If the holders of loanable funds are to be induced to give up their funds for a period, they must receive some compensation. This compensation is the higher purchasing power of the funds in the period in which they are returned and is necessary because, without it, the holders of funds have no incentive to forgo current consumption and, in addition, to be exposed to the risk of default. This compensation is termed the real return to the lenders of money.

If prices do not change, this return would represent the increase in the purchasing power of the loaned funds. But when prices are expected to rise and lenders are aware of this, they will demand compensation for inflation in order to protect the real rate of return. This demand will be met by including a factor for the expected rate of inflation in the interest rate. Thus, the interest rate will include a real return that increases the purchasing power of the loaned funds plus a return that offsets the loss of purchasing power due to inflation.

Link 2, between price-level changes and interest rate, implies that as the price level is expected to change (e.g., because of excessive money supply), the interest rate will change, so that changes in the nominal interest rate completely offset changes in prices, keeping the real rate of interest constant. The change in interest rates will thus be equal to the percentage change in expected price levels, which equals the rate by which the increase in the money supply exceeds the real needs of the economy.

It should be clear by now that if by the end of the period, prices have changed more than was expected, the rate of interest would have been underestimated and borrowers would have gained at the expense of lenders. Similarly, lenders would have gained if the price changes had been overestimated.

Given the process by which interest rate changes are determined in a national economy, how do differentials in interest rates between different countries come about? Two additional relationships, shown in Figure 2-2 as links 3 and 4, contribute to the explanation. Link 3 relates price-level changes in different countries to exchange rate changes; it is usually referred to as the purchasing power parity (PPP) theorem. The other link, which relates differences in interest rates, is sometimes referred to as the international Fisher effect to distinguish it from the relationship of price-level changes and interest rates in a closed economy.

The PPP theorem can be stated in different ways, but the most common representation links the changes in exchange rates to those in relative prices.[15]

The relationship is derived from the basic idea that in the absence of trade restrictions, changes in the exchange rate mirror changes in the relative price levels in the two countries. At the same time, under conditions of free trade, prices of similar commodities cannot differ between two countries, because arbitragers will take advantage of such situations until price differences are eliminated. This is known as the law of one price. (That is, the rate of change in the exchange rate equals the difference in inflation rates.) Thus, link 3 in Figure 2-2 relates expected changes in exchange rates to the expected differences in inflation rates. Of course, it must be recognized that this statement, like all simple relationships, is based on some strong assumptions (e.g., that consumers in all countries have the same consumption basket and that all goods are equally tradable, so that relative price changes are not possible within one country). If these conditions are not met, the postulated relationship between the

---

[15] For a comprehensive review of PPP, see Officer (1982).

respective inflation rates and the exchange rate is approximate at best, even after accounting for problems of measurement.

The relationship between the interest rates in two countries and the expected exchange rate changes has already been discussed in general terms. Now the linkage between these rates can be treated in a more formal manner. In the absence of effective controls on capital flows, risk-neutral investors will employ their funds wherever the (expected) return is the highest. Thus, if the interest rates between two countries are unequal, investors transfer their funds to the country with the higher interest rate. Will the higher interest rate not come down under the influence of these flows? According to the international Fisher effect, the interest rate differential will exist only if the exchange rate is expected to change in such a way that the advantage of the higher interest rate is offset by the loss on the forex transactions. An investor in the low-interest country can convert its funds into the currency of the high-interest country and expect to earn a higher rate of interest, but its gain (in terms of higher interest rate) will be offset by the expected loss because of forex rate changes.

This relationship is based on expectations only. However, it is possible to replace the expected future spot exchange rate with the forward rate, given certain specific assumptions. This forward rate, like interest rates, is a contractual rate; this leads to the interest rate parity theorem. According to this theorem, the observed differences in the interest rates will be equal to the premium or the discount of the forward exchange rate over the spot rate. This relationship is represented by link 5 in Figure 2-2, and its mechanics have been discussed in the context of the operation of the forex market.

The PPP theorem is based upon the assumption of perfect arbitrage in markets for goods and services. Goods markets are, however, far from perfect; costless and instantaneous arbitrage is usually not possible. Therefore, it is often argued that because of imperfections in the goods markets, PPP is at best a long-run tendency, and any test of the theorem should examine the behavior of deviation from PPP over an extended period. If there is a direct link between national price levels and exchange rates, deviations from PPP, over many periods, should not be significantly different from zero. Finally, there could be an indirect link between inflation and the exchange rate, owing to free movement of capital.

A test of this proposition reveals that deviations from PPP have been constant under both fixed and flexible exchange rate regimes.[16] Thus, there is some support for the notion that higher inflation rates would eventually lead to a change in the exchange rate, whereby the cause may not be arbitrage in goods markets but rather arbitrage by way of national money markets, which is less costly.

The implication is that deviations from PPP may not correct themselves over the long run, which substantially diminishes the usefulness of the PPP concept in exchange rate forecasting. Data in Figure 2-3 illustrate deviations from PPP during the 1980s for Germany, Japan, and South Korea relative to the United States.

In summary, interest rate differences and exchange rate changes are linked in two ways: (1) through the international Fisher effect, which is based on expectations and (2) through the interest rate parity theorem, which reflects an actual, arbitraged relationship in the market.

The integration of the ideas represented by the five links of Figure 2-2 can be summarized as follows:

---

[16] Adler and Lehmann (1983).

FIGURE 2-3

Currency and Purchasing Power Changes Affecting International Competitiveness

	1980	1981	1982	1983	1984	1985	1986	1987
Germany								
Actual DM/U.S. $	1.9590 (December)	2.2548 (December)	2.3765 (December)	2.7238 (December)	3.1480 (December)	2.4613 (December)	1.9408 (December)	1.6354 (November)
Rate implied by PPP	1.9590 (December)	1.9335 (December)	2.0139 (December)	2.0197 (December)	2.0334 (December)	2.0961 (December)	2.0992 (December)	1.9512 (November)
Wholesale price index	100 (December)	107.8 (December)	114.1 (December)	115.8 (December)	119.2 (December)	121.9 (December)	118.3 (December)	115.6 (September)
Japan								
Actual ¥/U.S. $	203.00 (December)	219.90 (December)	235.00 (December)	232.20 (December)	251.10 (December)	200.50 (December)	159.10 (December)	132.55 (November)
Rate implied by PPP	203.00 (December)	187.37 (December)	186.56 (December)	179.05 (December)	173.16 (December)	171.74 (December)	159.77 (December)	144.54 (November)
Wholesale price index	100 (December)	101.4 (December)	103.20 (December)	100.9 (December)	100.7 (December)	99.5 (December)	90.2 (December)	87.2 (August)
South Korea								
Actual W/U.S. $	659.90 (December)	700.50 (December)	748.80 (December)	795.50 (December)	827.40 (December)	890.20 (December)	861.40 (December)	796.40 (November)
Rate implied by PPP	659.90 (December)	734.47 (December)	756.91 (December)	749.65 (December)	737.78 (December)	748.33 (December)	752.29 (December)	722.59 (November)
Wholesale price index	100 (December)	120.4 (December)	126.0 (December)	126.3 (December)	127.2 (December)	128.3 (December)	125.5 (December)	125.5 (November)
United States								
Wholesale price index	100 (December)	109.1 (December)	111.3 (December)	112.7 (December)	115.4 (December)	114.9 (December)	111.5 (December)	116.0 (November)

1. Monetary theory links different rates of excess money supply and changes in price levels.

2. Changes in price levels and changes in interest rates are linked by the Fisher effect.

3. Changes in price levels and changes in forex rates are linked by the PPP theorem.

4. Changes in interest rates and forex rates are linked ex ante by the international Fisher effect.

5. Changes in interest rates and forex rates are linked ex post by the forward rate by means of the interest rate parity theorem.

Anyone familiar with economic theory will recognize that the precise nature of each of these relationships continues to be the subject of considerable controversy. Questions can be raised about both the assumptions and the empirical verification of these relationships. If these relationships hold at all, they do so only under the assumption that the markets for goods, capital, and currencies reasonably meet the requirements for perfect markets, especially with respect to governmental regulations and restrictions. However, at this point the concern is not so much with empirical validation as with presenting a simple, consistent, and comprehensive set of relationships that can serve as a point of departure for further analysis.

[7] Forecasting Exchange Rates and Managerial Implications

Observers of markets with competing private, profit-seeking traders have long recognized that prices are determined by the anticipations of demand and supply. The pursuit of profits in speculative markets requires that market participants take future prices into account in their current buying and selling decisions. They form opinions about future prices by continually searching for information and interpreting it in order to make predictions. Those that perform this task well grow and dominate the market; losers are eliminated. This concept of market efficiency is based on the notion that current prices reflect all available information, including market participants' expectations about future prices and, further, that all new information that is received by the market is analyzed and immediately incorporated into expectations about future prices. From these expectations, decisions to buy and sell are made, and thus the expected prices are converted into current prices.

These considerations apply to all organized asset markets, which include markets for spot and forward forex. The current spot rate reflects anticipated supply and demand conditions, and the forward rate contains information about the future spot rate. This is because as a contractual price, the forward rate offers opportunities for speculative profits for those that correctly assess the future spot price relative to the current forward rate.

Because expectations of future spot rates are formed on the basis of currently available information (historical data) and an interpretation of its implications for the future, they tend to be subject to frequent and rapid revision. As previously noted, the actual future spot rate may therefore deviate markedly from the expectation embodied in the present forward rate for that maturity. These deviations are in the nature of a forecast error that is known only after the fact, i.e., when the future has become the present. Formally, the forecast error is expressed as

$$F_{t,n} - S_{t+n} = e_{t,n}$$

where $F_{t,n}$ represents the forward rates in period t for maturity n, S_{t+n} represents the actual spot rates at period $t + n$, and e reflects the difference. Another view considers these errors to be speculative profits or losses. Can they be consistently positive or negative? It is reasonable to assume that this is not the case. Otherwise, one would have to explain why consistent losers do not quit the market or why consistent winners are not imitated by others or do not increase their volume of activity, thus causing adjustment of the forward rate in the direction of their expectation. Barring such an explanation, one would expect that the forecast error is sometimes positive, sometimes negative, alternating in a random fashion, and driven by unexpected events in the economic and political environment. Over sufficiently long periods allowing a large number of decisions, $e_{t,n}$ should average out to zero. This is the statistical basis for the view that the forward rate is an unbiased forecast of the future spot rate.[17]

However, this definition of efficiency leaves out sources of bias that may be known to market participants and may be incorporated, quite rationally, into the forward rate. Thus, there may be systematic deviations of the forward rate from the expected future spot rate that are compatible with market efficiency. The latter concept refers only to the processing of information, yet the relevant information may well contain factors that cause systematic deviations of forward rates from expected future spot rates. Forecasting errors can therefore be classified as random or systematic, leading to unbiased or biased forecasts. The latter, in turn, may be based on inefficient pricing processes or may be perfectly consistent with an efficient market. Two significant causes for bias can be identified: political risk and exchange risk.[18]

[8] Political Risk

The incidence of political interference in the market process by government is a different matter altogether. If, for example, the U.K. government was prone to interfere with the rights of nonresidents' sterling assets, one might expect that those that purchase sterling for forward delivery would demand a premium: more sterling for every dollar, other things being equal. By the same token, one would expect U.K. interest rates to be systematically higher than warranted on the basis of expected exchange rate changes alone.

To illustrate this point in terms of interest rates: Given a spot rate of $2 per pound, the 12-month forward is $1.92, while the expected future spot rate is assumed to be $1.94 under these conditions. Of course, the latter cannot be observed directly; the

---

[17] If the series of errors has a mean value of zero, it represents a martingale process. If the series $e_{t,n}$ is purely random, i.e., not correlated with any past or future value, it is referred to as white noise, which is the formal requirement for an efficient market. Tests of market efficiency on this basis involve testing two propositions jointly: (1) They test the underlying model that generates forex rates and (2) they test the proposition that participants indeed set the forward rate equal to the expected future spot rate. Thus, conclusive empirical verification of the existence of market efficiency is virtually impossible to achieve.

[18] A small source of bias or systematic differences is a technicality known in the literature as the Siegel paradox, which is based on a mathematical concept called Jensen's inequality. If residents of two countries consume a common basket of goods, the forex rate generally lies between the expectation of the future rate defined in terms of one currency and the expectation of the future rate defined in terms of the other currency. However, the practical significance of the Siegel paradox is negligible when the (expected) variance of the exchange rate is not excessive, and it disappears altogether when PPP holds. For a thorough analysis of this phenomenon, see Beenstock (1985).

only evidence would be an "undershooting" of the forward rate by $0.02, or, in terms of interest rates, an interest differential of 100 basis points per annum on average, provided that the political risk premium is constant over time and that participants do not make systematic errors in judging the future exchange rate of the pound.

While this example might clarify the effect of political risk on forward rates and interest differentials, it is much more difficult to estimate this premium. Even though this may be an intractable task, a modest contribution can be made by attempting to clarify conceptually the elements that comprise that catchall concept of political risk.

To begin, the term "political risk" is quite broad and cannot readily be made operational. The focus should probably be on current and potential effects of the political environment on investors' transactions. More precisely, one should be concerned with the probability that changes in the political environment will reduce returns to the point where investments would no longer be acceptable on the basis of predetermined criteria.[19] Obviously, exchange controls (i.e., quantitative restrictions on international flows of financial assets) that affect existing positions of nonresidents would fall under this category. What is less often recognized is that quantitative restrictions in domestic credit markets have the same effect: They add an additional constraining element to arbitrage.

Government actions that affect exchange rates or interest rates through markets, such as open-market operations by the central bank, are generally held to contribute to exchange risk, which can be taken fully into account by market participants in setting forward premiums and interest rate differentials, respectively. But the differentiation between quantitative restrictions and price fluctuations is not so clear.

Further, exchange rate fluctuations may themselves give rise to exchange controls if the body politic considers them excessive. In any case, market efficiency presupposes that prices are arrived at by competitive, profit-seeking participants. If a central bank is not motivated by profitability and if its actions are so massive that it succeeds in shifting prices from equilibrium points, the forward rate or interest differential will not be an unbiased predictor, nor will the market be efficient.

A further point of distinction is necessary. Risk refers to uncertainty, here, the uncertainty of future capital controls. It is therefore necessary to distinguish between interest differentials or premiums in the forward market that are caused by existing controls, which may place a taxlike burden on assets in a certain jurisdiction, and differentials that are due to expected, hence future, capital controls.[20]

[9] Exchange Risk

The analytical framework developed earlier suggests that exchange rates should not be affected by anything other than interest rates and inflation rates; thus, there should not be exchange risk premiums. However, that framework relies heavily on several very strong assumptions about economic behavior that may not be true in the real world.

One of the simplifying assumptions is that real interest rates are stable, so an unexpected change in monetary policy, for example, will affect only nominal rates. This assumes that prices of goods and services will adjust instantaneously to changes in

---

[19] Kobrin (1979).

[20] This point has been clearly made in Dooley and Isard (1980).

financial markets. This is obviously not the case. Prices for goods and services tend to be less flexible downward than prices of financial assets because of the existence of contractual relationships and, more prominently, the prevalence of market imperfections (e.g., unions, large corporations, and technological advantages). As a result, there will be transitory changes in real interest rates that may persist for some time when the change in monetary policy is not expected to last.

To illustrate, an unexpected increase (change from the expected trend) in the money supply leads to a drop in real interest rates. Prices (or price level) may increase or there may be a lag in the increase, depending on the elasticity of the prices. Output increases, but there is also a lag effect; output takes time to adjust to new levels. Exchange rates fall. Likewise, an unexpected decrease in the money supply leads to an increase in real interest rates. Prices may fall, but the magnitude and immediacy of the fall depends on the degree of price rigidity. Output also decreases, but there is a lag effect as well. Here, exchange rates rise.

Another assumption is the perfect substitutability of goods within a country and across borders, in effect, that all goods are homogeneous and there are no nontradable goods. This implies that both the law of one price and PPP hold. However, since PPP refers to the average price (i.e., price levels), it is possible, when arbitrage in goods' markets is imperfect, that PPP holds but the exchange rate changes. This would be the consequence of relative price changes in each country and the resultant impact on the commodity composition of trade. Conversely, it is possible for the exchange rate to remain unchanged while price-level changes differ at home and abroad.[21]

A final assumption in the equilibrium framework is the perfect substitutability of domestic and foreign financial assets. If domestic and foreign bonds are perfect substitutes, they must have the same expected real return; hence, differences in nominal interest rates can only mirror the expected exchange rate change.

The results of an equilibrium framework must be viewed as approximate, long-run tendencies only, since PPP may not hold for extended periods, the substitutability of assets may not be perfect, and the market for financial assets and real goods may not clear instantaneously.

When accounting for nonmoney assets, any investor in fixed-income investments faces a purchasing power risk because of the uncertainty of future inflation. As long as inflation rates are not perfectly positively correlated among countries, it pays to diversify portfolios internationally. In portfolio balance, therefore, it is theoretically possible that real return expectations differ between domestic and foreign securities because of residual purchasing power risk.[22] Put somewhat differently, systematic deviations from the international Fisher relationship are possible when a country has issued an excessive amount of government liabilities[23] relative to its share in the minimum variance, internationally diversified portfolio.[24] Accordingly, a premium above

---

[21] The conditions for the law of one price are therefore more stringent than those for PPP. It is frequently interpreted that the latter presumes that changes in price levels lead to changes in exchange rates, while the former allegedly implies that causation proceeds in the opposite direction. Both are equilibrium conditions, i.e., prices and exchange rates are simultaneously determined.

[22] There should be no residual exchange risk because there is a perfect negative correlation for deviation from PPP for any two currencies, guaranteeing, in principle, complete diversifiability.

[23] Government rather than private debt is necessary for a risk premium, for with private debt gains to borrowers will be losses to lenders, and the perfect negative correlation of such returns permits the complete elimination of this risk through an appropriate diversification strategy.

[24] See, e.g., Dornbusch (1980).

the expected depreciation could be explained as compensation for investors to increase their holdings of foreign currency assets, of which excessive amounts have been issued.[25]

The bottom line for management is that if such biases exist, they are not exploitable in a meaningful way. They are not recognizable before the fact, they are unstable, and they tend to be dominated by transaction costs and risks. This has important implications for corporate hedging and financing policies in an international context, but before attempting to deal with risk one must know what is exposed to exchange risk, and, in the context of a nonfinancial firm, this is not a trivial matter.

2.03 ASSESSING CORPORATE FOREIGN EXCHANGE RISK

The task of gauging the effect of forex rate changes on an enterprise begins with measuring its exposure to risk, i.e., the amount or value at risk. This issue is clouded by the fact that financial results for an enterprise tend to be compiled with methods based on the principles of accrual accounting. This means that the data provided are not those that are really relevant for business decision making, namely, future cash flows and their associated risk profiles. As a result, considerable efforts are expended, both by decision makers and students of exchange risk, in order to reconcile the differences between the effects of exchange rate changes on an enterprise in terms of accounting data, referred to as accounting or translation exposure, and the cash flow effects, referred to as economic (or sometimes transaction) exposure.[26]

[1] Accounting Exposure

The concept of accounting exposure arises from the need to translate accounts denominated in foreign currencies into the home currency of the reporting entity. (See Chapter 5 for more details.) The problem is most common when an enterprise has foreign affiliates that keep their books in the local currencies. For purposes of consolidation, these account records must somehow be translated into the reporting currency of the parent company. In this process, a decision must be made as to the exchange rate to be used for the translation of the various accounts. While income statements of foreign affiliates are typically translated at a periodic average rate, balance sheets pose a more serious challenge.

The underlying difficulties are revealed by the struggle of the accounting profession to agree on appropriate translation rules and the treatment of the resulting gains and losses. A comparative historical analysis of translation rules may best illustrate the issues at hand. Over time, U.S. companies have followed essentially four types of

---

[25] The foregoing considerations obscure the issue of diversifiable versus nondiversifiable risk in the broader context of an international capital asset pricing model. It would, for example, be risky to hold securities denominated in a currency whose value is positively correlated with that of other assets; the securities are afflicted with a risk that cannot be diversified away, and a risk premium would be required. But difficult questions arise as to the definition of "other assets" and the relevant consumption patterns of international investors.

[26] Many authors have referred to this conflict. For a well-focused report, see Showers (1988).

FIGURE 2-4

Methods of Translation for Balance Sheets

	Current/ Noncurrent	Monetary/ Nonmonetary	Temporal	Current/ Current
Assets				
Cash	C	C	C	C
Marketable securities (at market value)	C	C	C	C
Accounts receivable	C	C	C	C
Inventory (at cost)	C	H	H	C
Fixed assets	H	H	H	C
Liabilities				
Current liabilities	C	C	C	C
Long-term debt	H	C	C	C
Equity	Residual adjustment	Residual adjustment	Residual adjustment	Residual adjustment

Note: In the case of income statements, sales revenues and interest are generally translated at the average historical exchange rate that prevailed during the period; depreciation is translated at the appropriate historical exchange rate. Some of the general and administrative expenses as well as the cost of goods sold are translated at historical exchange rates; others are translated at current rates.

C: Assets and liabilities are translated at the current rate, or rate prevailing on the date of the balance sheet.

H: Assets and liabilities are translated at the historical rate.

translation methods, summarized in Figure 2-4. These four methods differ with respect to the presumed impact of exchange rate changes on the value of individual categories of assets and liabilities. Accordingly, each method can be identified by its manner of separating assets and liabilities into those that are exposed and, therefore, translated at the current rate (i.e., the rate prevailing on the date of the balance sheet), and those whose value is deemed to remain unchanged and that are therefore translated at the historical rate.

[2] Alternative Accounting Methods

The current/noncurrent method of translation divides assets and liabilities into current and noncurrent categories, using maturity as the distinguishing criterion; only current items are presumed to change in value when the local currency appreciates or depreciates vis-à-vis the home currency. Supporting this method is the economic rationale that forex rates are essentially fixed but subject to occasional adjustments upward or downward that tend to reverse in time. This assumption reflected reality, to some extent, in the industrialized countries during the fixed-rate system. However, with subsequent changes in the international financial environment, it has become outmoded, although this translation method is still being used in some European countries.

Under the monetary/nonmonetary method, all items explicitly defined in terms of monetary units are translated at the current exchange rate, regardless of their maturity. Nonmonetary items in the balance sheet, such as tangible assets, are translated at the historical exchange rate. The underlying assumption is that the value of such assets increases or decreases in local currency terms immediately after a devaluation or revaluation to a degree that compensates fully for the exchange rate change.

A similar but more sophisticated translation approach supports the so-called temporal method. Here, the exchange rate used to translate balance sheet items depends on the valuation method used for a particular item on the balance sheet. Thus, if an item is carried on the balance sheet of the affiliate at its current value, it is translated using the current exchange rate. Alternatively, items carried at historical cost are translated at the historical exchange rate. This method synchronizes the time dimension of valuation with the method of translation. As long as foreign affiliates compile balance sheets under traditional historical cost principles, the temporal method gives essentially the same results as the monetary/nonmonetary method. However, when current value accounting is used, i.e., when accounts are adjusted for inflation, the temporal method calls for the use of the current exchange rate throughout the balance sheet.

The temporal method provided the conceptual base for the Financial Accounting Standard Board's (FASB) Statement of Financial Accounting Standards (SFAS) No. 8, which came into effect in 1976 for all U.S.-based companies and for non-U.S. companies that had to adopt U.S. accounting principles if they intended to raise funds in the public markets of the United States.

The temporal method raises a more general issue: the relationship between translation and valuation methods for accounting purposes. When methods of valuation provide results that do not reflect economic reality, translation fails to remedy that deficiency but tends to make the distortion very apparent. To illustrate this point, companies with real estate holdings abroad financed by local currency mortgages found that under SFAS No. 8, their earnings were subject to considerable translation losses and gains. This came about because the value of their assets remained constant, as they were carried on the books at historical cost and translated at historical exchange rates, while the value of their local currency liabilities increased or decreased with every twitch of the exchange rate between reporting dates.

In contrast, U.S. companies whose foreign affiliates produced internationally traded goods (e.g., minerals) felt comfortable valuing all of their tangible assets on a dollar basis. These companies were the ones that did not like the transition of the current/current method where all assets and liabilities are translated at the exchange rate prevailing on the reporting date. They felt rightly that the assumption that the value of all assets denominated in the local currency of the given foreign affiliate changes in direct proportion to the exchange rate change did not reflect the economic realities of their businesses.

[3] Statement of Financial Accounting Standards No. 52

In order to accommodate the conflicting requirements of companies in different situations while maintaining a semblance of conformity and comparability, at the end of 1981 the FASB issued SFAS No. 52, replacing SFAS No. 8. (See Chapter 5.) SFAS No. 52 uses the current/current method as the basic translation rule. At the same time, it mitigates the consequences by allowing companies to move translation losses directly to a special subaccount in the net worth section of the balance sheet, instead of moving

FIGURE 2-5

Application of SFAS No. 52

In applying SFAS No. 52, a company and its accountants must make two decisions in sequence. First, they must determine the functional currency of the entity whose accounts are to be consolidated. For all practical purposes, the choice is between local currency and the U.S. dollar. In essence, there are a number of specific criteria that provide guidelines for this determination. As usual, extreme cases are relatively easily classified: A foreign affiliate engaged in retailing local goods and services has the local currency as its functional currency, while a "border plant" that receives the majority of its inputs from abroad and ships the bulk of the output outside of the host country has the dollar as its functional currency. If the functional currency is the dollar, foreign currency items on its balance sheet have to be restated into dollars and any gains and losses are moved through the income statement, just as under SFAS No. 8. If, on the other hand, the functional currency is determined to be the local currency, a second issue arises: whether the entity operates in a high-inflation environment. "High-inflation countries" is defined as those whose cumulative three-year inflation rate exceeds 100 percent. In that case, essentially the same principles as in SFAS No. 8 are followed. In the case where the cumulative inflation rate falls short of 100 percent, the foreign affiliate's books are to be translated using the current exchange rate for all items, and any gains or losses are to go directly as a charge or credit to the equity accounts.

SFAS No. 52 has a number of other fairly complex provisions regarding the treatment of hedge contracts, the definition of transactional gains and losses, and the accounting for intercompany transactions.

In essence, SFAS No. 52 allows management much more flexibility to present the impact of exchange rate variations in accordance with perceived economic reality; by the same token, it provides greater scope for manipulation of reported earnings and reduces the comparability of financial data for different firms.

---

them to current income. This provision may be viewed as a mere gimmick without much substance, providing at best a signaling function indicating to users of accounting information that translation gains and losses are of a different nature than that of items normally found in income statements.

A more significant innovation of SFAS No. 52 is the functional currency concept, which gives a company the opportunity to identify the primary economic environment of its foreign affiliate and to select the appropriate (functional) currency for each of the corporation's foreign entities. This approach reflects the official recognition by the accounting profession that the location of an entity does not necessarily indicate the relevant currency for a particular business. Thus, SFAS No. 52 represents an attempt to take into account the fact that exchange rate changes affect different companies in different ways and that rigid, general rules treating different circumstances in the same manner provides misleading information.

In order to adjust to the diversity of real life, SFAS No. 52 became quite complex. Figure 2-5 provides a brief guide to the logic of the standard.[27]

Even with the increased flexibility of SFAS No. 52, users of accounting information must be aware that there are three systematic sources of error that mislead those responsible for exchange risk management:

---

[27] Those interested in accounting aspects will find a number of useful publications by the large accounting firms. See, e.g., Price Waterhouse (1981).

1. Accounting data do not capture all commitments of the firm that give rise to exchange risk.

2. Because of the historical cost principle, accounting values of assets and liabilities do not reflect the contribution to total expected net cash flow of the firm.

3. Translation rules do not distinguish between expected and unexpected exchange rate changes.

Regarding the first point, it must be recognized that commitments entered into by the firm in terms of foreign currency, e.g., a contract involving the purchase or a sale of goods, are not normally booked until the merchandise has been shipped. At best, such obligations are shown as contingent liabilities if they are judged to be material.

More important, accounting data reveal very little about the ability of the firm to change costs, prices, and markets quickly. Alternatively, the firm may be committed by strategic decisions, such as investment in plant and facilities. Such commitments are important criteria in determining the existence and magnitude of exchange risk.

The second point surfaced in the previous discussion of the temporal method: If asset values differ from market values, translation, however sophisticated, will not redress this shortcoming. Thus, many of the perceived problems of SFAS No. 8 had their roots not so much in translation but in the fact that in an environment of inflation and exchange rate changes, the lack of current value accounting frustrates the best translation efforts.

Finally, translation rules do not take into account the fact that exchange rate changes have two components: (1) expected changes that are already reflected in the prices of assets and the costs of liabilities (relative interest rates) and (2) the unexpected deviations from the expected change that constitute the true sources of currency risk. The significance of this distinction is clear: Managers have already taken account of expected changes; risk management efforts must focus on the effect of unexpected changes, as expected changes are reflected in prevailing prices and costs.

[4] Economic or Cash Flow Exposure

The concept of economic exposure derives directly from the nature of the (nonfinancial) firm. Management in its entrepreneurial function perceives opportunities to generate profits, i.e., expected positive net cash flows. Those net cash flows are often subject to unexpected exchange rate changes. Since the firm claims its special expertise in the uncovering of market opportunities for real goods and services, its basic objective is to shield its net cash flows, and thus the value of the enterprise, from unanticipated exchange rate changes.[28]

This sketch of economic exchange risk has a number of significant implications, some of which seem to be at variance with ideas frequently found in the literature and apparent business practices. Specifically, there are implications regarding (1) the question of whether exchange risk originates from monetary or nonmonetary transactions; (2) a reevaluation of traditional perspectives such as transaction risk; and (3) the role of forecasting exchange rates in the context of corporate forex risk management.

---

[28] For specific suggestions on distinguishing between the effects of unanticipated exchange rate changes on the firm and other related events, see Hekman (1986).

[5] Contractual Versus Noncontractual Returns

Returns on contractual assets and liabilities of a firm are fixed in nominal, monetary terms. Such returns (e.g., earnings from fixed-income securities and receivables and the negative returns on various liabilities) are relatively easy to analyze with respect to exchange rate changes; when they are denominated in terms of foreign currency, their terminal value changes directly in proportion to the exchange rate change. Thus, with respect to financial items, the firm is concerned only about net assets or liabilities denominated in foreign currency, to the extent that maturities (or duration, to be precise) are matched.

For assets with noncontractual returns, it is much more difficult to gauge the impact of an exchange rate change. While conventional discussions of exchange risk focus almost exclusively on financial assets, for trading and manufacturing firms at least, it is equipment, real estate, buildings, and inventories that make the decisive contribution to the total cash flow of those firms and are therefore fundamental. And returns on such assets are affected in quite complex ways by changes in exchange rates. The most essential consideration is the reaction of the firm's prices and costs to an unexpected exchange rate change. For example, if prices and costs react immediately and fully to offset exchange rate changes, the firm's cash flows are not exposed to exchange risk, since they will not be affected in terms of the base currency. Thus, under those specific circumstances the value of noncontractual assets is not affected.

This point can be illustrated in the context of inventories. The value of an inventory (in a foreign subsidiary or at the parent) is determined not only by changes in the exchange rate but also by a subsequent price change of the product, to the extent that the cause of this price change is the exchange rate change. Thus, the dollar value of an inventory destined for export may increase when the currency of the destination country appreciates, provided that its local currency prices do not decrease by the full percentage of the appreciation.

The effect on the local currency price depends, in part, on competition in the market. The behavior of foreign and local competitors, in turn, depends on capacity use, market share objectives, the likelihood of cost adjustments, and a host of other factors.

Of course, firms are interested not only in the value change or the behavior of cash flows of a single asset but also in the behavior of all cash flows. Again, price and cost adjustments caused by an unexpected exchange rate change need to be analyzed. For example, a firm that requires components from abroad for production usually finds its stream of cash outlays rising whenever its local currency depreciates against foreign currencies. Yet, the depreciation may cause foreign suppliers to lower prices in terms of foreign currencies for the purpose of maintaining volume or mitigating or even neutralizing the effects of the currency change.

[a] **Currency Denomination.** In this context, it is worthwhile to distinguish between the currency in which cash flows are denominated and the currency that determines the size of the cash flows. In the example just mentioned, it does not matter whether, as a matter of business practice, the firm may contract, be invoiced in, and pay for each individual shipment in its own local currency. If foreign exporters do not provide price concessions, the cash outflow of the importer behaves just like a foreign currency cash flow; even though payments are made in local currency, they occur in greater

amounts. As a result, the cash flow, even while denominated in local currency, is determined by the relative value of the foreign currency.[29]

The choice of currency in which the accounting records are kept may complicate things further. For example, any debt contracted by the firm in foreign currency is always recorded in the currency of the country where the corporate entity is located. However, the value of its legal obligation is established in the currency in which the contract is denominated.

It is possible, therefore, that a firm selling in export markets may record assets and liabilities in its local currency and invoice periodic shipments in a foreign currency, and yet, if prices in the market are dominated by transactions in a third country, the cash flows received may behave as if they were in that third currency. To illustrate, a Brazilian firm selling coffee to Germany may keep its records in cruzeiros, invoice in deutsche marks, have deutsche mark–denominated receivables, and physically collect deutsche mark cash, only to find that its revenue stream behaves as if it were in U.S. dollars. This occurs because deutsche mark prices for each consecutive shipment are immediately adjusted to reflect world market prices, which, in turn, tend to be determined in U.S. dollars.[30]

[b] Time Dimension. An additional dimension of exchange risk involves the element of time. In the very short run, virtually all local currency prices for real goods and services (although not necessarily for financial assets) remain unchanged after an unexpected exchange rate change. However, over a longer period, prices and costs move inversely to spot rate changes; the tendency is for PPP and the law of one price to hold.

In reality, this price adjustment process takes place over a great variety of time patterns. These patterns depend not only on the products involved but also on market structure, the nature of competition, general business conditions, government policies such as price controls, and a number of other factors. Considerable work has been done on the phenomenon of pass-through of price changes caused by unexpected exchange rate changes.[31] And yet, because all of the factors that determine the extent and speed of pass-through are firm-specific and can be analyzed only on a case-by-case basis at the level of the operating entity of the firm, the strategic business unit, generalizations remain difficult.

The firm's foreign currency exposure is greatly influenced by the time frame within which management cannot react to unexpected rate changes by (1) raising prices; (2) changing markets for inputs and outputs; and/or (3) adjusting production and sales volumes. Sometimes, at least one of these reactions is possible within a relatively short time; at other times, the firm is locked in through contractual or strategic commitments

---

[29] The functional currency concept introduced in SFAS No. 52 is similar to the currency of determination, but not exactly. "Currency of determination" refers to revenue and operating expense flows, respectively; the functional currency concept pertains to an entity as a whole, and is, therefore, less precise.

[30] The significance of this distinction is that the currency of denomination is relatively readily subject to management discretion, through the choice of invoicing currency. Prices and cash flows, however, are determined by competitive conditions, which are typically beyond the immediate control of the firm.

[31] For a review of the literature, see Levi (1983), and, more recently, Flood and Lessard (1986). For recent illustrations, see "Dollar Drop Helps Those Who Help Themselves," Federal Reserve Bank of Chicago, *Chicago Fed Letter,* No. 7 (Mar. 1988).

extending considerably into the future. Again, firms that are free to react instantaneously and fully to adverse unexpected rate changes are not subject to exchange risk.

A further important implication is that exchange risk stems from the firm's position in the market for inputs and outputs, rather than from any specific international involvement. Thus, companies engaged only in domestic transactions that have dominant foreign competitors may notice the effect of exchange rate changes in their cash flows as much as or even more than some firms that are actively engaged in exports, imports, or foreign direct investment.

[6] Implementation of Economic Exposure Analysis

From this analytical framework, some practical implications emerge for the assessment of economic exposure. First of all, the firm must project its cost and revenue streams over a planning horizon that represents the period during which the firm is locked in, or constrained from reacting to unexpected exchange rate changes. It must then assess the impact of a deviation of the actual exchange rate from the rate used in the projection of costs and revenues. Thus, sensitivity analysis is called for with respect to the impact of unexpected exchange rate changes.

Subsequently, the effects on the various cash flows of the firm must be netted over product lines and markets to account for diversification effects where gains and losses could cancel out, wholly or in part. The remaining net loss or gain is the focus of economic exposure management. For a multiunit, multiproduct, multinational corporation, the net exposure may not be very large at all because of the many offsetting effects. In contrast, enterprises that have invested in the development of one or two major foreign markets are typically subject to considerable fluctuations of their net cash flows, regardless of whether they invoice in their own or in the foreign currency. The same holds for those that are exposed to competition from dominant foreign rivals. Figure 2-6 shows how exposure might be estimated using statistical techniques.

For practical purposes, three questions capture the extent of a company's foreign exchange exposure:

1. How quickly can the firm adjust prices in order to offset the effect of an unexpected exchange rate change on profit margins?

2. How quickly can the firm change sources for inputs and markets for outputs? Or how diversified are a company's factor and product markets?

3. To what extent do volume changes associated with unexpected exchange rate changes have an effect on the value of assets?

Normally, the executives within business firms who can supply the best estimates on these issues tend to be those directly involved with purchasing, marketing, and production. Forex specialists who focus exclusively on credit and foreign exchange markets may easily miss the essence of corporate forex risk.

[7] Critique of the Traditional View

The concept of forex exposure developed so far, while consistent with classical cash flow analysis, differs in significant respects not only from the accounting concept of exposure but also from the traditional view of transaction exposure.

FIGURE 2-6

A Statistical Perspective on Exposure

Since the essence of economic exposure of a business firm is the movement of its cash flows together with exchange rate changes, it can be represented using regression techniques.[a] A multiple linear regression of the future domestic currency market price on a set of forex rates for the corresponding periods will produce coefficients whose dimension is units of foreign currency. A coefficient can be positive, negative, or zero, depending on the nature of the relationship. The regression separates the net cash flow changes and the change in the market price of the firm into two components; one part is correlated to the movements in exchange rates and one part is independent of them. Hedging techniques can reduce the first component, which reflects economic forex exposure; hedging techniques cannot reduce the other part, which is randomly determined.

While the value of the firm is represented by the present value of its future cash flows after tax, the price of the firm's stock can be used as a proxy for this value. When changes in stock market price are regressed on a set of changes in forex rates for the same periods, coefficients associated with each currency indicate the amount of exposure in that currency. The t-statistic indicates whether the coefficient is statistically significant. The coefficient of determination (R^2) indicates the percentage of the total variability that is explained by the regression coefficients. These are indicators of the amount of total risk that can and cannot be hedged.

The regression equation is usually stated in the following form:

$$CF_t = a + bEXCH_t + u_t$$

where CF_t is the dollar value of cash flows during period t, $EXCH_t$ is the nominal exchange rate (dollar value of one unit of foreign currency) during period t, and u is the random error term with mean of zero.[b]

This model is designed to develop a hedge ratio appropriate to the firm's economic exposure. A crucial assumption in the model is stability of the underlying relationships, because it is the persistence of the comovement over time that makes the hedge effective.

The model can be refined as well to decompose the spot rate in expected and unexpected changes. This can be accomplished by measuring the change in exchange rate as the difference in the future rate (at $t - 1$) at the spot rate (at t).

While theoretically correct, this regression may be of little practical assistance if the t-values of the coefficients are small, i.e., when the standard deviation of the coefficient is large relative to the point estimate. This situation occurs when the firm has hedged its exposure by means of the currency denomination of its debt and/or the forward exchange market or both or when there are other causes of sampling error.[c]

---

[a] See M. Adler and B. Dumas, "Exposure to Currency Risk: Definition and Measurement," *Financial Management* (Summer 1984), pp. 41–50.

[b] See C.K. Garner and A.C. Shapiro, "A Practical Method of Assessing Foreign Exchange Risk," *Midland Corporate Finance Journal* (Fall 1984), pp. 6–17.

[c] See Maurice D. Levi, "Measuring Foreign Exchange Exposure From Regression Coefficients: A Practical Appraisal," Working Paper, University of British Columbia, July 1987.

Transaction exposure typically involves an export or import transaction giving rise to a foreign currency receivable or payable. On the surface, when the exchange rate changes, the value of this export or import transaction is affected in terms of the domestic currency. However, after careful analysis, it becomes apparent that the exchange risk results exclusively from a financial investment (the foreign currency receivable) or a foreign currency liability (the loan from a supplier) that is purely incidental to the underlying export or import transaction; it could have arisen in and of itself through independent foreign borrowing and lending. Thus, what is involved here are simply foreign currency assets and liabilities, whose value is contractually fixed in nominal currency terms.

While this traditional analysis of transactions exposure is correct in a narrow, formal sense, it is relevant only for financial institutions. Returns from financial assets and liabilities fixed in nominal terms can be shielded from losses with relative ease through cash payments in advance (with appropriate discounts), through the factoring of receivables, or by way of the use of forward exchange contracts, unless unexpected exchange rate changes have a systematic effect on credit risk.[32] However, the essential assets of nonfinancial firms have noncontractual returns (i.e., revenue and cost streams from the production and sale of their goods and services that can respond to exchange rate changes in very different ways). Consequently, these assets are characterized by forex exposure that differs significantly from that of firms with contractual returns.[33]

[8] Corporate Exchange Risk in a Theoretical Perspective

It may be useful to summarize the effect of unexpected exchange rate changes on the internationally involved firm by drawing on some well-known parity conditions. Given sufficient time, competitive forces and arbitrage neutralize the impact of exchange rate changes on the returns to assets; the relationship between rates of devaluation and inflation differentials leads these factors to neutralize the impact of the changes on the value of the firm as well. This simply reflects the principles of PPP and the law of one price operating at the level of the firm. On the liability side, the cost of debt tends to adjust as debt is repriced at the end of the contractual period in order to reflect (revised) expected exchange rate changes. And returns on equity also reflect required rates of return; in a competitive market, these are influenced by expected exchange rate changes.

In the long run, a firm operating in this setting will not experience increasing exchange risk. However, because of a variety of contractual or, more important, strategic commitments, these equilibrium conditions rarely hold in the short and medium term. Therefore, forex exposure and, significantly, its management are made relevant by these temporary deviations.

2.04 MANAGEMENT OF ECONOMIC EXPOSURE: MANAGEMENT AND HEDGING

Corporate forex exposure originates with the cash flows associated with the operations of the firm; that is, the analysis must begin with the asset side. For the trading or manufacturing firm, liabilities are secondary in the sense that such companies have liabilities only because they have assets, with all of the concomitant risks and headaches involved in ownership and operation of assets. However, before the problem

---

[32] Conventional forex management is concerned only with nominal gains and losses in the numeraire currency of the firm. Protection of returns in real terms involves more complex considerations.

[33] It is therefore good practice to segregate for analytical purposes the "finance company" business composed of purely financial assets, such as cash and receivables, and the associated financial liabilities from the remainder of the firm in order to focus on the "real" side of the business.

of appropriate asset and liability strategies can be tackled, the issue of forex rate forecasting must be addressed.

[1] Forecasting for Risk Control

Few firms commit real assets in order to take currency positions. Rather, they get involved with foreign currencies in the course of market competition. Rather than being based on currency expectations, competitive advantage is based on expertise in such areas as production, marketing, the organization of people, or technical resources. Any special expertise in forecasting forex rates can usually be put to use without incurring the risks and cost of committing funds to real assets. Thus, most managers of nonfinancial enterprises are in decision-making roles only because their employers produce and sell goods; they do not act principally as speculative forex traders.

Forecasting exchange rate changes, however, is important for planning purposes. To the extent that all significant managerial tasks are concerned with the future, anticipated exchange rate changes are a major input into virtually all decisions of enterprises involved in and affected by international transactions. However, the task of forecasting forex rates for planning and decision-making purposes, with regard to determining the most likely exchange rate, is quite different from attempting to beat the market in order to derive speculative profits.

Expected exchange rate changes are revealed by market prices when rates are free to reach their competitive levels. Organized futures or forward markets provide inexpensive information regarding future exchange rates, using the best available data and judgment. Thus, whenever profit-seeking, well-informed traders can take positions, forward rates, prices of future contracts, and interest differentials for instruments with similar risk levels (but denominated in different currencies) provide good indicators of expected exchange rates. In this fashion, an input for corporate planning and decision making is readily available in all currencies where there are no effective exchange controls. The advantage of such market-based rates over in-house forecasts is that they are both less expensive and likely to be more accurate. Market rates are determined by those that tend to have the best information and track record; incompetent market participants lose money and tend to be removed as market participants over time.

The nature of the market-based expected exchange rate should not lead to confusing notions about the accuracy of prediction. In speculative markets, all decisions are based on the interpretation of past data; however, new information surfaces constantly. Therefore, market-based forecasts rarely come true. The actual price of a currency will either be below or above the rate expected by the market. Any predictable, economically meaningful bias would be corrected by the transactions of profit-seeking transactors.[34]

The importance of market-based forecasts in determining the forex exposure of the firm is that of a benchmark against which the economic consequences of deviations must be measured. This can be put in the form of a concrete question: How will the expected net cash flow of the firm behave if the future spot exchange rate is not equal

---

[34] See supra section 2.03.

to the rate predicted by the market when commitments are made? The nature of this kind of forecast is completely different from an attempt to outguess the forex markets.

[2] Financial Versus Operating Strategies

When operating cash inflows and contractual outflows from liabilities are affected by exchange rate changes, a general principle suggests itself: Any effect on cash inflows and outflows should cancel out as much as possible. This can be achieved by maneuvering assets, liabilities, or both. Among the operating policies are the shifting of markets for output, sources of supply, product lines, and production facilities as a defensive reaction to adverse exchange rate changes. It is obvious that such measures will be very costly, especially if undertaken over a short span of time. Therefore, operating policies designed to reduce or eliminate exposure are undertaken only as a last resort, when less expensive options have been exhausted.[35]

It is not surprising, therefore, that exposure management focuses not on the asset side, but primarily on the liability side of the firm's balance sheet. The asset side is largely determined by broad strategic decisions, for instance, regarding in which market the company should sell its products; changes in the asset side can only be made slowly. Changes in the liability side are comparatively easy to make. To be precise, corporate forex management becomes a matter of choosing the appropriate currency denomination of debt (and financial assets) and a suitable maturity structure in terms of the interest period.[36]

[3] Debt Denomination: Strategy Versus Tactics

Each unit of corporate debt must be denominated in one currency or another. When international debt markets are not distorted in a systematic fashion by exchange or credit market controls, the interest differentials closely reflect the expected appreciation or depreciation of the currency over the period during which the interest rate is contractually fixed. Thus, the expected cost of debt denominated in all currencies for which competitive international markets exist is the same for all debts. However, when future currency values differ from the expected value, the realized cost of debt in different currencies varies. The principle of exposure management is to cause this variance to offset any impact of this currency on the asset side.

If simulations for expected forex values (deviations from the expected rate) over a reasonable range of outcomes show that the firm may not have sufficient capacity for debt to hedge fully against a large swing in cash flows, the firm could use phantom debt (i.e., forward contracts or currency swaps).

This raises the issue of the appropriate role of forward contracts in exposure management. It must be recognized that forward contracts in exposure management are simply tools to change the currency of denomination of financial assets or liabilities. For this reason, some of the literature on foreign currency risk management carefully distinguishes between covering and hedging. Covering a transaction means simply to

---

[35] See Srinivasulu (1981).

[36] It is necessary to distinguish here between maturity of the interest period and maturity with respect to the availability of funds. On floating rate loans, the former is considerably shorter than the latter.

change its effective currency denomination. Whether such a change will also hedge a position depends entirely on the nature of the exposure. For example, an importer with a foreign currency payable may cover it with a forward contract, which makes it, in effect, a domestic currency liability. If, however, the pricing of the imported products follows the foreign currency (currency of determination), the cover operation exposes its expected net cash flow to exchange risk.

Debt denomination therefore is the overriding strategic consideration. It can be achieved either through outright borrowing in the desired currency or indirectly by the use of forward contracts and swaps. For example, foreign currency debt can be turned into U.S. dollar debt by entering into a commitment to purchase the foreign currency at a future point in time, taking interest and principal into account. Also, dollar debt can be turned into foreign currency debt by contracting to deliver foreign currency in the future in return for dollars.

Once management has decided, based on exposure analysis, on the appropriate currency denomination of its debt, it must choose the method of implementing that decision. It can choose its denomination directly, through borrowing, or indirectly, through forward contracts; in choosing, it must assess such factors as government restrictions that may limit access to markets, transaction costs, tax factors, accounting practices, and financial public relations (the maintenance of certain financial ratios). Further differences in liquidity and flexibility must be considered.[37] But these are tactical decisions; the strategic decision involves the determination of the appropriate currency denomination of debt.

Of course, when markets are controlled, the decision to borrow may give rise to arbitrage opportunities that can be exploited by means of swaps and parallel loans, resulting in special gains or the avoidance of excess interest costs. If the achievement of such gains does not conflict with the desired debt denomination from an exposure point of view, the decision is clear. If, however, exposure analysis calls for debt denomination in, e.g., U.S. dollars, but because of capital market controls or subsidization, particularly inexpensive local currency loans are available while forward markets are nonexistent, the firm is faced with a painful trade-off between the expected (but uncertain) gains from borrowing the "cheap" currency, and a net cash flow exposure to the vagaries of the exchange rate.

Only after all avenues of debt policy have been explored does the firm resort to these types of operating, or asset, strategies if the remaining exposure is unacceptably large. The reason is simply that changes in debt denomination are relatively inexpensive to implement.

The following is a summary of the steps involved in managing economic exposure:

1. Estimation of the planning horizon, as determined by the reaction period

2. Determination of the expected future spot rate

3. Estimation of the expected revenue and cost streams, given the expected spot rate

4. Estimation of the effect on revenue and expense streams of unexpected exchange rate changes

5. Choice of the appropriate currency for debt denomination

6. Estimation of the necessary amount of foreign currency debt

---

[37] For an extensive analysis of debt denomination under various conditions, including the incidence of taxes, see Jacque and Lang (1987).

7. Determination of the average interest period of debt

8. Selection between direct or indirect debt denomination

9. Decision on the trade-off between arbitrage gains and exchange risk stemming from exposure in markets where rates are distorted by controls

10. Decision about "residual" risk; considering adjustments to business operations and strategy

Realistically, a nonfinancial firm should not expect that exchange risk can be hedged completely with debt denomination, either direct or indirect. This is because of the nature of its assets; while a firm with a portfolio consisting only of assets with contractual returns can hedge ("immunize") its value in nominal terms, an enterprise whose assets yield, for the most part, noncontractual returns cannot hedge its exchange risk perfectly by way of appropriate debt denomination. This is because a given exchange rate change has a different effect on the return of (noncontractual) assets than on (contractual) liabilities. Still, this residual exchange risk should be reasonably small in most circumstances, and it does not detract from the importance of debt denomination as the lowest-cost hedging policy. Figure 2-7 explains in technical terms the effects of exchange rate changes on contractual and noncontractual cash flows.

[4] Foreign Currency Options and Exchange Risk Management

Contractual cash flows denominated in a foreign currency can be hedged against unexpected changes of the exchange rate through the use of forward contracts and swaps. However, a company may often be confronted with contingent cash inflows or outflows denominated in foreign currencies. The most common case is when a company submits a bid for a foreign project; should the firm win the bid and complete the project, it would receive a certain amount of foreign currency. In this case, the forward contract is a perfect hedge instrument only if the firm is certain of winning the bid for the project. If the firm loses the bid, it will still be obliged to perform under the forward contract.

Suppose that a U.S. company bids for a project in the United Kingdom, with payments to be received in pounds. If the company does not hedge this contingent open position and the bid is awarded, the actual dollar cash inflow will be less if the future pound-dollar exchange rate is lower than expected at the time the bid was submitted. Thus, the firm must hedge this contingent open position against unexpected downward changes in the exchange rate. If certain instruments would give the firm the right to sell pounds for dollars at a predetermined rate, subject to the condition of winning the contract, this contingent open position could be perfectly hedged.

In fact, such instruments do exist in part, in the form of put and call foreign exchange options. In the preceding case, the firm would buy a call option on dollars, that is, the equivalent to a put option on pounds, which would give the firm the right to buy dollars at a predetermined rate (exercise price) on a predetermined date (maturity date) subject to the firm's winning the contract. Figure 2-8 summarizes the hedging policies that should be undertaken when a firm is exposed to contingent and fixed open positions. Unfortunately, options are usually written only on the value of the currency, not on the award of the contract. Thus, the firm still has exposure with respect to the value of the option, determined largely by the change in the expected volatility of the currency over the remaining life of the option.

FIGURE 2-7

Debt Denomination and Uncertain Cash Flows

The cash flows of a firm can be divided into both noncontractual and contractual components. Cash flows generated by operating assets fall in the former category; cash flows from liabilities belong to the latter. In terms of corporate forex exposure analysis, this difference is important. Indeed, a further distinction must be made with respect to noncontractual cash flows, which behave either deterministically or nondeterministically in response to exchange rate changes.

The following symbols are used to analyze the implications of these distinctions:

C = contractual cash flows fixed in terms of foreign currency
$\tilde{C}$ = random cash flows in terms of foreign currency
$\tilde{S}$ = random exchange rate
H = amount of liabilities used for hedging against exchange risk

For simplicity, it is assumed that each random variable ($\tilde{C}$ and $\tilde{S}$) can take only two values in the illustration that follows.

1. Contractual Cash Flows

At the end of the period, C units of foreign currency (FC) are received, where their total value in terms of domestic currency (DC) is $C \times \tilde{S}$. In this case, exchange risk can be perfectly hedged by having liabilities equal to C at the end of the period.

	End-Of-Period Cash Flow	
	FC	**DC**
Cash flow	C	$C \times \tilde{S}$
Hedging policy ($H = -C$)	$-C$	$-C \times \tilde{S}$
Exposed position	0	$0 \times \tilde{S}$

2. Noncontractual Cash Flows

When foreign currency cash flows are uncertain, it is not possible to hedge perfectly against exchange rate variations by denominating liabilities. This can be illustrated under two different sets of circumstances.

a. $\tilde{C}$ is a deterministic function of S (i.e., $C(\tilde{S})$).

	End-Of-Period Cash Flow	
	FC	**DC**
Cash flows	$C(S_1)$	$C(S_1) \times S_1$
	$C(S_2)$	$C(S_2) \times S_2$
Hedging policy	$-H$	$-H \times S_1$
		$-H \times S_2$
Exposed position	$C(S_1) - H$	$S_1[C(S_1) - H]$
	$C(S_2) - H$	$S_2[C(S_2) - H]$

It must be recognized that the exposed position is not always equal to zero and there is the possibility that some foreign currency cash flow will not be exactly offset by the cash outflow on the liability side, because the cash flow from $-H$ is fixed, while cash inflows $C(\tilde{S})$ fluctuate.

FIGURE 2-7   (*continued*)

b. C is a nondeterministic function of S (i.e., $C(\bar{S}) + \tilde{\epsilon}$, where $\tilde{\epsilon}$ is the random part that is independent of the exchange rate.

	End-Of-Period Cash Flows	
	FC	DC
Cash flows	$C(S_1) + \epsilon_1$	$[C(S_1) + \epsilon_1]S_1$
	$C(S_1) + \epsilon_2$	$[C(S_1) + \epsilon_2]S_1$
	$C(S_2) + \epsilon_1$	$[C(S_2) + \epsilon_1]S_2$
	$C(S_2) + \epsilon_2$	$[C(S_2) + \epsilon_2]S_2$

	End-Of-Period Cash Flows	
	FC	DC
Hedging policy	$-H$	$-H \times S_1$
		$-H \times S_2$
Exposed position	$C(S_1) + \epsilon_1 - H$	$[C(S_1) + \epsilon_1 - H]S_1$
	$C(S_1) + \epsilon_2 - H$	$[C(S_1) + \epsilon_2 - H]S_1$
	$C(S_2) + \epsilon_1 - H$	$[C(S_2) + \epsilon_1 - H]S_2$
	$C(S_2) + \epsilon_2 - H$	$[C(S_2) + \epsilon_2 - H]S_2$

In this case, the possibility of an exposed position is much greater; as a result, debt denomination would be a less effective policy for exchange risk management. Unfortunately, case b better represents reality and thus illustrates the limitations of exchange risk management by debt denomination alone.

An exchange risk management policy that includes changes in the operations of the firm can be characterized as changing the functional relationship existing between the cash flow, $\bar{C}$, and the exchange rate, $\bar{S}$. Thus, finding a perfect exchange risk policy usually involves actions on the liability side as well as the asset side of the firm.

FIGURE 2-8

Foreign Currency Cash Flows

Source: I.H. Giddy, "The Foreign Exchange Option as a Hedging Tool," Midland Corporate Finance Journal, Vol. 1 (Fall 1983).

	Outflow	Inflow
Amount known	Buy forward	Sell forward
Amount unknown	Buy call option	Buy put option
Amount partially known	Hedge known portion with forward contracts and remainder with options	

2.05 CORPORATE PRACTICE AND THE RELEVANCE OF CURRENCY HEDGING

Two major issues remain to be addressed: (1) the variance of corporate practice with the normative model just developed and (2) whether forex risk management should be a legitimate concern of management in light of recent developments in corporate finance and capital market theory. The first issue is considered from the perspective of the practitioner; the second issue is from the perspective of the theory of finance.

[1] Corporate Exchange Risk Management Practice

Corporate forex decisions tend to be highly political. Governments generally take offense at corporate expression of a lack of confidence in the purchasing power of a local currency by the taking of short positions, and speculation has a strong negative connotation everywhere. Most important, because forex decisions are easy to criticize with hindsight, such decisions tend to be highly sensitive in a corporate political environment. This is accentuated by the natural tension that exists between managers responsible for operating decisions and those responsible for financing decisions. Last but not least, the decision-making process may be obscured by motives other than the pure optimization of shareholder wealth.[38]

A glance at corporate policies reveals a disproportionate concern with accounting exposure, although most of the corporate financial staff have been well educated on the difference between accounting and economic measures of exposure. This preoccupation with accounting exposure would be understandable if the evidence on stock market performance indicated that stock prices are influenced by reported translation losses and gains. However, in contrast to analysts' reports, the evidence suggests that stock market activity is based not on the accounting results reported but on the cases where translation losses and gains coincide with real losses and gains and situations where the two are at variance.[39]

There are a number of explanations that make corporate practice quite rational. First of all, economic exchange risk is reasonably complex. All relevant data must be estimated, and are therefore difficult to audit and to justify to a critical audience. Accounting losses, on the other hand, are very visible and can be determined precisely. Along the same lines, accounting-based foreign exchange management is straightforward and almost mechanical; translation rules indicate which assets and liabilities are exposed; the firm must then project its balance sheet to the end of the reporting period and ensure that exposed assets are funded with exposed liabilities or that net-exposed positions are covered with a forward contract. If these policies are not feasible because of capital market controls, various asset strategies can be used to reduce exposed assets: factoring of local currency receivables, conversion of monetary assets into real ones (and vice versa), and similar machinations.

While the tools are very much the same as in economic exposure management,

---

[38] For an incisive analysis of the managerial issues in corporate forex risk management, see Lessard and Nohria (1989).

[39] Yeater, "The Impact of Statement of Financial Accounting Standard No. 8 on Corporate Value," Ph.D. Thesis, Cornell University, 1978; J. Williams, "Capital Market Reaction to Financial Accounting Standards Board Statement No. 8," Ph.D. Thesis, Pennsylvania State University, 1978; R. Dukes (1978).

accounting exposure will often be different in amount and often in direction; a given exchange rate change may have a negative effect on accounting exposure but a positive effect on expected future cash flows.[40] However, for a multiproduct, multimarket company, economic exposure and, therefore, cash flow variability may be relatively small.

In contrast, the necessity for an explanation of excessive earnings variability owing to translation gains and losses may be of concern to the manager selected for decision-making skills rather than analytical, expository capabilities. The pressure to make the visible effects of exchange rate changes disappear is even stronger when incentive compensation is tied to reported earnings. Furthermore, the reporting system in many companies seems to highlight forex gains and losses much more than the interest expense typically incurred in balance sheet hedging.

Also, a considerable amount of speculation seems to be occurring without due regard for the nature of markets. Rarely do financial executives appear to inquire as to the markets in which positive payoffs over the long run can result from forecasting efforts. Judging by the criterion of currencies covered by commercial forecasting services, the demand seems to be greatest for the major currencies where well-informed traders are most active because governments interfere least with transactions. This is difficult to explain, and the observation that speculation at the corporate level is usually quite modest relative to the size of the firm suggests that perhaps the true function of these activities is to keep the minds of treasury staff sharply focused on markets so they can better identify any market imperfections that can be exploited.

[2] Relevance of Managing Corporate Exchange Exposure

Recent developments in the theory of finance suggest that the management of corporate forex exposure may be neither an important nor a legitimate concern.[41] It has been argued, in the tradition of the Modigliani-Miller theorem, that investors themselves can hedge corporate exchange exposure by taking out forward contracts in accordance with their share in the firm. But apart from transaction costs, which are typically greater for individuals than for firms, there are more serious reasons why forex risk should be managed at the firm level. Again, the assessment of economic exposure requires detailed estimates of the susceptibility of net cash flows to unexpected exchange rate changes. Operating managers can make such estimates with much more precision than shareholders, which typically lack the detailed knowledge of markets and technology. Furthermore, the firm has considerable advantages in obtaining relatively inexpensive debt at home and abroad by taking maximum advantage of interest subsidies and minimizing the effect of taxes and political risk.

Another line of reasoning suggests that forex risk management does not matter because of the functioning of PPP and the international Fisher effect. However, as pointed out previously, deviations from PPP can persist for considerable periods. And such deviations can be especially pronounced at the level of the individual firm. The resulting variability of net cash flows is of significance, as it can cause the firm to incur the costs of financial distress or default. The same argument supports the importance of corporate exchange risk management against the claim that only systematic risk mat-

---

[40] See Dufey (1972).

[41] Dufey and Srinivasulu (1983).

ters. To the extent that forex risk represents unsystematic risk it can, of course, be diversified (hedged), provided again that investors have the same quality of information about the firm as management. However, there is one task that the firm cannot perform for shareholders: To the extent that individuals face unique exchange risk as a result of their different expenditure patterns, they must themselves devise appropriate hedging strategies. After all, corporate financial management is only able to protect expected nominal returns in the reference currency.[42]

Suggested Reading

Adler, M., and B. Lehman. "Deviations From Purchasing Power Parity in the Long Run." *Journal of Finance,* Vol. 38 (Dec. 1983), pp. 1471–1488.

Aliber, Robert Z., ed. *The Handbook of International Financial Management.* Homewood, Ill.: Dow Jones-Irwin, 1989.

"Banking Gets 'in the CHIPS.' " *Morgan Guaranty Survey* (May 1975), pp. 12–14.

Beenstock, M. "Forward Exchange Rates and Siegel's Paradox." *Oxford Economic Papers,* Vol. 37 (1985), pp. 298–303.

Biger, N., and J. Hull. "The Valuation of Currency Options." *Financial Management,* Vol. 12 (Spring 1983), pp. 24–28.

Business International Money Report (Oct. 28, 1977), pp. 339–340.

Coninx, Raymond G.F. *Foreign Exchange Dealer's Handbook.* New York: Pick Publishing, 1982.

———. *Foreign Exchange Today.* New York: John Wiley & Sons, Inc., 1978.

Cornell, B. "Inflation, Relative Price Changes, and Exchange Risk." *Financial Management,* Vol. 9 (Autumn 1980), pp. 30–34.

———. "Spot Rates, Forward Rates, and Exchange Market Efficiency." *Journal of Financial Economics,* Vol. 5 (1977), pp. 55–65.

Deardorff, Alan V. "One-Way Arbitrage and Its Implications for the Foreign Exchange Markets." *Journal of Political Economy,* Vol. 87 (1979), pp. 351–364.

Dooley, M.P., and P. Isard. "Capital Controls, Political Risk and Deviations From Interest Parity." *Journal of Political Economy,* Vol. 88 (Mar./Apr. 1980), pp. 370–384.

Dornbusch, R. "Exchange Rate Economics: Where Do We Stand?" *Brookings Papers on Economic Activity,* Vol. 1 (1980), pp. 143–185.

———. "Expectations and Exchange Rate Dynamics." *Journal of Political Economy,* Vol. 84 (Dec. 1976), pp. 1161–1176.

Dufey, G. "Corporate Finance and Exchange Rate Variations." *Financial Management,* Vol. 1 (Summer 1972), pp. 51–57.

Dufey, G. and I. Giddy. "International Financial Planning: The Use of Market-Based Forecasts." *California Management Review,* Vol. 12 (Fall 1978), pp. 69–81.

Dufey, G., and S.L. Srinivasulu. "The Case for Corporate Management of Foreign Exchange Risk." *Financial Management* (Winter 1983), pp. 54–62.

---

[42] Eaker (1981).

Eaker, M.R. "Covering Foreign Exchange Risks: Comment." *Financial Management,* Vol. 9 (Winter 1980), pp. 64–65.

————. "The Numeraire Problem and Foreign Exchange Risk." *Journal of Finance,* Vol. 36 (May 1981), pp. 419–427.

Fisher, Irving. *The Theory of Interest.* New York: Macmillan, 1980.

Flood, E., Jr., and D.R. Lessard. "On the Measurement of Operating Exposure to Exchange Rates: A Conceptual Approach." *Financial Management,* Vol. 15 (Spring 1986), pp. 25–36.

"Focus: The Foreign Exchange Markets." *Columbia Journal of World Business* (Winter 1979).

Foreign Exchange and Money Market Operations. Swiss Bank Corporation. Zurich: June 1987.

"The Forex Market Goes West." *Euromoney* (Aug. 1983), p. 59.

Frankel, J. "On the Mark: A Theory of Floating Exchange Rates Based on Real Interest Differentials." *American Economic Review,* Vol. 69 (Sept. 1979), pp. 610–622.

————. *A Test of the Existence of the Risk Premium in the Foreign Exchange Market vs. the Hypothesis of Perfect Substitutability.* Federal Reserve System, International Finance Discussion Papers No. 149. Aug. 1979.

Frenkel, J. "A Monetary Approach to the Exchange Rate: Doctrinal Aspects and Empirical Evidence." *Scandinavian Journal of Economics,* Vol. 78 (June 1978), pp. 255–276.

Frenkel, J.A., and R.M. Levich. "Covered Interest Arbitrage: Unexploited Profits?" *Journal of Political Economy,* Vol. 83 (Apr. 1975), pp. 325–338.

Fukao, Mitsuhiro. "The Risk Premium in the Foreign Exchange Market." Ph.D. Dissertation, University of Michigan, 1981.

Giddy, I.H. "Exchange Risk: Whose View?" *Financial Management,* Vol. 7 (Summer 1977), pp. 23–33.

————. "Foreign Exchange Options." *The Journal of Futures Markets,* Vol. 3 (1983), pp. 143–166.

————. "An Integrated Theory of Exchange Rate Equilibrium." *Journal of Financial and Quantitative Analysis,* Vol. 11 (Dec. 1976), pp. 883–892.

————. "Measuring the World Foreign Exchange Market." *Columbia Journal of World Business* (Winter 1979), pp. 36–48.

Goedhuys, Diederik, ed. *The Foreign Exchange Market in the 1980s: The Views of Market Participants.* New York: Group of Thirty, 1985.

Hacche, G., and J.C. Townsend. "A Broad Look at Exchange Rate Movements for Eight Currencies, 1972–80." *Bank of England Quarterly Bulletin* (Dec. 1981), pp. 489–509.

Hekman, C.R. "Don't Blame Currency Values for Strategic Errors: Protecting Competitive Position by Correctly Assessing Foreign Exchange Exposure." *Midland Corporate Finance Journal,* Vol. 4 (Fall 1986), pp. 45–55.

————. "Foreign Exchange Exposure: Accounting Measures and Economic Reality." *Journal of Cash Management* (Feb./Mar. 1983), pp. 34–45.

Henderson, Dale W. *The Dynamic Effects of Exchange Market Intervention Policy: Two Extreme Views and a Synthesis.* Federal Reserve Board, International Finance Discussion Papers No. 142, June 1979.

Hilley, J.L., C.R. Beidleman, and J.A. Greenleaf. "Why There Is No Long Forward Market in Foreign Exchange." *Euromoney* (Jan. 1981), pp. 94–103.

Isard, Peter. *Exchange Rate Determination: A Survey of Popular Views and Recent Models.*

Princeton University, International Finance Section, Studies in International Finance No. 42. Princeton, N.J.: May 1978.

Jacque, L.L. "Management of Foreign Exchange Risk: A Review Article." *Journal of International Business Studies,* Vol. 12 (Spring/Summer 1981), pp. 81–101.

Jacque, L.L., and P. Lang. "Currency Denomination in Long-Term Debt Financing and Refinancing: A Cross-Hedging Paradigm." *Journal of the Operational Research Society,* Vol. 38 (1987), pp. 173–182.

Kobrin, S.J. "Political Risk: A Review and Reconsideration." *Journal of International Business Studies,* Vol. 10 (Spring–Summer 1979), pp. 67–80.

Kohlhagen, Steven W. *The Behavior of Foreign Exchange Markets—A Critical Survey of the Empirical Literature.* New York University, Monograph Series in Finance and Economics, Monograph No. 3. New York: 1978.

Kolb, Robert W., ed. *The International Finance Reader,* 2nd ed. Miami: Kolb Publishing, 1993.

Kubarych, Roger M. *Foreign Exchange Markets in the U.S.,* rev. ed. New York: Federal Reserve Bank of New York, 1983.

Lessard, Donald R., ed. *International Financial Management: Theory and Application,* 2nd ed. New York: John Wiley & Sons, Inc., 1985.

Lessard, Donald R., and Nitin Nohria. "Rediscovering Functions in the MNC: The Role of Expertise and the Emergent Matrix in Firms' Responses to Shifting Exchange Rates," *Managing the Global Corporation,* Bartlett, Doz, and Hedlund, eds. London: Routledge, 1989.

Levi, Maurice. *Financial Management and the International Economy.* New York: McGraw-Hill, 1983.

Logue, D.E., and G.S. Oldfield. "Managing Foreign Assets When Foreign Exchange Markets Are Efficient." *Financial Management,* Vol. 6 (Summer 1977), pp. 16–22.

Mandich, D.R., ed. *Foreign Exchange Trading Techniques and Controls.* Washington, D.C.: American Bankers Association, 1976.

McCormick, F. "Covered-Interest Arbitrage: Unexploited Profits: Comment." *Journal of Political Economy,* Vol. 87 (Apr. 1979), pp. 411–417.

Officer, Lawrence. *Purchasing Power Parity and Exchange Rates: Theory, Evidence and Relevance.* Greenwich, Conn.: JAI Press, 1982.

———. "The Purchasing-Power-Parity Theorem of Exchange Rates: A Review Article." *IMF Staff Papers* (Mar. 1976), pp. 1–60.

Price Waterhouse. *Foreign Currency Translation: Understanding and Applying FASB 52.* New York: 1981.

Reier, S. "Wall Street Muscles In on Foreign Exchange." *Institutional Investor,* international ed. (Jan. 1984), pp. 133–134.

Report on Exchange Restrictions. Washington, D.C.: International Monetary Fund (annual).

Revey, P.A. "Evolution and Growth of the United States Foreign Exchange Market." *Quarterly Review.* Federal Reserve Bank of New York (Autumn 1981), pp. 32–33.

Riehl, Heinz, and Rita M. Rodriguez. *Foreign Exchange and Money Markets.* New York: McGraw-Hill, 1983.

Rodriguez, R.M. "Corporate Exchange Risk Management: Theme and Aberrations." *Journal of Finance,* Vol. 36 (May 1981), pp. 427–439.

———. *Foreign Exchange Management in U.S. Multinationals.* Lexington, Mass.: D.C. Heath, 1980.

Shapiro, A.C. *Multinational Financial Management,* 3rd ed. Boston: Allyn and Bacon, 1989.

Shapiro, A.C., and D.P. Rutenberg. ''Managing Exchange Risks in a Floating World.'' *Financial Management,* Vol. 5 (Summer 1976), pp. 48–58.

————. ''What Does Purchasing Power Parity Mean?'' *Journal of International Money and Finance* (Summer 1983), pp. 295–318.

Showers, Janet. *Hedging the Currency Exposure of Foreign Subsidiaries: Strategic Issues.* Salomon Bros. Bond Portfolio Analysis Group. New York: Oct. 1988.

Stein, J.L., M. Rzepczynski, and R. Selvaggio. ''A Theoretical Explanation of the Empirical Studies of Futures Markets in Foreign Exchange and Financial Instruments.'' *The Financial Review,* Vol. 18 (Feb. 1983), pp. 1–32.

Stulz, R.M. ''Optimal Hedging Policies.'' *Journal of Financial and Quantitative Analysis,* Vol. 19 (1984), pp. 127–140.

Chapter 3

International Financial Markets

Anant Sundaram

3.01 Introduction 64

3.02 Regular and Direct Securities 64
[1] International Bonds 64
   [a] Eurobonds 66
   [b] Fixed-Rate Eurobonds 67
   [c] Floating-Rate Notes 67
   [d] Zero-Coupon Bonds 68
   [e] Dual-Currency Bonds 68
   [f] Equity-Linked Eurobonds 68
   [g] Foreign Bonds 69
[2] Euro Commercial Paper 70
[3] Euro Medium-Term Notes 70
[4] Euro Syndicated Credits 70
[5] Euroequity 71
[6] Currency Mix of Direct Securities . . . 71

3.03 Derivative Securities 72

[1] Currency Forwards 73
[2] Currency Futures 74
[3] Currency Options 76
[4] Interest Rate Futures 77
[5] Interest Rate Options 78
[6] Caps and Floors 78
[7] Forward Rate Agreements 79
[8] Interest Rate Swaps 80
[9] Currency Swaps 81
   [a] Example of a Currency Swap 81
   [b] Valuation of Swaps 82
[10] Swaptions 82

**3.04 Future Market Evolution and Potential
Regulation** 83

Suggested Reading 85

The author recognizes the outstanding research assistance of Diego Ferro and Thomas Hudson in the preparation of this chapter.

3.01 INTRODUCTION

International financial markets offer the fastest-growing and, in many cases, the most liquid source of debt and equity capital as well as financial hedging instruments to major corporations, financial institutions, sovereign nations, and supranational entities. The 1980s witnessed dramatic growth in the value, volume, range, and sophistication of cross-border financial transactions in direct underlying securities (e.g., debt and equity) as well as derivatives on these direct securities (e.g., options, futures, swaps, and swaptions).

The growth was fueled by a number of factors. On the demand side, the driving forces include underlying product-market needs derived from growth in cross-border trade and direct investment, increased volatility in interest and exchange rates resulting in the need for better financial risk management tools, and a diversification of the investor base resulting from firms' search worldwide for lower costs of capital. On the supply side, the driving forces include deregulation and privatization (perhaps along with the renaissance of conservative political movements in the United States and Europe), innovation resulting from better research, technology that helped propagate these innovations, the shift in the structure of financial market competition from traditional relationship-oriented to transaction-oriented financial services, and the breakdown of cross-border barriers to funds flows as reflected in the growth of Euromarkets and the emergence of nearly 24-hour trading in foreign exchange markets.

Data from the Bank for International Settlements (BIS) reports end-of-year net stocks for international bond financing at $1.65 trillion in 1991, up from $700 billion in 1986 and $286 billion in 1982. Annual volume of international bond issues approached $300 billion in 1991 alone, a sum that nearly equals the total funds raised through private-sector, domestic bond issues in the United States during that year. It is estimated that cross-border trade in equities grew at a rate of 28 percent per year from 1980 to 1990, with annual volumes now approaching $1.5 trillion per year. Annual gross new international equity offerings increased from $17.3 billion in 1987 to $18.9 billion in 1991.

Indeed, as Figure 3-1 shows, the volume of cross-border trade in bonds and equities has increased by impressive amounts in all the major economies: in the United States, for example, such trade accounted for less than 3 percent of the gross national product (GNP) in 1970; 20 years later, it approached 92.5 percent. In Japan and the United Kingdom, these increases are even more dramatic. In addition, daily trading volumes in foreign exchange markets now approach $1 trillion. Finally, the growth in volume of derivatives has been equally impressive: Even as recently as 1986, the stock of major derivatives (options, futures, and swaps) was $1.1 trillion; by 1991, it was nearly $7 trillion.

3.02 REGULAR AND DIRECT SECURITIES

[1] International Bonds

International bonds can be divided into three broad groups: Eurobonds, foreign bonds, and global bonds. (See Figure 3-2.) Eurobonds are long-term bonds issued and sold outside the country of the currency in which they are denominated; they can be further subdivided into fixed-rate, floating-rate, and equity-linked Eurobonds. Foreign bonds are long-term bonds issued outside of the issuers' home country and denominated in

FIGURE 3-1

Cross-Border Transactions in Bonds and Equities

Source: Annual Report, *Vol. 62, Bank for International Settlements (Basel, Switzerland: 1992)*

Country	1970	1975	1980	1985	1990
United States	2.8%	4.2%	9.3%	36.4%	92.5%
Japan	NA	1.5	7.0	60.5	118.6
Germany	3.3	5.1	7.5	33.9	57.5
France	NA	NA	8.4[a]	21.4	53.3
Italy	NA	0.9	1.1	4.0	26.7
United Kingdom	NA	NA	NA	367.5	690.1
Canada	5.7	3.3	9.6	26.7	63.8

Note: Gross purchases and sales of securities between residents and nonresidents as a percentage of gross domestic product.

[a] Data are from 1982.

FIGURE 3-2

Estimated Net Financings in International Markets

Source: Institutional Investor *(various issues) (international bond and equity data);* Annual Report, *Vol. 62, Bank for International Settlements (Basel, Switzerland: 1992) (net international bank lending, ECP, and EMTN data)*

Components of Net International Financing	1987	1988	1989	1990	1991	1992[a]
International bonds	$164.4	$199.5	$227.3	$225.1	$299.8	$177.9
Foreign bonds	23.2	18.6	18.7	65.9	54.7	28.6
Global bonds	NA	NA	NA	NA	14.3	11.4
Eurobonds	141.2	180.9	208.6	159.2	230.8	137.9
Straight fixed-rate issues	86.3	123.8	114.7	77.3	165.5	56.7
FRNs	15.6	20.5	18.5	49.2	31.3	16.9
Equity convertible bonds	14.9	6.9	7.3	10.6	7.5	1.7
Bonds with equity warrants	24.4	29.7	68.1	22.1	26.5	62.6
International equities	17.3	8.2	12.2	12.0	18.9	15.2
Net international bank lending	320.0	260.0	410.0	465.0	85.0	NA
ECP[b]	33.3	53.2	58.5	70.3	79.6	NA
EMTNs[b]	2.6	5.6	9.6	21.9	38.5	NA

Note: Annual market volume in billions of U.S. dollars.

[a] Data are through June 1992.

[b] Figures show outstandings at year-end.

the currency of the foreign country. The global bond is a relatively recent security, a Eurobond that is simultaneously issued in multiple markets. (However, until recently, the term referred to a temporary debt certificate issued by a Eurobond borrower, representing the borrower's total issue size; they would usually be subsequently replaced by Eurobonds.)

As of the end of 1991, there were over $1.6 trillion in international bonds outstanding

FIGURE 3-3

Euromarket Issue Volumes and Redemption Schedule

Source: Euromoney *Supplement (Sept. 1992)*

Issue Volumes	1989	1990	1991	1992[a]	1993	1994	1995	1996	1997
Totals	$220.4	$181.9	$277.9	$199.4	—	—	—	—	—
Japanese equity JWBs[b]	65.3	19.1	24.3	5.1	—	—	—	—	—
Volume excluding JWBs	155.1	162.8	253.6	194.3	—	—	—	—	—
Scheduled redemptions All issues	43.0	65.4	101.2	161.0	$226.0	$158.1	$161.7	$178.6	$130.7
Redemptions of JWBs	1.4	1.6	8.1	30.2	74.3	28.4	20.6	8.8	0.2
Redemptions less JWBs	41.6	63.8	93.2	130.8	151.7	129.7	141.2	169.9	130.5
New issues less redemptions	177.4	116.4	176.7	38.4	—	—	—	—	—
Above less JWBs	113.5	98.9	160.5	63.5	—	—	—	—	—

Note: U.S. dollars in billions.

[a] Data are through August 24, 1992.

[b] Japanese warrant bonds.

worldwide: $1,160 billion in international fixed-rate bonds, $210 billion in international floating-rate bonds, and $272 billion in international equity-linked bonds.

[a] Eurobonds. Since Eurobonds were introduced in 1963 as a means of avoiding U.S. tax and disclosure regulations, the market has grown from $75 million at the end of 1963 to over $230 billion in annual new issuance by 1991, with $137.8 billion in new issuance in just the first half of 1992. (See Figure 3-2.) The first issue was lead-managed by the U.K. investment bank S.G. Warburg, denominated in U.S. dollars, and issued in London on behalf of the Italian firm Autostrada.

Eurobonds are typically issued in denominations of $5,000 and $10,000, pay interest annually (based on a 30/360-day count), are held in bearer form, are traded over the counter (usually in London), and are often rated by agencies such as Moody's Investors Service, Inc. or Standard & Poor's (S&P). The all-in-cost (i.e., the yield to maturity after accounting for transaction costs) of issuing Eurobonds is often lower owing to decreased documentation needs (relative to domestic issues) and, in the case of the United States, owing to the fact that the bonds need not be registered with the Securities and Exchange Commission (SEC).

New issuing activity was up substantially in the first half of 1992 owing partially to the large number of international bond redemptions. This trend is likely to continue through the mid-1990s, since scheduled redemptions were expected to increase to $190 billion in 1992 and $270 billion in 1993. (See Figure 3-3.) One quarter of the bonds maturing in the period 1993–1995 are Japanese equity-linked debt that has not been converted owing to the depressed stock prices of many Japanese companies. A second cause of the increase in new issuing activity in 1991 and the first half of 1992 was the fall in interest rates to historically low levels in many countries. Many issuers, expecting interest rates to rise after the global recession, apparently decided to refinance high-coupon debt, an issuing trend that has also been mirrored in the U.S. domestic bond markets.

Issuers of Eurobonds include large, well-known corporations, financial institutions, sovereign nations, and supranational entities such as the European Community. Historically, the Japanese have been the largest issuers of Eurobonds. Despite recent deregulation, the domestic issuance cost of Japanese debt continues to remain high owing to Ministry of Finance regulations and the underwriting oligopoly formed by Japan's largest security firms. However, the market is increasingly becoming dominated by sovereign and state-related issues and bonds of supranational organizations. New corporate credit issuance was down in the first half of 1992. This trend is probably a result of credit scares in the Euromarkets from the bankruptcies of corporations such as Olympia and York Developments Ltd., Polly Peck International plc, Heron International plc, Bond Corporation Holdings Ltd., and Maxwell Communication Corporation plc. Further, the need for capital in some countries with restored credit ratings (e.g., Mexico, Brazil, and Argentina) is so great that they increasingly account for a larger share of new issues.

[b] Fixed-Rate Eurobonds. Fixed-rate Eurobond new issues grew by over 100 percent in 1991 with secondary trading, which had fallen in recent years, rising to historic levels. Factors contributing to this (as seen by market participants) include (1) investors that sought to lock in low interest rates and capture capital gains as interest rates declined into 1992; (2) the increased use of international markets by sovereign nations; and (3) the decline in Japanese stock prices forcing many Japanese companies to issue fixed-rate debt, not only to abandon their heavy use of equity-linked debt but also to raise funds for the likely redemption of such debt issued previously.

[c] Floating-Rate Notes. Floating-rate notes (FRNs) have coupon payments that are usually paid every six months, based on a spread over some predetermined reference rate such as the London interbank offered rate (LIBOR).

The first Euro FRN was issued by the Italian state electric company in 1970. The market grew rapidly in the late 1970s during a period of particularly high interest rate volatility. Banks, governments (notably in Latin America), and government agencies replaced traditional sources of capital with FRNs in order to match their funding costs to prevailing lending rates.

The market continued to grow through the 1980s, peaking in 1990 with new issues totaling $49.2 billion. Since then, new FRN issuance fell to $31.3 billion in 1991, probably owing to investors' (correct) belief that interest rates on many currencies would fall in 1992. In additional, financial institutions, which account for over two thirds of Euro FRN issues, found it increasingly difficult to locate receptive investors as their credit quality declined owing to increased competition and declining profit margins in the industry.

FRNs, which were developed to decrease the interest rate risk of financial intermediaries created by borrowing short term and lending long term, enhanced credit risk, since interest rate volatility was transferred to borrowers. The pitfalls of such attempts at risk transference were evidenced by the developing-country debt crisis, which largely resulted from these countries' having to repay debt at historically high interest rates in the early 1980s because they had borrowed at floating interest rates when they were low in the 1970s.

[d] Zero-Coupon Bonds. Zero-coupon bonds pay no coupons during the term of the bonds. At maturity, the bondholder receives the original issue price of the bond plus accrued interest. Most zero-coupon bonds are sold at a deep discount and are redeemable at par at maturity, although some are issued at par and redeemable at par plus accrued interest. Total return is calculated on the basis of the difference between the purchase price and the repayment price of the bonds at maturity.

The investor clientele for zero-coupon bonds was dominated by Japanese companies (in particular, insurance companies), owing to favorable tax treatment that allowed the accrued interest on zero-coupon bonds to be taxed at the lower capital gain rate. Recent changes in Japan's tax codes have eliminated the preferential tax status of zero-coupon bond interest and have resulted in almost no new issuance of these bonds.

[e] Dual-Currency Bonds. Dual-currency bonds are issued in one currency and pay coupons, or repay principal at maturity, in a different currency. These bonds combine a straight bond with a forward currency contract. The forward currency contract allows the borrower to know, at issuance, the future currency cash flow payments over the bonds' maturity by fixing the rate of exchange used to calculate interest or principal repayment. This allows corporations, in particular, to match known future cash flows that are denominated in a currency different from that of their current borrowing needs. Dual-currency bonds allow borrowers to lock in exchange rates up front over longer periods than do standard currency options, forwards, or futures contracts. Typically, investors are compensated for the transfer of exchange rate risk from borrower to investor with a higher coupon interest rate.

Dual-currency bonds against the yen were particularly popular in the 1980s with Japanese insurance companies whose regulatory status led them to have a preference for yen income over capital gains. Most insurance companies in Japan are mutual and not stock companies, and, consequently, they pay dividends to policyholders; thus, dividends are an important basis for competition among these firms. Laws in Japan permit these companies to pay their dividends only out of current income and not out of capital gains. As a result, many of these firms had a preference for securities that would pay higher coupons, even if they would result in a capital loss at maturity (resulting from the expected loss built into the principal on the bond via a forward exchange rate that would be favorable to the issuer of the dual-currency bond).

[f] Equity-Linked Eurobonds. Equity-linked Eurobonds include convertible bonds and bonds with equity warrants. Convertible bonds are bonds that, in addition to paying a coupon, can be exchanged for some other asset, usually stock of the issuer's company, at a fixed exchange ratio. Convertible bonds from U.S. issuers are typically issued with conversion premiums of 15 percent to 20 percent. Bonds with equity warrants combine a straight bond with the option of buying a fixed number of shares, usually in the issuer's company, at a fixed price until a certain date. Warrants are often separated from the originally issued bond and traded independently in the secondary market.

The market for equity-linked debt grew from a net stock of $17 billion in 1982 to $272.4 billion by the end of 1991. While total outstandings grew each year, new issuance

FIGURE 3-4

Japanese Warrant Bonds

Source: "A Survey of International Finance," The Economist (Apr. 27, 1991), p. 31. Reprinted with permission.

Stranded Issues				Maturing Issues		
Price Relative to Exercise Price	Value	Number of Issues		Maturity	Value	Number of Issues
Over 50% below	$ 5.7	18		1991	$ 2.5	54
20%–40% below	62.1	225		1992	20.4	185
0%–20% below	32.3	187		1993	64.1	284
0%–20% above	14.3	129		1994	27.9	107
20%–50% above	5.1	65		1995	3.7	20
Over 50% above	0.7	31		1996–1998	1.6	5
Total	$120.2	655		Total	$120.2	655

Note: Data as of February 18, 1991. Values expressed in billions of U.S. dollars.

peaked in 1989 at $75.4 billion and fell to $34 billion in 1991. The decrease in net new issuance came in the wake of the prolonged decline in the Tokyo stock market. Japanese companies dominated the issuance of equity-linked debt and still account for over 75 percent of total issuance. In 1991, Japan issued $24.3 billion of new equity warrant bonds with scheduled redemptions in 1991 of $8 billion of equity warrant bonds, for a net increase of $16.3 billion of equity warrant bonds. During 1992 and 1993, Japan's scheduled redemptions of these bonds was expected to increase to $30.2 billion and $74.3 billion respectively. (See Figure 3-4.) With Japanese share prices and interest rates falling, companies switched to issuing straight fixed-rate debt securities to cover scheduled redemptions and raise additional capital.

Major investors of equity-linked debt include portfolio managers, pension funds, and other institutions managing discretionary accounts.

[g] Foreign Bonds. Foreign bonds are bonds issued outside the issuer's home country and denominated in the currency of the foreign country. Countries usually make a legal distinction between foreign-issued bonds and bonds issued by domestic borrowers. These distinctions can include regulatory differences for registration, tax treatment, disclosure requirements, and restrictions limiting investment to certain classes of investors. Foreign bonds are usually rated by S&P or Moody's, pay interest semiannually, and are registered.

New issuance of foreign bonds increased from $23.2 billion in 1987 to over $54.8 billion in 1991, with $28.6 billion of gross new issuance in the first half of 1992. (See Figure 3-2.)

Foreign bonds issued in some countries are given names that denote the country of original issue. For example, foreign bonds issued in the United States and denominated in U.S. dollars are called Yankee bonds, Japan's foreign bonds denominated in yen are called Samurai bonds, and foreign bonds issued in the United Kingdom and denominated in sterling are called Bulldog bonds.

[2] Euro Commercial Paper

Euro commercial paper (ECP) is a short-term debt instrument, maturing within a year and sold at a discount to par. The market, which started in 1985, has grown from $3 billion in outstandings to $79.6 billion in 1991. (See Figure 3-2.)

Currently there are 10 major dealers, with the majority of business concentrated among 6 securities firms. However, many dealers (e.g., Merrill Lynch, Credit Suisse First Boston, and S.G. Warburg) left the market in 1989, citing lack of profitability. The same year also saw the first defaults on ECP, including companies such as Integrated Resources, Inc., Lomas & Nettleton Mortgage Investors, and Wang Laboratories, Inc. Unlike the U.S. commercial paper market, where almost all paper is rated, until 1989 only about 50 percent of ECP was rated. Differences in European accounting standards and the reluctance of some companies to disclose previously confidential financial information led many issuers to issue unrated debt. Issuers have had to obtain ratings or drop their ECP programs because of the greater cost of funding due to higher perceived credit risk.

[3] Euro Medium-Term Notes

Euro medium-term notes (EMTNs) are debt obligations issued continuously through dealers, with a variety of maturities typically determined by the investor. Original maturities range from 9 months to 30 years, and notes are usually noncallable and nonrefundable and have either a fixed or floating coupon paid annually. Merrill Lynch established the first EMTN program in April 1986 for the U.S. firm First Interstate Bancorp.

Total outstandings rose from an estimated $350 million at the end of 1986 to $38.5 billion in 1991. Major issuers of EMTNs include companies such as General Electric (GE), which has established a $4 billion global facility. For example, in the first half of 1992 GE completed three tranches of financing, including a two-year, 75 million European currency unit (ECU) tranche; a five-year, £70 million tranche; and a five-year, Can$150 million tranche. Investors include insurance companies, central banks, commercial banks, corporations, and pension funds, all of which need to match their liabilities with specific maturities.

The major factors behind this growth are convenience and cost. From a single set of documentation, an issuer can choose a wide range of currencies, maturities, and structures. The cost of establishing an EMTN program is approximately the same ($50,000 to $100,000) as the cost to document just one custom Eurobond issue. Once a program is in place, the cost of documenting an underwritten EMTN goes down even further, and is typically between $5,000 and $10,000.

[4] Euro Syndicated Credits

Euro syndicated credits are bank loans that are underwritten by a lead manager and then syndicated among participating banks. During the late 1980s, this method of finance was used heavily by U.S. and U.K. companies involved in merger and acquisition activity. By 1991, the shift away from highly leveraged transactions reduced the new volume of issuance for these activities from $62 billion in 1989 to $29 billion in 1990 and less than $5 billion in 1991. Total investment in new facilities declined 14 percent in 1991 to $137 billion.

The decline is attributed to the credit crunch caused by the recession in the industrial world. Lending restrictions increased, spreads rose to historic levels, and the average lending maturities declined to a little over five years. Banks required added lending covenants and stronger financial ratios from corporate borrowers. Although 1991 saw a decline in new facilities overall, there was net new lending to developing countries. Organization for Economic Cooperation and Development (OECD) countries received two thirds of new financing, and major financings were arranged for lower- and middle-income countries such as Indonesia, South Korea, Mexico, and Thailand. Moreover, in terms of volume outstanding, Euro syndicated credit is still the single largest source of capital, with a total stock of $3.6 trillion at the end of 1991.

[5] Euroequity

Euroequity is equity placed simultaneously in several different countries, with or without a listing on a stock exchange in that country. Annual new issuance of Euroequity increased from $17.3 billion in 1987 to $18.9 billion in 1991; however, in the first half of 1992 there was $15.2 billion in new issuance. The largest issuers include the governments of the United Kingdom and France, which have both used it to place equity of recently privatized firms. More recently, Argentina and Mexico have gained access to Euroequity markets in their privatization efforts.

It is well known that when international capital markets are "segmented"—i.e., less than fully integrated, in the sense that risk-equivalent securities may have different prices in different markets—international portfolio diversification can lower the systematic risk of a portfolio compared to a fully diversified domestic portfolio. Firms issuing international equity are primarily motivated by the lower cost of equity that they would presumably need to pay resulting from the benefits of such international portfolio diversification.

There are other motivations as well; these include illiquidity in home country equity markets (this is perhaps more true of the smaller markets), dispersion of ownership to reduce potential takeover threats, dispersion of ownership to prevent nationalization (or renationalization after privatization), making available the option of securities-based rather than cash-based financing of acquisitions in the host country, lower regulatory burdens, and disclosure requirements. Finally, there is even perhaps the ability to enhance host country visibility in the firm's product market.

The disadvantages of Euroequity include the potential problem of flowback (or the tendency for the stock to be resold in home markets), particularly during bear spells; different clientele expectations on matters such as reporting, management, and investor relations; and having to subscribe to reports in different languages and different accounting standards.

[6] Currency Mix of Direct Securities

Figure 3-5 summarizes the trends in the currency denomination of the major types of direct securities. In the case of fixed-rate issues (accounting for over $1 trillion in stocks outstanding as of the end of 1991), U.S. dollars account for about 30 percent of the issues, followed by the yen, whose share has fluctuated between 12 percent and 18 percent in the last few years. Between 1988 and 1991, the share of ECU bonds rose substantially (from 7 percent to 12 percent), but since then, the European currency

FIGURE 3-5

Type and Currency Structure of International Bond Issues

Source: Annual Report, *Vol. 62, Bank for International Settlements (Basel, Switzerland: 1992)*

Sectors and Currencies	Announced Gross New Issues and Currency Breakdowns								Stocks at Year-End 1991
	1988	%	1989	%	1990	%	1991	%	
Straight fixed-rate issues	$160.8		$150.2		$165.9		$255.2		$1,158.5
U.S. dollar	47.3	29	54.6	36	52.2	31	74.3	29	349.7
Yen	18.8	12	23.1	15	30.2	18	39.1	15	193.4
Swiss franc	18.2	11	5.7	4	15.5	9	13.5	5	117.7
Deutsche mark	21.2	13	9.4	6	7.3	4	12.1	5	114.1
ECU	10.7	7	11.7	8	15.1	9	30.2	12	92.8
U.K. pound	11.8	7	11.9	8	9.5	6	17.2	7	78.2
Canadian dollar	13.2	8	10.9	7	6.3	4	22.5	9	60.1
French franc	2.3	1	4.6	3	7.8	5	16.4	6	38.9
Other	17.3	11	18.2	12	21.9	13	30.1	12	113.5
FRNs	24.4		27.3		42.5		19.1		210.5
U.S. dollar	7.0	29	10.2	37	15.0	35	4.5	24	110.8
U.K. pound	11.5	47	9.3	34	10.8	25	7.6	40	48.2
Deutsche mark	1.4	6	2.6	10	8.2	19	2.8	15	23.7
Other	4.5	18	5.3	19	8.4	20	4.2	22	27.9
Equity-related issues	42.0		85.2		33.1		42.4		272.4
U.S. dollar	29.0	69	65.1	76	19.5	59	24.8	58	184.8
Swiss franc	8.3	20	13.6	16	8.2	25	7.0	17	54.3
Other	4.7	11	6.5	8	5.4	16	10.6	25	43.2

Note: U.S. dollars in billions.

crises of 1992 and the resulting uncertainty over the common European currency and European central bank have led to a dramatic decline in new ECU issues.

The U.S. dollar share of FRN issues (stocks outstanding at over $200 billion) has fallen from a high of 37 percent in 1989 to 24 percent in 1991. The leading currency for FRN issues is the U.K. pound, although its share has declined from nearly 50 percent in 1988 to about 40 percent in 1991 as the deutsche mark has become the most attractive currency for FRNs. The reasons for this appears to be the decline in U.S. interest rates since 1990 coupled with the rise in German interest rates during the same period.

The two favored currencies in the case of equity-related bonds (stocks outstanding at over $270 billion) are the U.S. dollar and the Swiss franc, the dollar accounting for about 60 percent of issues and the franc for about 20 percent. The high share of U.S. dollars is probably explained by the fact that a majority of these bonds have been issued by Japanese companies looking for dollar funds; the significant share of francs is probably accounted for by the fact that Swiss investors are major clientele for these securities.

3.03 DERIVATIVE SECURITIES

The development and growth of derivative contracts (i.e., contracts whose value depends on the value of another underlying asset or direct security) in the last 20 years has been one of the most extraordinary and important features of the global financial marketplace: The outstanding nominal value of derivative contracts in the international financial markets reached nearly $7 trillion by the end of 1991.

Although commodity forwards and futures contracts have been traded since the beginning of this century, it was not until 1972 that the modern derivatives market was born. In that year, the Bretton Woods agreement, the postwar pact that instituted a fixed-rate regime for the world's major nations, collapsed when the United States suspended the dollar's convertibility into gold. Exchange rate volatility followed, and consequently, interest rate volatility.

Two months prior to the Bretton Woods collapse, the Chicago Mercantile Exchange (CME) launched the world's first successful exchange-traded currency futures contracts. Today, this market, like the rest of the derivatives market, is mature. There are liquid markets in exchange-traded contracts on all the major commodities and currencies, on the most important fixed-income instruments, and on many of the key stock indexes. Further, over-the-counter (OTC) markets offer two-way prices in a range of swaps and option products on an even wider range of underlying assets.

The following sections provide a brief description of some of the most important derivative products in international financial markets, their uses, and key institutional features.

[1] Currency Forwards

When two parties enter into a currency forward contract, the buyer of the contract assumes an obligation to buy foreign currency from the seller at a specified price, on an agreed future date. In other words, a price for the foreign currency, called the forward exchange rate, is agreed on today, and this agreed-on exchange rate is the one at which the contract will be settled at the prespecified future date. No money actually changes hands until the date of contract maturity. In foreign exchange markets, there are reasonably liquid markets in forward exchange rates for most of the heavily traded currencies, with maturities of typically up to one year. Even for currencies and maturities for which forward prices are not readily observable, such prices can be easily derived, at least in principle, through the interest rate parity theorem (IRPT).

Currency forward contracts are traded in the interbank market in connection with spot foreign exchange rates. Although banks will quote "outright forwards" (i.e., forward prices quoted without reference to the spot exchange rate) to corporate customers, banks trade among themselves in the form of swaps (not to be confused with interest rate and currency swaps), which involve both a spot and a forward contract with simultaneous agreements for the purchase and sale of identical amounts of a currency at different value dates. Thus, most forward rates in interbank markets are quoted by reference to spot rates. It is estimated that approximately 35 percent of the $1 trillion in daily currency trading volume is accounted for by swaps and less than 2 percent by outright forwards.

If a foreign currency has a greater forward value than spot value (in terms of the domestic currency), the foreign currency is said to be at a forward premium (which implies that the domestic currency is at a forward discount); this simply means that a greater number of units of the domestic currency would have to be put out to buy one unit of the foreign currency at a future point in time. If the forward value of a foreign currency is less than the spot value, the foreign currency is at a forward discount (which implies that the domestic currency is at a premium). Because forward exchange is traded at a premium or discount to spot exchange, forward rates are quoted in terms of the premium or discount that is to be added to the spot rate. Such premiums or discounts are determined by a no-arbitrage condition, the IRPT, or covered interest parity condition, which establishes a relationship between risk-equivalent domestic and foreign nominal interest rates and spot and forward exchange rates.

Consider a spot exchange rate, e_0 (expressed as the number of units of domestic currency it takes to buy each unit of the foreign currency, or the "direct quote") with a forward exchange rate e_t (where t is the period) and domestic and foreign nominal interest rates on risk-equivalent securities for period t r_d and r_f, respectively. The IRPT says that given the spot exchange rate and the domestic and foreign nominal interest rates, in the absence of arbitrage opportunities, the forward rate must be exactly determined by

$$e_t = [e_0][(1 + r_d)/(1 + r_f)]$$

An approximate version of the same relationship follows:

Forward premium rate $= (e_t - e_0)/e_0 \approx r_d - r_f$

The reasoning behind this relationship is as follows: Agreeing to buy a foreign currency forward contract today at the forward exchange rate e_t is equivalent to borrowing a certain amount of domestic currency at interest rate r_d, converting it into foreign currency at today's spot exchange rate e_0, and investing these foreign currency proceeds at the foreign interest rate, r_f. The returns from these two transactions must be the same; otherwise, there would be an arbitrage opportunity in well-functioning markets.

It turns out that the interbank markets actually use this formula (adjusted for transaction costs) to derive forward exchange rates, and, as a result, quoted prices often reflect the "true" no-arbitrage price suggested by the formula (this offers an interesting example of a theoretical model driving real-world behavior).

Financial institutions and corporations are heavy users of forward currency contracts. Their main objective is financial risk management, i.e., to hedge currency exposure.

[2] Currency Futures

Although there are some important institutional differences between forward and futures contracts, futures contracts are conceptually similar to forward contracts in that they too, in theory, obligate the buyer of the contract to buy foreign currency from the seller at a specified price at a specified future date.

The first exchange-traded foreign currency futures contract was introduced on the International Monetary Market, now part of the CME, in 1972. Seven currencies were traded, and since then, others have been added. The CME remains the most active market in these contracts, although a number of other exchanges have launched their own contracts, e.g., the Philadelphia Board of Trade, the Singapore Monetary Exchange, and the Sydney Futures Exchange. In 1991, nearly 30 million currency futures contracts were traded, and the total value of open positions as of the end of 1991 was about $18 billion. (See Figure 3-6.)

Foreign exchange futures markets usually price currencies in terms of the number

FIGURE 3-6

Derivative Financial Instruments Traded on Organized Exchanges Worldwide

Source: Annual Report, *Vol. 62, Bank for International Settlements (Basel, Switzerland: 1992)*

Instrument	Annual Turnover of Contracts[a]					Open Positions at Year-End 1991[b]
	1987	1988	1989	1990	1991	
Futures on short-term interest rate instruments	$ 29.40	$ 33.70	$ 70.20	$ 75.80	$ 84.80	$1,907.50
Futures on long-term interest rate instruments	116.30	122.60	130.80	143.30	149.70	250.70
Total interest rate futures	$145.70	$156.30	$201.00	$219.10	$234.50	$2,158.20
Interest rate options and options on interest rate futures	29.30	30.50	39.50	52.00	50.80	1,072.40
Currency futures	20.80	22.10	27.50	29.10	29.20	17.80
Currency options and options on currency futures	18.20	18.20	20.70	18.80	21.50	59.40
Total	$214.00	$227.10	$288.70	$319.00	$336.00	$3,307.80
United States	$161.40	$165.30	$198.10	$205.70	$199.70	$2,004.30
Europe	27.20	32.60	49.00	61.00	84.20	680.20
Japan	18.30	18.80	23.70	33.60	30.00	390.50

[a] U.S. dollars in millions.
[b] U.S. dollars in billions.

of U.S. dollars per unit of foreign currency. Although futures appear similar to forward contracts, there are substantial differences:

- Futures contracts are marked to market, which means that there are daily cash flows. In a forward contract, no money changes hands until the contract expires, and, as a result, interest rate volatility is a potential source of valuation differences between forwards and futures.

- In futures contracts, both amounts and maturities are standardized. This is not the case with forwards, which can be tailored contracts.

- Futures are traded on organized exchanges; forwards are traded on the OTC market.

- Futures have a secondary market; forwards typically do not have a secondary market.

- Futures are delivered at expiration only in about 5 percent of the cases; forwards are delivered in about 90 percent of the cases.

- Futures are used more frequently for speculative purposes (i.e., betting on the directions of futures price movements), and forwards for hedging purposes.

Although foreign exchange futures contracts offer liquid and transparent tools for hedging and speculating on foreign exchange movements, their inflexibility and the difficulties involved in managing basis risk (i.e., the risk that the movements in spot and futures prices is not one for one) make them somewhat more difficult than forward contracts to use for specific hedging purposes.

[3] Currency Options

Options contracts give the buyer of the contract the right but not the obligation to buy or sell something. The holder (buyer) of a currency option has the right but not the obligation to exchange a fixed amount of one currency for another at a fixed exchange rate (the strike or exercise price) on or before a predetermined future date. An option to buy foreign currency is called a call option (as in "I call it in"), and an option to sell, a put option (as in "I put it to you"). (See Chapter A9 in the *Handbook of Modern Finance* and Chapter 9 in the *Handbook of Financial Markets*.) Since all foreign exchange transactions involve buying one currency by selling another, a call option on the foreign currency is the same as a put option on the domestic currency.

Options that can only be exercised at maturity are called European options, and those that can be exercised any time up to (and including) maturity are called American options. This right to exercise the option comes with an option premium or option price (usually paid two working days after the deal) and represents the maximum loss to the buyer and thus also the maximum profit to the seller.

The Philadelphia Stock Exchange was the first to list traded currency options, at the beginning of the 1980s. At the same time, banks started to quote option prices to each other, and the secondary OTC market was born. In 1985, standard terms and conditions for London OTC options were devised, and these conventions soon became internationally accepted. In 1991, over 20 million currency option contracts were traded, for a year-end open position of nearly $60 billion. (See Figure 3-6.) The market for currency options and futures, taken together, grew from $49 billion in 1986 to $77 billion in 1991. (See Figure 3-7.)

There are three basic types of currency options:

1. *Options on spot*. These are options to buy or sell spot foreign currency and can be either American or European options.

2. *Options on futures*. These are options to go long (call) or short (put) an exchange-traded currency futures contract, and are typically American options.

3. *Futures-style options*. These are basically speculative contracts where investors are speculating on the direction of the option price: The buyer agrees to pay (or receive) a daily cash flow equal to any decrease (or increase) in the market value of the option, in addition to which there is an option to buy or sell the underlying currency. Premiums are paid only at exercise and are marked to market daily.

There are well-known models (e.g., the Black-Scholes model and its variants) to price each type of option, and these can be found in any textbook on international finance (this model will not be developed here, since it would require considerable digression and substantial notation). For readers who are already familiar with the Black-Scholes model in the context of equity options, an important point to note is that, unlike the traditional model, the option pricing model for foreign currencies requires the use of two interest rates rather than one: domestic and foreign interest rates (recall the connection between the two interest rates from IRPT).

A wide range of products is now available, and more are being researched and

FIGURE 3-7

Expansion of Selected Derivative Markets

Source: Annual Report, *Vol. 62, Bank for International Settlements (Basel, Switzerland: 1992)*

Instrument	1986	1987	1988	1989	1990	1991
Exchange-traded instruments	$ 583	$ 724	$1,300	$1,762	$2,284	$3,518
Interest rate options and futures	516	609	1,174	1,588	2,054	3,231
Currency options and futures	49	74	60	66	72	77
Stock index options and futures	18	41	66	108	158	210
OTC instruments	500	867	1,330	2,402	3,451	4,080[a] [b]
Interest rate swaps	400[a]	683	1,010	1,503	2,312	2,750[a] [b]
Currency and interest-currency swaps[c]	100[a]	184	320	449	578	700[a] [b]
Other[c] [d]	NA	NA	NA	450	561	630[a] [b]

Note: Notional principal amounts outstanding at year-end in billions of U.S. dollars.

[a] Estimated data.

[b] Data as of June 1991.

[c] Data adjusted for reporting of both currencies.

[d] Caps, collars, floors, and swaptions.

developed. Various payoff structures, each with several names, have been developed to get over investors' unwillingness to pay up-front premiums. These can delay the premium payment until maturity (e.g., Boston options), reduce the premium by giving up some of the benefit (e.g., participating forwards), or get rid of it all together (cylinder options). Nearly all of these more complex instruments are just combinations of call and put options (and sometimes spot and forward currencies) in varying amounts and/ or different exercise prices.

The OTC market is the largest market for currency options. This market consists of banks, securities firms, and corporations. The two major exchange-listed markets are Philadelphia, where the stock exchange lists options on spot foreign currency, and Chicago, where the CME lists options on its currency futures contracts.

[4] Interest Rate Futures

The increased volatility of interest rates that followed the abandonment of fixed exchange rates and interest rates led to a need for new ways to hedge exposure to this source of volatility. One of the most successful products that has emerged in the process is the exchange-traded interest rate futures contract. (See Chapter A10 in the *Handbook of Modern Finance* and Chapter 10 in the *Handbook of Financial Markets.*) The first traded interest rate future was the Government National Mortgage Association collateralized depository receipts contract that opened on the Chicago Board of Trade (CBT) in 1975. Since then, over 50 futures and options exchanges have opened worldwide. As of 1991, over $2 trillion in notional principal value of short-term and long-term bonds was covered by interest rate futures contracts. (See Figure 3-6.)

In an interest rate futures contract, the underlying asset is a short-term or long-term bond. Contracts are normally traded for March, June, September, and December deliveries or settlements. Long-term interest rate futures contracts generally specify physical delivery. They often oblige the buyer to purchase a specified fixed-income instrument at maturity if the contract is not closed by an equal and offsetting transaction in the market. On the other hand, short-term interest rate futures contracts are usually settled with cash on the expiring date.

Interest rate futures contracts are used for both hedging and speculation. Company treasurers, fixed-income fund managers, and banks are the typical users of these instruments. Futures contracts are off-balance sheet transactions, with high liquidity. However, some OTC instruments can be used to replicate the hedging function provided by interest rate futures contracts; these include interest rate and currency swaps and forward rate agreements (FRAs).

[5] Interest Rate Options

Given the inverse relationship between interest rates and bond prices, interest rate options are usually traded as options on bonds. Bond options were developed in response to the success of interest rate futures contracts. A number of U.S. exchanges have developed bond, note, and bill options covering virtually the entire range of the Treasury yield curve. In addition, dozens of futures and option exchanges have been set up around the world, and many list at least one bond option among their products. The most heavily traded of these is the CBT's option on U.S. Treasury bond futures.

The majority of options on bonds are options on bond futures (futures options). The buyer of the option buys the right to buy a bond future at a specified price at a specified time in the future. However, a few bond options contracts are options on the underlying cash instrument. The holder of this type of contract has the right to buy or sell the bond directly. Bond options are used to speculate or hedge against interest rate movements. The major advantage of options is that instead of locking in a specific bond price or interest rate, the the option allows the holder to retain the ability to benefit from any moves in its favor (until the option is exercised).

The bond options market is largely used by financial institutions: Banks use it for asset and liability management; providers of OTC products use it to hedge their positions; dealers in government bonds and Eurobonds use it to hedge positions both secondary markets and related to bids placed in auctions and related to the underwriting of new issues; arbitrage departments of banks and investment banks use it for speculation. As of the end of 1991, there were interest rate options and futures contracts on international bonds with a notional principal amount totaling over $3.2 trillion. (See Figure 3-7.)

[6] Caps and Floors

Caps and floors are interest rate options on FRNs. In an interest rate cap, the seller (writer) contracts to pay the buyer the difference between an actual (reference) interest rate and a cap interest rate level, should the chosen reference rate exceed the cap's interest rate level. In other words, the buyer of a cap need not pay any more than the cap rate (equivalent to the exercise price on an option), regardless of where the actual interest rate is. Thus, a cap is equivalent to a series of call options on the interest rate, where the exercise price is the cap interest rate (a series of options because, during the maturity of the FRN, the reference rate would be periodically reset a number of times). In an interest rate floor, the seller agrees to pay the buyer should the reference interest rate fall below the strike price. Thus (as in the case of caps' being calls), a floor is equivalent to a series of put options on the interest rate, where the exercise price of the put is the floor interest rate. In both cases, the seller receives a premium for taking on the risk.

The market for interest rate caps and floors began in 1985, when a group of 20 large banks in the United States issued $2.75 billion of floating-rate notes. These notes contained options that capped the corporate issuers' floating-rate exposure at a maximum level. As a means of reducing the issuer's borrowing cost, the banks then stripped (i.e., unbundled) these caps and sold them in the market for an up-front fee. In the 1980s, U.S. savings and loans institutions, concerned about hedging their short-term borrowing costs against their returns on their longer-terms loans, emerged as the largest buyers of caps.

Corporations and financial institutions use caps and floors to hedge exposure to adverse movements in interest rates. In many cases, these products offer substantial advantages over other hedging alternatives. Caps and floors are OTC options that the user may customize to fit a specific financial need. For example, a cap gives the buyer the additional flexibility of benefiting from lower rates—being able to borrow at less cost—while maximizing the exposure to rates moving higher. Although hedging such exposure through swap or futures contracts may be cheaper, the borrower is not locked into a fixed rate for the entire transaction.

While the market for U.S. dollar caps and floors developed the most rapidly, options denominated in other currencies have experienced similar growth patterns. Having participated in the U.S. dollar caps and floors markets, London dealers extended their trading capacity to include these instruments denominated in U.K. pounds. The market for deutsche mark caps and floors received a boost during the early period of German unification in the fall of 1990. The yen market expanded mainly as a result of banks' and trusts' selling these options to speculate.

Caps and floors are now traded in a large and liquid market. The increasing number of financial institutions entering the market as active traders accounts for much of this expansion. Most markets now provide liquidity for bonds with maturities of up to 10 years, although the 1-to-5-year maturities trade most actively.

[7] Forward Rate Agreements

The FRA market began to develop in 1983, as activity in financial futures markets and the incentives to hedge exposure to volatile interest rates grew. Standard terms for FRA dealing were published by the British Bankers' Association in August 1985, and these terms are generally accepted throughout the market.

An FRA enables a firm to protect itself against interest rate risk. It fixes the effective interest rate on a future borrowing (or deposit) in advance of the intended borrowing (or deposit) date. In an FRA contract, the parties agree to exchange the difference between the market rate of interest on the contract's effective date and the agreed-on fixed rate, decided on the date of the execution of contract.

FRAs are available in a wide range of the primary trading currencies and are available in all major financial centers. Though an FRA is an OTC product, it is usually transacted in standard deal sizes for standard periods. In the U.S. dollar segment, the size of interbank deals is commonly $50 million, and $10 million is considered the smallest marketable size. In terms of maturities, an FRA usually covers only one interest period (usually 3, 6, or 12 months), and this period can be fixed up to 18 months ahead of time; other terms can only be reached by negotiation.

[8] Interest Rate Swaps

An interest rate swap is a contractual agreement between two parties to exchange a series of payments for a stated period. In a typical interest rate swap, one party issues fixed-rate debt while another issues floating-rate debt, and the two swap interest payment obligations based on a notional principal amount (the principal itself is not exchanged). Since its beginnings in the late 1970s, the interest rate swap market has grown into a market where in excess of $3 trillion in securities has been swapped. (See Figure 3-7.)

The market for swaps is organized by market makers, usually large commercial banks, which take the opposite side of any reasonable swap transaction. Swaps done in one side will be warehoused until they can be done on the other. Interest payments are made on the basis of a notional principal amount, which is itself not paid nor received.

The price of a swap, its all-in cost, is quoted as the rate the fixed-rate payer will pay to the floating-rate payer. It is quoted on a semiannual basis, either as an absolute level or as a basis-point spread over the Treasury yield curve. The fixed-rate payer receives floating interest and is said to be long or to have bought the swap. The long side has conceptually purchased a floating-rate note (because it receives floating interest) and issued a coupon bond (because it pays out fixed interest at periodic intervals).

There are several forms of interest rate swap besides the traditional one described:

- *Off-market swap*. Any swap set up with a nonzero initial value is "off market," and at some point a compensating up-front payment from one party to the other or a lower-than-market coupon will be required to bring the net value to zero.

- *Zero-coupon swap*. A zero-coupon swap is an extreme case of an off-market swap, in which one of the counterparties makes a lump-sum payment instead of periodic payments over time.

- *Basis swap*. A basis swap is a swap between two floating-rate indexes. An example is when LIBOR interest payments are swapped against interest payments based on the CP index on the same notional amount.

- *Asset swaps and synthetic securities*. Swaps are used not only for managing liabilities but also for engineering cash flows from assets into desired formats. For example, a floating-rate asset can be converted into a synthetic fixed-rate asset using an interest rate swap.

- *Forward swap*. A forward swap is one in which there is a delay between the date on which the swap is traded or committed to and the settlement or effective date of the swap. It is like a forward contract to enter into a swap.

- *Currency swap*. In a currency swap, one party agrees to make periodic payments in one currency to a counterparty, which in turn makes periodic payments to the other in a different currency.

Swaps are generally used in an attempt to reduce either fixed-rate or floating-rate costs, to guarantee liquidity, and to convert fixed-rate borrowing to floating. It has become a widely used tool by all manner of firms—financial and nonfinancial, sophisticated and not-so-sophisticated—the world over. Since its inception, the swap market has grown to a multi-billion-dollar global market. Its huge liquidity currently enables almost any combination to meet investors' needs. Although the most common swaps have maturities of up to 5 to 10 years, some deals have included maturities of up to 30 years. These are maturities that go well beyond those of other markets, such as the forwards, futures, or options markets.

[9] Currency Swaps

As with interest rate swaps, the currency swap market arose from earlier parallel and back-to-back loan structures that were developed in the 1970s. These structures involved companies in one country simultaneously lending in their domestic currencies to companies in another country and in turn being lent money by the counterparty. They enabled companies (or financial institutions) to circumvent regulations in countries with foreign exchange controls or to provide medium and long-term instruments where none existed.

There are many uses for currency swaps. Borrowers with funding advantages in different markets can exchange these benefits to gain attractive funding costs in non-domestic currencies. Swaps can also be useful in the management of existing liabilities and assets; hedging currency exposure associated with acquisitions, divestitures, and management of subsidiaries abroad; and circumventing foreign exchange regulations.

Cross-currency swaps currently undertaken do not involve currency loans like their predecessors. Instead, one party typically agrees to make periodic payments, based on either fixed or floating interest rates, to a counterparty, who in turn makes periodic payments to the other in a different currency. The payments are based on notional principal amounts that are fixed at the initiation of the swap. Unlike interest rate swaps, in a currency swap the principal amount is generally exchanged at the beginning of the transaction and reexchanged at maturity. A currency swap is therefore often a complete swap of liabilities.

Unlike exchange-traded instruments or forwards, swap markets are liquid for up to around 10 years, and swaps dated as long as 30 years are not unheard of. Also, because there is a liquid 2-way market, cross-currency swaps can be tailored to meet the requirements of almost any counterparty. Major corporations, financial institutions, governments, and governmental entities worldwide currently use these instruments.

[a] **Example of a Currency Swap.** Suppose a French company would like to borrow floating-rate U.S. dollars to finance a foreign investment but is not very well known outside of France. There is a similar U.S. company that would like to borrow fixed-rate French francs.

An intermediary may get involved in putting the two companies together through a currency swap: The French company issues a fixed-rate franc bond, turns the franc proceeds over to the U.S. company, and agrees to pay the U.S. company its dollar coupon on principal obligations on a U.S. dollar FRN that the U.S. company would issue (and whose proceeds would be turned over to the French company). In this case, since the U.S. company has the fixed-rate payment commitment in the swap deal, it is said to be long the swap (while the French company, which has a floating-rate payment commitment in the swap deal, is said to be short the swap).

[b] Valuation of Swaps. The value of a swap at any time is simply the value of the portfolio that is long one bond and short the other; that is, it is the difference between the values of the two bonds. In a currency swap, the change in this value is dependent on two factors: interest rate changes and exchange rate changes.

The general effects of these changes are as follows:

- A change in interest rates would primarily affect the long side of the swap, since that is the side that has a fixed payment obligation; the value of FRNs is affected to a far lesser degree by interest rate changes (since coupon payments on an FRN change as the interest rate changes). For example, an increase in interest rates would make the long side better off, since that party is committed to making lower fixed-coupon payments than what the market currently requires; similarly, a decrease in interest rates makes the long side worse off, since it is locked into paying a higher fixed coupon than what the market currently requires.

- A depreciation of one of the currencies makes the party that is getting the coupon payments in that currency worse off; on the other hand, an appreciation makes that party better off.

Consider the long side in the previous example, the U.S. firm. Suppose U.S. dollar interest rates fall and nothing happens to franc interest rates. Since the U.S. firm has a dollar FRN asset, its asset value does not change (approximately speaking); on the other hand, since franc interest rates do not change, the value of its fixed-rate franc liability does not change either. Therefore, in this instance, the value of the swap does not change because of the interest rate change. However, suppose the dollar depreciates against the franc. This depreciation must mean that the party receiving the dollar coupons and paying the franc coupons—i.e., the U.S. firm—is made worse off to the extent of the depreciation.

[10] Swaptions

Options associated with swaps are often termed swaptions. Swaption contracts give the right to enter into a swap agreement, or to exit out of a swap, under specified terms and conditions. A swaption call gives the buyer the right but not the obligation to receive fixed payments based on a fixed interest rate and to pay a floating interest rate. That is, the swaption call gives the buyer the right to go short a swap. A swaption put gives the right (but not the obligation) to pay a fixed rate and receive a floating rate, i.e., the right to go long a swap.

Swaptions are an OTC product: The strike price, the maturity, the size, and the structure can be tailored to suit the particular needs of individual clients. Both American- and European-style swaptions are available.

There are two main categories of users of the swaption market, each having different expectations and each assuming varying degrees of risk. Corporate treasurers use swaptions to hedge an existing or anticipated exposure while still being able to profit from a beneficial movement in interest rates. The cost of the swaption represents the total possible loss on the transaction for the buyer, while leaving its profit potential unlimited. Financial institutions use swaptions to manage the complex and dynamic risks of an option portfolio.

3.04 FUTURE MARKET EVOLUTION AND POTENTIAL REGULATION

The 1980s witnessed a revolutionary shift in the scope, depth, and sophistication of international financial markets, fueled to a significant degree by the growth of derivatives. Many types of risk management tools that are commonplace today came into existence less than a decade ago. The financing and risk management choices available to a chief financial officer operating in the global marketplace today are impressive.

That decade also witnessed a steady decline in the role of regulation, in part out of choice (e.g., the ascendence of conservative political philosophies in the U.K. and U.S. financial markets and the role of economic integration in the continental European markets) but also in part out of necessity (e.g., the slower pace of changes in the Japanese markets and the range and sophistication of financial instruments, as well as the role of technology in moving money across borders in seconds, which put these markets beyond the reach of regulators). Many types of restrictions on prices, quantities, types of products, and controls over geographical bases of operations were abolished, and this wave of deregulation found its way to the developing world as well (notably Latin America and, increasingly, Asia).

Yet, the 1980s was also the decade in which the range of financial crises paralleled that of financial instruments. Beginning with the lesser developing country (LDC) debt crisis in the early part of the decade (a problem that appears to be on its way to resolution), the 1980s saw a globally transmitted stock market crash, the crisis in the savings and loan industry in the United States, the collapse of the high-yield bond market, spectacular bank failures such as the Bank of Commerce and Credit International (BCCI) and Banco Ambrosiano affairs, insider stock and bond trading scandals, the collapse of property markets in the industrialized world, the 60 percent secular decline in the Tokyo stock market after an equally impressive rise, the rise and fall of the ECU bond market, and a European currency crisis, to name a few of the more important events. However, there was no crisis in the derivatives markets.

The financial services sector (notably the banking sector) underwent significant changes. The first type of change, common to all of the industrialized countries, was the growing institutionalization of savings. For example, in the United States, according to the BIS, financial institutions held about 20 percent of household financial assets in 1980, a figure that grew to over 30 percent in 1990. Similar figures for Japan are 15.6 percent and 26.4 percent; for Germany, 22.6 percent and 35.1 percent; for France, 10.6 percent and 36.3 percent; and for the United Kingdom, 41.5 percent and 58.6 percent. The second change was the growing competition, the increased role of securitization, and the increased off-balance sheet exposures of the banking sector. Bank profit margins dropped, and noninterest income as a proportion of total income grew significantly for banks in most of the OECD countries. The third major change was the growing indebtedness of the private sector in the industrialized world. Finally, from the standpoint of the regulators, the fourth major change was the increasing opaqueness of cross-border financial transactions: Traditional statistics that purported to measure a country's external capital transactions, such as the balance of payments accounts, were effectively rendered useless from the standpoint of policy formulation and implementation. This opaqueness was also perhaps extended to the less sophisticated (and retail) consumers of these financial services.

Each of these changes offers some potential clues to the shape of things to come. The growing institutionalization of savings suggests even greater activity in financial markets, since it is generally believed that financial institutions trade far more often than individual investors. The increased off-balance sheet incomes of the banking sector suggest a shift in the structure of the banking industry away from their traditional borrowing and lending activities (activities that are inherently more retail- and relationship-oriented in nature) toward those that are more information- and innovation-intensive (activities that are inherently more wholesale- and transaction-oriented in nature). Shrinking profit margins suggest that banks will seek new avenues to increase their returns, avenues that are likely to be therefore riskier; further, it is likely that banks will attempt to combat the increased product-market competition through more attempts at mergers and consolidation. In addition, while securitization has become a mature activity in the United States, it is still a relatively open field in other parts of the world. There may yet be growth in securitization in non-U.S. markets and the development of derivative securities around such securitized products. The growth in private-sector indebtedness suggests a possible shift away from debt-type instruments toward equity-type instruments.

Clearly, the development in the growth and sophistication of derivatives is a trend that is likely to continue through the 1990s. We may, however, see the emergence of derivatives on securities traded in emerging equity markets, notably those in Asia and Latin America. In addition, while the market for debt-for-asset, debt-for-equity, and debt-for-debt swaps in Latin American countries is mostly stagnant (because of the improved performance of these economies), such transactions may be on the verge of a take-off in Eastern Europe and the former Soviet Union.

Perhaps the most uncertain aspect of the future evolution of the financial services sector is the potential for new types of regulation. It is evident that regulators are concerned by the range of financial crises of the 1980s and their sense of the increasing opaqueness of financial markets resulting from the roles of innovation and technology, as well as their own sense of inability. In its 1992 annual report, the BIS expresses this concern:

> [T]hese changes [in the financial services sector] have heightened the importance of payment and settlement arrangements and of market risks, have vastly increased the speed with which turmoil can spread and have heightened the role of liquidity provision as the lifeblood of financial activity. They have also complicated the resolution of problems by rendering markets and institutions more opaque and participants less homogeneous.

The report also expresses concern at the "unprecedented intraday liquidity and credit exposures" in banks, and the potential risk of "domino effects."

One source of concern is the information problem that is inherent in any large-scale financial activity: While any particular institution has sufficient information on its own exposures, there is an information problem (compounded by lack of comprehensive and timely statistics) concerning systemwide exposures. As is well known in the economics literature (e.g., in relation to the LDC debt crisis), one of the problems that could be induced by the individual-versus-collective-information asymmetry is over-commitment to particular types of securities (and derivatives) in particular markets. In the international context, this potential information problem is exacerbated by these facts: (1) There is an absence of commonly accepted and enforced regulatory standards among countries and (2) even if there were common standards, there is a void at the intersection of sovereign boundaries in terms of cross-border design and enforcement of regulations (e.g., in the BCCI case). There is some evidence that regulators in the leading economies are collectively attempting to develop common regulatory, prudential, and supervisory standards, as reflected in the activities of organizations such as the International Organization of Securities Commissions or the application of a common set of capital adequacy standards (the Basel Standards) for banks worldwide. There is also movement toward the development of some common standards for cross-border claim settlement rules, although, in the absence of common bankruptcy codes among countries (even among countries in the European Community), it is doubtful whether any significant progress will be made in this area. The one area where regulation is likely to increase is in the timely disclosure of off-balance sheet and derivatives transactions for both financial and nonfinancial firms.

In short, the decade of the 1990s (and beyond) promises to be at least as exciting as the last decade in terms of the continued development of direct securities and derivatives, as well as the possible reemergence of regulation in newer and cross-border forms.

Suggested Reading

Crossan, R., and M. Johnson. *The Guide to International Capital Markets*. London: *Euromoney* Publications, 1992.

Freedman, R. "A Theory of the Impact of International Cross-Listings." Working Paper, Stanford University, 1989.

French, K., and J. Poterba. "Investor Diversification and International Equity Markets." *American Economic Review*, Vol. 81 (May 1991), pp. 222–226.

Grabbe, Orlin. *International Financial Markets*, 2nd ed. New York: Elsevier Science Publishing, 1991.

Howe, J.S., and J. Madura. "The Impact of International Listings on Risk: The Implications for Capital Market Integration." *Journal of Banking and Finance*, Vol. 14 (Dec. 1990), pp. 1133–1142.

International Financial Corporation. *The Emerging Stock Markets Factbook: 1991*. Washington, D.C.: World Bank, 1992.

Internationalization of the Securities Markets. Division of Corporate Finance, Securities and Exchange Commission. Washington, D.C.: 1990.

Jayaraman, N., K. Shastri, and K. Tandon. "The Impact of International Cross-Listings on Risk and Return: The Evidence From American Depository Receipts." *Journal of Banking and Finance*, Vol. 17 (Feb. 1993), pp. 91–104.

Kim, Y., and R. Stulz. "The Eurobond Market and Corporate Financial Policy: A Test of the Clientele Hypothesis." *Journal of Financial Economics*, Vol. 22 (Dec. 1988), pp. 189–205.

Marr, W., J. Trimble, and R. Varma. "On the Integration of International Capital Markets: Evidence From Euroequity Offerings." *Financial Management*, Vol. 20 (Winter 1991), pp. 11–21.

Marshall, J.F., and K.R. Kapner. *Understanding Swap Finance*. Cincinnati: Southwestern Publishing Co., 1990.

Mason, R. *Innovations in the Structure of International Securities*. London: Credit Suisse First Boston Research, 1986.

Nix, W.E., and S.W. Nix. *Dow Jones-Irwin Guide to International Securities, Futures, and Options Markets*. Homewood, Ill.: Dow Jones-Irwin, 1988.

Parker, William E. *A Banker's Guide to Capital Markets Products*. Boston: The John Colet Press, 1991.

Pavel, C., and J.N. McElravey. "Globalization in the Financial Services Industry." *Economic Perspectives.*, Vol. 14. Chicago: Federal Reserve Bank of Chicago, May-June 1990, pp. 3–18.

Solnik, Bruno. *International Investments,* 2nd ed. Reading, Mass.: Addison-Wesley, 1991.

Stern, Joel M., and Donald H. Chew Jr., eds. *New Developments in International Finance.* New York: Basil Blackwell, 1988.

Wheatly, S. "Some Tests of International Equity Integration." *Journal of Financial Economics*, Vol. 21 (Sept. 1989), pp. 177–212.

Chapter 4

International Banking

ROBERT GROSSE

SIVAKUMAR VENKATARAMANY

4.01 **Introduction** 89

4.02 **Historical Perspectives** 92

4.03 **Current Perspectives** 93

4.04 **International Banking Activity in Selected Countries** 95
  [1] Canada 98
  [2] Germany 99
  [3] Hong Kong 100
  [4] Japan 100
  [5] Switzerland 101
  [6] United Kingdom 102
  [7] United States 102
  [8] Brazil 104

4.05 **Foreign Exchange Markets** 104
  [1] Basic Market Characteristics 104
  [2] Foreign Exchange Trading 106
  [3] Brokers' Market 108
  [4] Foreign Exchange Rate Quotations 108
  [5] Forward Market 108
  [6] Arbitrage in Foreign Exchange Markets 109

4.06 **Euromarkets** 111
  [1] Scope of the Markets 111
  [2] Key Role of the Markets 112
  [3] Bases of the Markets 112
  [4] Eurocurrency Interest Rates 114
  [5] Instruments of the Euromarkets 116
  [6] Criticisms of the Euromarkets 117
  [7] European Community 117

4.07 **Trade Financing** 119
  [1] Export-Import Transactions 119
  [2] Traditional Forms of Trade Finance 121

  [3] Government Loans and Loan Guarantees 124
  [4] Countertrade 124
  [5] Factoring 127
  [6] Forfaiting 127
  [7] Leasing 128

4.08 **Cross-Border Credit Extension** 128
  [1] Interbank Lending 129
  [2] Commercial Lending to Foreign Clients 129
  [3] Credit to Government Borrowers 130
  [4] Instruments in Cross-Border Lending 131
    [a] Syndicated Loans 131
    [b] Project Financing 132
    [c] Debt-To-Equity Swaps 133

4.09 **Cross-Border Liabilities** 134
  [1] Petrodollars 135
  [2] International Corporate Deposits 136
  [3] Personal Banking 136

4.10 **Other International Banking Services** . 137
  [1] Information Services 137
  [2] Electronic Banking Services 138
  [3] Corporate Cash Management 138
  [4] Interest Rate Swaps 138

4.11 **Managerial Issues** 140
  [1] Risk Management 140
  [2] Country Risk 140
    [a] Nature of Country Risk 140
    [b] Measuring Country Risk 141
    [c] Dealing With Country Risk 141
  [3] Competitive Strategy 142
  [4] Lending Strategy 143
  [5] Funding Strategy 144
  [6] Organizational Structure 146

[7] Marketing International Services 148

**4.12 Other International Banking
Structures** 149

[1] Offshore Banking Centers 149

[2] International Banking Facilities 150

4.13 Future of International Banking 150

Suggested Reading 150

4.01 INTRODUCTION

The basic business of commercial banking consists of financial intermediation and provision of noncredit services such as risk management and investment information. In addition, because banks must manage their own funds, it involves concerns similar to those of a corporate treasury, with the major difference being that the bank's sales and costs are based primarily on use of financial instruments rather than goods or services. Thus, banking involves provision of financial services to clients and management of financial instruments for the institution itself.

International banking is commercial banking that involves transactions crossing national borders or national currencies. While the basic concerns are still extension of credit, attraction of deposits and other funding sources, risk management, and provision of information, the instruments, clients, and rules differ widely.

International banking involves transactions such as loans to clients in countries other than that of the lender; deposits received from clients residing in countries other than that of the receiving institution; foreign exchange (forex) provisions for carrying out international transactions; issuance of letters of credit and other risk management instruments to protect clients from various international business risks; and provision of noncredit financial services, such as trust advising, treasury management, and check clearing, to foreign clients.

The main participants in international banking are the commercial banks from dozens of countries, central banks that set the rules of the game in each country, and nonbank clients that utilize the banks' services. The international client base is quite different from that of domestic banks. For one thing, international banking tends to be much more of a wholesale business, with large transactions constituting much more of the activity. Interbank dealings for millions of U.S. dollars per transaction are common in the Euromarkets and in the foreign exchange market; indeed, these make up the bulk of the value of international banking transactions. International loans to governments and companies are generally much larger than loans to domestic clients, which also include retail borrowers. The large size of the market should not be overstated, however; certainly the bulk of the *number* of transactions in international banking are financing of exports and imports and small-scale forex dealings with clients. Nonetheless, the *value* of transactions in the market just as clearly demonstrates that the interbank, large transactions dominate the total business.

The size of international banking can be measured in many ways. Figure 4-1 offers a view of the size of some key parts of international banking business and comparisons with other relevant aggregates. The Eurocurrency market worldwide is larger than any national money supply, and it amounts to a value similar to gross domestic product (GDP) in the world's largest economy. While these comparisons must be judged with care—since, for example, the Eurocurrency market is not part of the basic money supply (defined as cash plus demand deposits), and gross national product (GNP) involves real production, while financial transfers are only movements of financial assets from one owner to another—nonetheless it is quite striking to see the huge size of international banking markets and important to understand their implications.

The importance of international banking can be seen from another view, namely its significance to the banks that participate in these activities. Bank surveys from 1980 onward have shown consistently that the world's largest banks actively participate in international activities and earn substantial portions of their total income from such business. International business is a primary focus of several of the largest banks. Figure 4-2 lists the largest banks ranked by their tier one capital, consisting of paid-

FIGURE 4-1

Size of International Banking

Source: Morgan Guaranty Trust Company, World Financial Markets; *Federal Reserve Bank of New York,* Quarterly Review *(Summer 1984);* The Wall Street Journal; *Organization for Economic Cooperation and Development,* International Financial Trends; Federal Reserve Bulletin; *Bank for International Settlements*

	Value					
Type of Activity	**1970**	**1980**	**1983**	**1986**	**1987**	**1992**
Eurocurrency market: gross value of deposits at year-end	$110	$1,524.0	$ 2,278		$4,461.0	$6,100.00
Net value of deposits	35	477.0	479		959.0	1,408.00
Percentage of U.S. dollars	76%	75%	81%		66%	77%
Foreign exchange markets: monthly turnover						
New York			$ 456.0[a]	$1,325.3[b]		$4,695.56[a]
Tokyo			183.0[a]			
Singapore			118.0[a]			
Value of cross-border loans of commercial banks by home country						
United States			$ 590.2[c]		$ 647.6[c]	$ 720.30[c]
United Kingdom			192.9[c]		253.9[c]	1,061.30[c]
West Germany			191.2[c]		347.9[c]	523.50[c]
Japan			707.2[c]		1,552.1[c]	767.90[c]
France			244[c]		375.5[c]	523.50[c]
Value of banker's acceptances outstanding (trading in New York market)			$ 78.3[c]		$ 70.6[c]	
Value of deposits in international banking facilities			$ 167.9[c]		$ 306.0[c]	
Money supply of United States			$ 525.3[c]		$ 751.1[c]	$1,011.40[c]
GNP of United States			$3,405.7		$4,488.6	$6,031.50

Note: U.S. dollars in billions.
[a] April.
[b] March.
[c] Year-end.

up share capital and disclosed reserves. The largest banks earn major portions of their income from international activities (which include the domestic banking business of these banks' overseas affiliates). These data need to be interpreted carefully, since the vast majority of banks in the industrial countries, as well as in less developed nations, operate primarily in the domestic market.

International banking is largely a legal and cultural phenomenon, totally dependent on government policy to determine the structure and functioning of markets where it takes place. Banks develop services in response to clients' needs, but they only can

FIGURE 4-2

International Bank Scoreboard (1992)

Source: Euromoney (June 1992)

Bank	Country	Tier One Capital	Assets	Capital-To-Asset Ratio	Profit	Profit/Capital Ratio (%)	Return on Assets (%)
1. Sumitomo Bank	Japan	$15,217	$406,107	3.75	$1,024	6.73	0.25
2. Dai-Ichi Kangyo Bank	Japan	13,599	425,509	3.20	649	4.77	0.15
3. Fuji Bank	Japan	13,257	396,450	3.34	716	5.40	0.18
4. Sanwa Bank	Japan	13,019	400,740	3.25	801	6.15	0.20
5. Union Bank of Switzerland	Switzerland	12,858	183,911	6.99	897	6.98	0.49
6. Mitsubishi Bank	Japan	12,010	380,439	3.16	724	6.03	0.19
7. Barclays Bank	United Kingdom	11,676	263,708	4.43	529	4.53	0.20
8. Sakura Bank	Japan	11,550	405,953	2.85	609	5.27	0.15
9. Deutsche Bank	Germany	11,230	298,158	3.77	912	8.12	0.31
10. Compagnie Financiere De Paribas	France	11,067	199,727	5.54	211	1.91	0.11
11. Industrial and Commercial Bank of China	China	10,593	179,688	5.90	2,537	23.95	1.41
12. National Westminster Bank	United Kingdom	10,371	232,097	4.47	134	1.29	0.06
13. Credit Lyonnais	France	9,651	306,334	3.15	787	8.15	0.26
14. Citicorp	United States	9,489	216,922	4.37	457	4.82	0.21
15. Industrial Bank of Japan	Japan	9,431	287,941	3.28	467	4.95	0.16
16. Swiss Bank Corp	Switzerland	9,183	152,731	6.01	761	8.29	0.50
17. Caisses D'Epargne Ecureuil (Cencep)	France	9,121	174,965	5.21	553	6.06	0.32
18. ABN-AMRO Bank	Netherlands	8,973	242,686	3.70	898	10.01	0.37
19. Bank of China	China	8,190	140,153	5.84	1,179	14.40	0.84
20. Caisse Des Depots Et Consignations	France	8,091	74,965	10.79	682	8.43	0.91
21. BankAmerica Corp.	United States	8,063	115,509	6.98	1,124	13.94	0.97
22. Rabobank Nederland	Netherlands	7,612	126,901	6.00	594	7.80	0.47
23. Tokai Bank	Japan	7,442	247,853	3.00	310	4.17	0.13
24. Long-Term Credit Bank of Japan	Japan	7,379	213,108	3.46	264	3.58	0.12
25. Chemical Banking Corp.	United States	7,281	138,930	5.24	154	2.12	0.11

Note: U.S. dollars in millions.

offer these services with the permission of governments in the countries involved. Each time governments change the rules, banking competition changes, and often institutions swing from strong to weak positions or vice versa. (For example, the International Banking Act of the United States in 1978 permitted foreign banks to establish U.S. offices under essentially the same rules as domestic banks. This led to large-scale participation of foreign banks such as HongKong Bank, Barclays Bank, Industrial Bank of Japan, and many others in U.S. financial markets.)

Another consideration is the importance of such activity to the economies of the countries involved. Just how significant are the international loans and deposits undertaken through the banking system to economic development, efficient functioning of financial and real markets, and the ability of governments to pursue their economic policies? There are no simple answers, although one can make the general argument that by opening financial markets to foreign participation, international banking makes the process of uniting lenders and borrowers more efficient than they would be in a solely domestic context. Also, it could be argued that the commercial banks are the primary vehicles through which financial disaster was avoided during the Organization of Petroleum Exporting Countries (OPEC) oil crises of the 1970s, when the banks recycled hundreds of billions of dollars earned by the oil-exporting countries and the major industrial countries suffered recessions and reduced demand for loaned funds. The commercial banks also played a supportive role toward developing and reconstructing Eastern Europe after 1989. (For example, Hungary received capital inflow of $700 million during 1991, leading to a huge current account surplus of $600 million. As a result, the country had no need to borrow abroad.) Just as plausibly, one could argue that the growth of international lending in the last 20 years has created a much greater instability in the global financial system, with huge swings in interest and exchange rates and massive loans to sovereign borrowers out of proportion to their abilities to service the debts. In sum, the economic significance of international banking cannot be denied, but the balance of its positive and negative aspects is highly debatable.

4.02 HISTORICAL PERSPECTIVES

In the period just after World War II, international banking was largely confined to financing exports and imports among the industrial countries, not yet including Japan. The loans had merchandise for collateral, and they were relatively stable and routine in their handling. The International Monetary Fund (IMF) was established in 1944, and subsequently the fixed exchange rate system eliminated most exchange risk. Competition certainly existed, but at that time it took place mainly from the banks' home offices, since few institutions had overseas affiliates.

Interest rates were relatively stable until the 1970s, and the financial markets were generally characterized by excess liquidity. Banking laws around the world severely restricted interest rate movements, and many of today's major international banking activities simply did not exist under that regulatory regime. It still remained for the dollar overhang to lead to the collapse of the Bretton Woods system, floating exchange rates to become the norm for the industrial countries, and the oil shocks to upset the international financial system and lead to the volatility that characterizes today's environment. It is clear that the problems of the 1990s do not differ greatly from those of the previous decades and centuries of international banking.

4.03 CURRENT PERSPECTIVES

Probably the most critical condition in international banking today is the *volatility* of the markets for international credit and foreign exchange. The central currency in the system, the U.S. dollar, experienced swings of more than 50 percent in value relative to the other main industrial country currencies during the 1980s. This phenomenon had an impact everywhere on pricing (and quantities sold) of exports, borrowing to finance trade deficits and domestic budget deficits, and even company decisions to locate production facilities (i.e., to choose low-cost locations that change as exchange rates change).

Commercial banks responded to this situation by designing new instruments and offering services to new clients that extend credit further and offer more risk protection than at any time in the past. Forex markets burgeoned to such a size and degree of sophistication that clients have access to foreign exchange 24 hours a day in dozens of currencies with transaction dates as far forward as 5 or 10 years. Credit markets developed to enable financing of huge projects through syndicated loans, to service clients in blocked-currency countries through forfaiting and countertrade, and to serve many other special purposes with credit forms that are limited primarily by the creativity of the bankers.

Another major problem of international banking in the 1980s was the *external debt crisis*, mainly suffered by the Latin American countries but also extending to Asian countries, such as Korea and Indonesia, and Eastern European countries, such as Poland. This crisis originated with the OPEC cartel's successful effort to raise oil prices in 1973–1974 and 1979–1980, causing a massive transfer of purchasing power to member countries. (These price increases were followed by very little reduction in demand, which resulted in a large transfer of funds to the OPEC members from oil-importing nations.) By obtaining the funds from importers, OPEC created a transfer problem that required the importing countries to generate new exports or to increase financing of their oil imports through the banking system. OPEC members did spend some of the new income on increased imports, thus partially carrying out the necessary transfer of real resources to pay the oil bill. Given OPEC's collective inability to absorb additional purchases from abroad, however, much of the income went into deposits in international banks during the 1970s and early 1980s.

This situation does not inherently create a problem, since new owners of bank deposits generally use them for purposes similar to those of their predecessors. The crisis arose when the global recession of 1974–1976 left the banks with inadequate demand for their funds among traditional borrowers in the developed countries. The banks then were forced to look to nontraditional borrowers, such as governments and private firms in Latin America. While these borrowers had no greater ability than before to generate income to repay international indebtedness (except for the oil exporters Mexico, Venezuela, and Ecuador), they were offered much greater amounts of money. This fact, coupled with very low or negative real interest rates (U.S. inflation exceeded nominal dollar interest rates for most of the 1970s after 1973), attracted the Latin American borrowers to take advantage of the new funding. Figure 4-3 shows the growth of foreign borrowing by the largest lesser developed country (LDC) debtors during the 1970s and 1980s.

The debt crisis was exacerbated by the global recession of 1981–1983, which led to lower imports by Latin American exporters' main customers and more restrictions on international trade. This period was also characterized by a return to positive, and for a while very high, real interest rates on U.S. dollar loans—which again exacerbated

FIGURE 4-3

Foreign Debt of Major LDC Borrowers

Source: World Bank, World Debt Tables (various years)

Year	Argentina	Brazil	Indonesia	South Korea	Mexico	Venezuela
1973	$ 6.4	$ 13.8	$ 5.7	$ 4.6	$ 8.6	$ 4.6
1974	8.0	18.9	7.1	6.0	12.8	5.3
1975	7.9	23.3	8.9	7.3	16.9	5.7
1976	8.3	28.6	11.0	8.9	21.8	8.7
1977	9.7	35.2	12.8	11.2	27.1	12.3
1978	12.5	48.4	14.5	14.8	33.6	16.3
1979	19.0	57.4	17.0	20.5	40.8	23.7
1980	27.2	71.0	21.0	29.5	57.4	29.3
1981	35.7	80.6	22.8	33.0	78.2	32.1
Average annual growth rate during 1973–1980	24.0%	24.7%	18.9%	27.9%	31.8%	27.5%
1982	$38.0	$ 88.2	$21.0	$35.8	$ 82.0	$31.3
1983	45.9	98.3	30.0	40.4	93.0	38.3
1984	48.9	105.3	31.9	42.1	94.8	36.9
1985	50.9	106.0	36.7	47.1	96.9	35.3
1986	52.5	113.6	43.0	46.7	100.9	34.3
1987	58.5	123.7	52.1	39.8	109.5	34.7
1988	58.7	115.7	52.8	35.7	100.8	34.9
1989	64.8	111.3	54.6	32.8	95.4	32.5
1990	61.1	116.2	67.9	34.0	96.8	33.3
Average annual growth rate during 1982–1990	6.1%	3.5%	15.8%	−0.6%	2.1%	0.8%

Note: Current U.S. dollars in billions.

the situation for the borrowers. By the end of the 1980s, dollar interest rates had plunged in nominal terms and returned to pre-1973 real terms, so the burden on borrowers became much more manageable.

The remaining Latin American debt problem is a transfer problem, because the borrowers have incurred foreign-currency debt, which requires a transfer of real purchasing power to repay. It is no longer a crisis, because a combination of debt restructurings and conversions, as well as debt reductions through such vehicles as privatization of state-owned firms (especially in Argentina)—along with a high, positive rate of real growth in Latin America since 1989—have broken the cycle of nonpayments and renegotiations of the early and mid-1980s. The arrangements in the late 1980s for trading loans for equity investments in Latin American countries (especially Chile and Mexico) through debt-to-equity swaps provided another safety valve for alleviating the crisis. In addition, the relatively orderly process that arose for selling Latin American loans at a discount in the secondary market in New York has enabled individual lenders to restructure their portfolios and eliminate Latin American exposure if they choose, albeit at a loss. The net result of these conclusions is that the transfer probably will be partially carried out through trade surpluses and foreign direct investment, partially financed for an indefinite period, partially inflated away, and partially renounced by the borrowers (especially through debt-to-equity swaps and loan repurchases)—very much like the experience with German reparations in the 1920s and Latin American debt in the 1930s.

Latin America was, of course, not the only region of borrowers hurt by the OPEC shocks of the 1970s. The industrial countries of the Triad incurred very large debts to finance their continued oil imports during this period. How has their transfer problem been resolved? The historical record shows that some form of default and ultimate write-down of loan values has been the rule rather than the exception during major crises in this century. However, these countries do seem to be the exception, since they emerged without defaulting. The industrial nations accomplished this by increasing their exports and selling other assets of real value, such as ownership of domestic companies and real estate, as well as by continuing to finance the unpaid part of their oil bills with new borrowing. One could argue that the United States has not really escaped the transfer problem, because its international indebtedness has now grown to a size greater than all of the Latin American countries combined! The U.S. problem has arisen from a number of factors beyond the OPEC crises, so it is considered as a separate issue.

A third concern that today threatens the normal functioning of international banking markets is the *U.S. foreign debt*. By 1987, the United States had become the largest debtor country in the world. This situation is untenable in principle, because at some point lending countries will demand some real resources instead of financial claims to be paid by U.S. borrowers. The situation is complicated, because the U.S. Treasury prints the currency that is generally used to settle international claims. Unless another currency replaces the dollar in international business, the U.S. government will continue to reap seignorage benefits by its special ability to print the means of payment.

The unification of Germany, the attempts to have a single currency for the countries in the European Community (EC), the breakup of the Soviet Union into different independent sovereign states, and the formation of democratic governments in Eastern Europe have opened new opportunities for and threats to international banking. These turbulent developments have increased the competition in the financial services industry because new players have started staking claims. While concepts of deregulation and liberalization were the theme of the 1980s, financial conglomeration and increased trends in reduction of cross-border restrictions dictate the performance of international banking in the 1990s. Banks have experienced lower asset quality and declining profitability owing to heavy writing off of bad debts. All of these problems have rendered the banks financially fragile and have produced a regulatory response to establish higher minimum capital requirements and to pursue other increased prudential controls.

4.04 INTERNATIONAL BANKING ACTIVITY IN SELECTED COUNTRIES

International banking activity depends wholly on the regulatory structure in any country. The least restrictive countries tend to be the industrial nations of the first world;

FIGURE 4-4

Current Restrictions on Foreign Commercial Bank Entry

Source: Report to Congress on Foreign Government Treatment of U.S. Commercial Banking Organizations, U.S. Department of the Treasury (Washington, D.C.: 1979); National Treatment Study, U.S. Department of the Treasury (Washington, D.C.: 1986 and 1990); Business International Corporation, Financing Foreign Operations

Country	No Foreign Presence	No New Foreign Commercial Bank Entry	No Foreign Commercial Banking Except Representative Office	No Foreign Commercial Bank Branches	No Equity Interest in Indigenous Commercial Banks	No Controlling Interest in Indigenous Commercial Banks	No Restrictions Found	Comment
Argentina		a					X	
Australia		a					X	
Austria						X	X	
Bahamas							X	
Belgium							X	
Brazil		b			X	X		
Canada						X		
Cayman Islands							X	
China					X	X		
Colombia							X	
Costa Rica				X	X	X		
Cuba	X	X		X				
Czechoslovakia					X	X		
Denmark					X	a		
Federal Republic							X	
France								
Germany								
Hong Kong							X	
Hungary							X	

Country					Comments
India		X	X		
Israel	X	X			
Japan	X	X			
Mexico [c]					
Netherlands	X				
New Zealand	X				
Norway	X				
Panama	X				
Philippines	X				Under consideration
Poland		X	X	X	
Singapore					No new branches and no automated teller machines
South Korea		X	X		
Spain		X			
Sweden	X		X	X	
Switzerland		X [d]	X		
U.S.S.R.	X	X	X		
United Kingdom		X	X	X	
Venezuela		X	X	X	Reciprocity
Yugoslavia		X	X	X	

[a] In practice, authorities very rarely approve foreign bank entry.

[b] No new entry is permitted except minority acquisition of nonbank financial institutions.

[c] Under the North American Free Trade Agreement, the United States and Canada may form 100 percent foreign-owned subsidiaries in Mexico.

[d] Entry is permitted as newly formed subsidiary.

the most restrictive were the formerly Communist countries of the second world, many of which have opened their economies extensively, while others remain highly restrictive. Ranging between these extremes are most of the LDCs of the third world. Figure 4-4 describes some of the limitations on foreign bank entry and operation in selected host countries.

In all of the countries shown, some form of foreign bank presence is permitted. The formerly Communist countries initially tended to limit foreign bank activity to the operation of representative offices, which are not allowed to carry out commercial banking functions but only to serve as channels of information between other offices of the bank and local clients. In the early 1990s, these restrictions have been relaxed in many of the former Soviet-bloc nations. Currently, it is very common to see EC-style rules in these countries—although foreign banks have been slow to enter these very economically depressed markets. LDCs have tended to limit foreign bank acquisition of domestic banks and often to preclude full-service foreign banking offices, but they generally have permitted foreign banks to lend locally and provide other financial services (other than deposit taking). In the early 1990s, they too have opened up the commercial banking sector to foreign participation. Industrial countries during the 1980s moved to open their regulatory environments, permitting full-service foreign-owned banks but sometimes limiting foreign acquisitions of existing domestic banks. The rest of this section illustrates the international banking environments in eight countries, six of which are the world's largest economies as measured by their GDPs of 1990, plus Switzerland and Hong Kong, because of their strategic locations as centers of the international market for currency and banking.

This review of international banking conditions in selected countries is intended only to sketch some of the broad characteristics of these markets. Because both economic conditions and regulatory policies change frequently, the accuracy of the descriptions is only temporary, although it is hoped that it gives a useful idea of the relative situations between countries and a basic understanding of some of the reasons for these policies.

[1] Canada

Canada ranks seventh of all countries, with a GDP of $570 billion in 1991. Canada's deregulation movement in the 1980s resulted in the opening of the commercial banking business to foreign banks. As a group, however, foreign banks are limited to a maximum of 12 percent of the Canadian banking system's assets. The 10 chartered banks (all owned by Canadian interests) still account for well over 90 percent of total banking assets today, and foreign banks are prohibited from acquiring any of them. Although the rules on domestic versus foreign banks do not bar the foreign entrants from specific activities, they do impose some additional requirements on the foreign banks. For example, foreign banks are limited to lending 20 times authorized capital, while the chartered banks have no such restriction. The trend in the late 1980s was toward still greater opening of the market to foreign banks and there are now 56 foreign banks operating in Canada. Under the U.S.-Canada Free Trade Agreement, U.S. banks are no longer subject to the "foreign" restrictions. The 1991 Bank Act Revision permits foreign shareholdings in securities firms of up to 100 percent.

The leading international banks in Canada are listed in Figure 4-5. As can be seen in the figure, the six largest chartered banks of Canada far outpace the foreign banks,

FIGURE 4-5

Leading International Banks in Canada

Source: Business International Corporation, FFO Canada (May 1992)

Banks	Assets
1. Royal Bank of Canada	$136,600
2. Canadian Imperial Bank of Commerce	128,200
3. Bank of Montreal	104,200
4. Bank of Nova Scotia	95,300
5. Toronto-Dominion Bank	70,100
6. National Bank of Canada	39,800
7. Hongkong Bank of Canada	10,600
8. Citibank Canada	6,032
9. Credit Suisse Canada	3,560
10. Barclays Bank of Canada	3,241
11. Swiss Bank Corp (Canada)	2,361
12. Banque Nationale de Paris (Canada)	2,312
13. Union Bank of Switzerland (Canada)	1,996
14. Credit Lyonnais Canada	1,930
15. Societe Generale (Canada)	1,911
16. The Bank of Tokyo Canada	1,688
17. Morgan Bank of Canada	1,517
18. National Westminster Bank of Canada	1,357

Note: Canadian dollars in millions.

although Hongkong Bank, Citibank, and others have multi-billion-dollar asset positions in the Canadian market.

[2] Germany

Germany ranks third, with a GDP of $1,488 billion. Foreign commercial banks in Germany are now permitted to offer the same services as domestic banks, although their access to Bundesbank credit facilities is restricted. Because foreign banks do not have access to central bank discounting, they must raise their funds in the money market, in the commercial and retail deposit-taking markets, or outside of Germany. The opening of the German financial system to extensive participation of outside banks was a product of the 1980s, and foreign banks still do not have substantial local deposit bases. On the other hand, they do hold a large share of the Eurocurrency deposit market in Frankfurt. Foreign investors can operator freely in the country's security market.

Germany's banking system is dominated by the three big banks, Deutsche Bank, Dresdner Bank, and Commerzbank, and their more than 3,000 branches throughout the country. German banks combine the roles of commercial and investment banks and thus act as brokers to private and institutional clients. The 112 foreign banks established through subsidiaries and the 60 others that operate through branches and representative offices accounted for DM236 billion as of 1990. They tend to specialize in trade financing, Euromarket activity, forex, and financing of large corporate clients, including subsidiaries of foreign multinational firms, i.e., in international business.

[3] Hong Kong

As a British colony (until 1997), Hong Kong uses a U.K.-type legal framework to regulate the banking industry, and historically it has been very open to foreign participation. With a GDP of $60 billion in 1991, Hong Kong ranks thirty-first among countries. Foreign banks are numerous in the small island economy: There are 134 foreign commercial banks (including 20 from the United States), and 30 domestic commercial banks in Hong Kong, which ranks among the largest Eurocurrency centers in the world today. The principal limitations on foreign bank activities are practical; because most foreign banks have few local branches compared with Hong Kong's domestic banks, they are relatively weak in attracting local deposits. The law permits foreign banks to operate branches, and while several of them have significant networks, such as Standard Chartered Bank's 116 branches, Citibank's 28, and Chase Manhattan Bank's 12, these networks do not approach the 405 branches of HongKong Bank, or the Bank of China's 254. In all, local banks hold about 70 percent of local deposits in the Hong Kong banking system. In the Eurocurrency market, on the other hand, foreign banks dominate as a group, although HongKong & Shanghai Banking Corporation still leads all of the others. Hang Seng Bank and the British Bank of the Middle East are the other two largest banks.

Hong Kong has no central bank, and thus far the Commissioner of Banking has controlled financial institutions through the banking ordinance. Presently, the Office of the Exchange Fund and the Commissioner of Banking are being brought under one agency called the Hong Kong Monetary Authority, which will develop a central bank culture to oversee money market management, handling of reserves, banking supervision, and banking policy. The issue of notes and clearing of checks will remain with banks. The new authority will not provide retail banking services to the government.

Hong Kong has 40 domestic banks, most of which have some degree of foreign shareholding. These banks tend to concentrate in the retail parts of the business (except for HongKong Bank), and they are large net lenders into the Eurocurrency market. The 122 foreign banks operating in Hong Kong tend to concentrate in international business and in financing the large industrial clients in Hong Kong. At present, the prospects of Hong Kong's banking system are dependent on the country's political situation with China. The Bank of China group, with 13 banks in Hong Kong, is an aggressive player at present and is expected to operate in all levels of banking by 1997, even though it is at present engaged only in retail banking and mortgages.

[4] Japan

Japan ranks second in the world in economic size, with a GDP of $2,942 billion in 1991. Among the industrial countries, Japan ranked first in restrictiveness of foreign bank activity during the 1970s and 1980s. Until 1985, foreign banks were not permitted to operate full-service branches in Japan. Since this permission was granted, 81 foreign banks have set up branches. The regulatory structure and business practice today still make Japan the most difficult industrial market for foreign banks to enter. Foreign banks interested in establishing new offices or in expanding operations in Japan must obtain approval from the Ministry of Finance. Foreign entities are prohibited from simultaneously participating in both commercial banking and securities issuance and trading, so they are at somewhat of a disadvantage relative to their domestic competitors. Foreign banks' activities are almost routine functions of letters of credit (LOC) operations, forex dealing, interbank trading, and offering short-term yen credits. Presently, there are 87 foreign banks operating in Japan, and combined they account for a meager 3 percent market share.

As with most other industries in Japan, foreign banks are greatly hindered from entering and building business in Japan by cultural preferences of Japanese people for dealing with other Japanese and excluding foreigners. Even Barclays (United Kingdom) and Citicorp (United States) have not been able to make inroads into the tight Japanese market. A second, equally serious disadvantage facing foreign banks is their funding base for Japanese operations; because they lack domestic deposit bases that will require time and/or acquisitions of Japanese institutions to build, their cost of funds is inevitably higher. Together, these kinds of problems will continue to keep Japanese banks ahead of their foreign competitors in the local market for the foreseeable future.

[5] Switzerland

Switzerland ranks seventeenth among countries, with a GDP of $225 billion in 1991. Swiss law permits foreign banks to establish local branches, subsidiaries, and other types of offices, subject only to reciprocal treatment of Swiss banks in the foreign jurisdiction. The banking environment has been open to foreign participation longer than that in many of the other European countries, and, as a result, many foreign banks have extensive presences in Switzerland. There are 146 foreign banks in Switzerland, which have combined assets of Sfr107 billion; the four leading domestic universal banks have assets of Sfr543 billion. Foreign banks hold only about 10 percent of all commercial banking assets in the country, and they are especially active in trust activity, accounting for about 40 percent of that function. Both foreign branches and domestic Swiss banks offer the same provisions of secrecy to their clients.

The foreign banks tend to operate in wholesale activities such as Eurocurrency deposits and loans and interbank foreign exchange dealing, as well as commercial finance with large industrial firms. The additional market segment of wealthy foreign individuals who hold depository accounts with the foreign banks is much larger than in the other countries discussed here, primarily because of the secrecy laws and the tradition of safety in handling these deposits. While the foreign presence is quite significant, the Swiss banking system is dominated by the four largest institutions: Swiss Bank Corp, Union Bank of Switzerland, Credit Suisse, and Schweizerische Volksbank. Together, they hold nearly half of Swiss banking assets and participate actively in businesses such as forfaiting, securities underwriting and trading, and even (through their holding companies) owning shares of industrial corporations.

[6] United Kingdom

The United Kingdom ranks sixth, with a GDP of \$975 billion in 1991. U.K. banking deregulation during the 1980s placed foreign banks on a more equal footing with their local counterparts, although participation in the main clearing association, the Banker's Clearing House, is still restricted to U.K. banks, with only a handful of exceptions. Foreign banks may enter the United Kingdom with full-service operations, subject to regulatory control by the Bank of England. They have access to funding from the Bank of England, just as the domestic banks do.

London has attracted over 263 foreign banks (331 including multiple affiliates) and "licensed institutions" (which are allowed to take deposits but not to rediscount their paper with the Bank of England). These entities account for over 80 percent of the Eurocurrency market in London, whereas in the domestic market they are far less active than the six largest U.K. clearing banks. The EC banks account for 27 percent of total cross-border business. The foreign banks tend to operate in the wholesale market, funding their operations through the money market and lending in the inter-bank market and to prime corporations. U.K. regulations and practices continue to lessen the limitations on foreign banks' activities, so that they (especially Citibank and the Bank of Boston) are becoming involved in retail banking and branching in the United Kingdom.

[7] United States

The United States has the largest economy in the world, with a GDP of \$5,392 billion in 1991. The U.S. government places very few restrictions on foreign bank entry or operation in the United States. Federal regulation is primarily aimed at creating an equal, competitive footing for domestic and foreign banks, and most restrictions apply to all commercial banks, regardless of ownership. The current regulatory structure was established through the International Banking Act of 1978 and the revision of the Edge Act in 1979, each of which eliminated some of the limitations on foreign bank activities in the U.S. market. The International Banking Act also took away a loophole in the regulatory structure that had permitted foreign banks to operate deposit-taking branches in more than one state while domestic banks were limited to receiving deposits in only one state. Today, the regulatory structure facing foreign banks that seek to operate in the United States is virtually identical to that for domestic banks.

The rules do not stop at the federal level, however. Each state has the authority to regulate banks within its jurisdiction, and many states have placed restrictions on foreign banks in general and on banks from countries that do not offer reciprocal treatment of U.S. banks there. For example, 39 states do not permit foreign banks to operate branches, and another 33 states do not permit foreign bank agencies. Since U.S. law permits banks to use federal or state charters, any foreign bank that meets normal Federal Reserve rules for all banking institutions can establish a federally chartered subsidiary in any state that it chooses.

As waves of deregulation continue to wash through the system, today foreign (and domestic) banks can branch within regions of the United States where interstate pacts permit such activity; foreign banks can operate branches or subsidiaries in several states if they received "grandfather" protection of multistate offices established before the International Banking Act; and they can bid to purchase failed banks and savings

FIGURE 4-6

Foreign Banks With the Most Assets in the United States (September 1992)

Source: The Banker *(Feb. 1993)*

U.S. Ranking	Bank	Country	Business Overseas (%) (1991)[a]	Business Overseas (%) (1992)[a]	Total Assets	Assets in United States
1.	Mitsubishi Bank	Japan	34.8	26.2	$424,102	$40,381
2.	Fuji Bank	Japan	37.0	35.0	418,956	32,103
3.	National Westminster	United Kingdom	44.3	43.5	229,272	28,179
4.	Sumitomo Bank	Japan	35.0	32.0	427,102	26,804
5.	Dai-Ichi Kangyo Bank	Japan	36.0	39.3	445,707	25,913
6.	Swiss Bank Corporation	Switzerland	53.1	52.4	152,564	21,491
7.	HSBC Holding	United Kingdom	79.8	81.9	160,355	20,152
8.	Bank of Montreal	Canada	38.5	37.1	77,309	20,007
9.	Credit Lyonnais	France	36.5	38.8	306,335	18,517
10.	UBS	Switzerland	56.4	57.9	183,911	17,973
11.	Sakura Bank	Japan	39.2	29.7	420,348	17,910
12.	Bank of Nova Scotia	Canada	40.0	38.7	71,822	16,839
13.	ABN-Amro	Netherlands	34.0	34.0	242,686	15,851
14.	Banque Nationale de Paris	France	43.8	42.1	275,876	14,371
15.	LTCB	Japan	23.6	21.8	221,035	14,366
16.	Barclays Bank	United Kingdom	37.0	37.2	258,339	13,800
17.	CIBC	Canada	28.5	28.8	100,916	10,121
18.	Banco Santander	Spain	29.1	27.0	60,256	7,299
19.	Asahi Bank	Japan	17.9	17.8	212,382	6,602
20.	Deutsche Bank	Germany	20.2	19.9	296,226	5,740
21.	Istituto B.Sao Paolo	Italy	27.3	19.9	178,243	5,225
22.	Royal Bank of Canada	Canada	22.1	21.0	111,445	5,035
23.	Westpac Banking Corp.	Australia	35.9	33.9	74,882	4,766
24.	Credit Suisse	Switzerland	52.6	53.5	162,661	4,643
25.	Toronto-Dominion	Canada	22.1	20.0	56,300	4,350

[a] As of September or December 1991.

and loan associations from the Federal Deposit Insurance Corporation (FDIC) when such entities are sold to solvent financial institutions.

The amount of foreign bank activity in the United States is shown in Figure 4-6, which lists the largest foreign banks in the country. At present, 744 foreign bank branches, subsidiaries, and other types of offices are operating in the United States. During the 1980s, Japanese banks replaced those from Western Europe and Canada as the leading foreign investors in U.S. banking, and Japanese banks now account for about 40 percent of all foreign bank assets in the United States.

[8] Brazil

In comparison with the rest of the countries surveyed here, Brazil, with a GDP of $414 billion in 1991, ranking ninth, presents by far the most restrictive environment for foreign banks. The number of foreign banks permitted in the country is fixed, so new entry must be through acquisition of an existing foreign bank or by exception to the rule. Added to this constraint, Brazil is an LDC with $116 billion (U.S.) in foreign debt and major problems of unemployment, inflation, and other macroeconomic imbalances. The environment is quite forbidding.

The other side of the coin is that Brazil constitutes about half of the Latin American economy, the country has seen annual GDP growth near that of Japan's during much of the past two decades, and the natural resource base is bountiful and probably only marginally tapped so far. Brazil has often been cited as the country of the future, and many international banks continue to seek entry into the already immense market. The debt crisis, however, has caused interest in new entry to wane during the past decade.

The number of foreign banks in Brazil is now 24, and their market share in most activities is very small. The government-owned Banco do Brasil alone controls about one quarter of the domestic deposit base and half of the (legal) forex trading. Banco Bradesco and Banco Itau are the largest banks after Banco do Brasil. As may be expected, the foreign banks tend to concentrate on wholesale business, funding large corporate clients, and borrowing in the interbank market. Because the central bank closely controls the foreign exchange market, foreign banks are not able to provide services that differ significantly from those of domestic banks. Similarly, trade financing techniques are limited by law, so foreign banks are not able to be nearly as innovative in Brazil as in the other countries studied here.

4.05 FOREIGN EXCHANGE MARKETS

[1] Basic Market Characteristics

Along with the Eurocurrency market, the other major financial market that distinguishes domestic from international finance is the foreign exchange market. In most industrial countries, the forex market is a combination of several separate markets in which specific types of transactions are carried out. Futures markets are generally operated by stock or commodities exchanges. Physical currency exchange is often undertaken by exchange houses that are not banks. Corporations may buy forex from

FIGURE 4-7

U.S. Foreign Exchange Submarkets

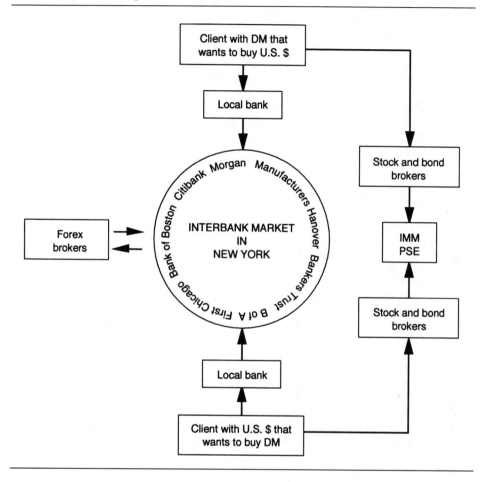

local banks, which in turn buy it from money center banks. In all, the forex market is a linked set of submarkets, as shown in Figure 4-7 for the United States.

The main participants in most forex markets are commercial banks. Whether or not a country's central bank imposes exchange controls, commercial banks are usually the market makers for purchases and sales of foreign currency. Since most of the world's forex dealing takes place in the main financial centers of leading industrial countries and involves commercial banks on one or both sides of the market, this section emphasizes the interbank market for forex transactions. This is not to say that other participants are not important; central banks are crucial to the market, since they set the rules of operation and they participate as buyers and sellers of foreign currencies; also, corporations and individuals account for thousands of transactions every day, although these are for much less value than the interbank transactions.

However, the primary activity of commercial banks in foreign exchange dealings is in the interbank market.

The instruments of forex include actual currency, bank deposits denominated in different currencies, forward and futures contracts, options, swaps, and quite a few others. Most transactions in the interbank market are carried out through telephone calls between banks directly or with brokers involved, and they are cleared through electronic account debits and credits between the buying and selling banks. That is, no physical currency is involved, nor do any other instruments change hands except confirmations of the transactions. This is a far cry from the forex market facing a traveler who wants to exchange a few hundred dollars in cash for local currency in another country, but it represents over 75 percent of the value of forex dealings in the industrial countries today. The size and diversity of the U.S. forex market is depicted in Figure 4-8.

[2] Foreign Exchange Trading

Commercial banks deal in the interbank forex market through their traders, who carry out transactions via telephone with other banks around the world. Transactions are relatively large, normally for values between $1 million and $10 million (U.S.). Traders in each bank that chooses to deal in forex attempt to sell high and buy low in their transactions while they purchase and sell currencies for the bank's commercial clients. That is, forex traders operate as buyers and sellers even without clients' accounts, when they try to locate cheap sources of foreign currencies and opportunities to sell those currencies for a profit. This situation leads banks to establish limits on forex dealing as to the amounts they are willing to have their traders long or short during the trading day, the amounts they are willing to leave on their books overnight, and the mismatching of maturities of transactions that are booked.

When operating as agent for a commercial client, the forex trader needs only to go to the telephone, contact various other banks that deal in the currency of interest, and close a deal at the best exchange rate offered. The client is then charged a small spread over the cost of this purchase; the spread tends to be smaller on the larger transactions and those of large corporate clients (since the client sometimes may have alternative access to forex and the bank may take a low profit in order to keep the good customer relationship).

When acting on his or her own account, the trader may take long or short positions (i.e., buy more of a currency than needed to cover clients' requests or sell more of a currency than needed to eliminate a long position), speculating that the currency will move either up or down later in the day or in the near future. Banks typically apply strict limits to each trader's ability to create exposures to long or short positions, so that potentially large forex losses are avoided if the trader guesses wrong. Traders frequently buy and sell currencies during the day to keep abreast of market tendencies and create long or short positions as they see tendencies toward revaluation or devaluation, respectively. Such trading clearly is based on observations of supply and demand conditions from minute to minute, rather than on economic fundamentals, such as purchasing power parity or the international Fisher relationship, which relate to longer-term exchange rate determination (over weeks, months, or years).

Forex trading in the 1990s is a 24-hour-a-day business, with the interbank market functioning in regular business somewhere around the globe all the time. When the New York market reaches its 3:00 P.M. closing time, there are still 3 hours of trading

FIGURE 4-8

Forex Turnover in the U.S. Market (April 1992)

Source: Federal Reserve Bank of New York, U.S. Foreign Exchange Turnover Survey *(Apr. 1992)*

Type of Transaction	Amount
Spot	
Direct with banks in the United States	$ 27,508
Direct with banks abroad	38,343
With nonreporting counterparties	28,854
Through brokers	32,404
Total	$127,109
Swaps	
Direct with banks in the United States	$ 15,840
Direct with banks abroad	25,402
With nonreporting counterparties	17,371
Through brokers	24,795
Total	$ 83,408
Outright forwards	
Direct with banks in the United States	$ 1,999
Direct with banks abroad	3,582
With nonreporting counterparties	8,046
Through brokers	528
Total	$ 14,155
Options	
Direct with banks in the United States	$ 2,931
Direct with banks abroad	7,051
With nonreporting counterparties	4,624
Through brokers	8,109
Total	$ 22,715
Interbank transactions	
Direct with banks in the United States	$ 48,278
Direct with banks abroad	74,378
With nonreporting counterparties	58,895
Through brokers	65,836
Derivatives	10,760
Total interbank transactions	$209,869

Note: U.S. dollars in millions.

left in San Francisco, to which banks can shift their trading activities (if the bank operates an office there). When San Francisco is approaching the close of the business day, banks can shift their trading activity to offices in Honolulu, where it is only noon. At the end of the trading day in Honolulu, forex positions can be moved to Tokyo, where it is 10:00 A.M., or Hong Kong, where it is 9:00 A.M., and trading is just getting under way. Similarly, trading activity moves to Bahrain, then to continental Europe (Frankfurt, Zurich, and Paris), to London, and finally back to New York. A bank without offices around the world can still participate in these other forex trading centers in different time zones by arrangement with banks that do have trading centers or simply by having traders work odd hours on the telephone to deal with the foreign markets. It is not uncommon for a New York forex trader to close a deal at 5:00 A.M. through a London affiliate.

[3] Brokers' Market

Another facet of large-scale forex trading in the major financial centers is the brokers' market. About half a dozen forex brokerage firms make markets for a wide variety of currencies, creating transactions similar to those in the interbank market. In fact, brokered transactions are often discussed together with direct interbank forex deals, since brokers function only as intermediaries and do not buy or sell for their own account, leaving banks as the principals in both cases.

The key differences from the direct interbank market are that the brokers bring together currency buyers and sellers without taking any position themselves, deal simultaneously with many banks, and offer both buy and sell positions to clients (whereas a bank may wish to operate only one side of the market at any particular time). Also, the brokers deal "blind," offering rate quotations without naming the potential seller or buyer until a deal has been negotiated. In the New York forex market, brokered transactions account for about half of the total value of interbank activity.

[4] Foreign Exchange Rate Quotations

Exchange rate quotations in the interbank market are two-digit numbers, bid and ask, with the preceding numbers assumed. A deutsche mark quote of 50/92 on May 7, 1993, means the following actual prices: a DM1.5750 bid to buy \$1 (U.S.) and a DM1.5792 ask to sell \$1 (U.S.). The bank is offering (bidding) to buy dollars for DM1.5750 per dollar and also offering (asking) to sell dollars for DM1.5792 per dollar. Of course, the actual transaction will involve \$1 million or more, to be exchanged at those prices.

Rates are typically quoted on the continental basis, as units of forex per dollar, everywhere. U.S. banks have traditionally used the U.S. basis, quoting U.S. dollars per unit of forex. Clearly, whether the quote is DM2.0 per dollar or \$0.50 per deutsche mark, the value is the same.

Another means that is used to distinguish the two ways of presenting an exchange rate is to call a quotation of units of domestic currency per forex unit an indirect quote. Conversely, a quotation of units of forex per domestic currency unit is called a direct quote. This system has more general applicability to any pair of currencies, whereas the U.S. and continental systems only relate to rates involving the U.S. dollar.

[5] Forward Market

The forward forex market offers banks, companies, governments, and individuals the opportunity to contract today for a specific forex transaction in the future at a fixed price (i.e., exchange rate). Forward contracts are negotiated between the offering bank and the client as to size, maturity, and price. The interbank forward market is sufficiently active that regular rate quotations are offered by major trading banks for forward dates of one, three, and six months. In addition, it is quite common to see quotes of one-year forward dates in the major trading currencies.

The rationale for forward contracts in currencies is analogous to that for futures contracts in commodities: The firm can lock in a price today to eliminate uncertainty about the value of a future receipt or payment of foreign currency. When a firm obtains an account receivable denominated in a foreign currency, it can immediately contract with a commercial bank to sell that currency and buy domestic currency at a price fixed now for actual payment at the future date. Similarly, a foreign currency account payable would require the firm to obtain that currency in the future; the purchase can be contracted now through a forward contract at a fixed price for actual transaction at the future date.

The bank that offers this service to commercial clients must either find a counterpart to each forward contract such that exchange risk is not held by the bank or speculate and simply leave the position open. Generally, the bank would prefer to balance its foreign currency position, so a client's forward purchase of forex would lead the bank to buy that currency forward simultaneously from another bank for the same maturity and value, thus eliminating its exchange risk. The interbank market for forward contracts operates analogously to the spot market, though the volume of contracts is far less in the forward market.

Forward markets exist in any currencies and for any maturities that banks are willing to offer. Most of the forward contracts used in the United States involve exchanges of U.S. dollars for deutsche marks, U.K. pounds, Canadian dollars, Swiss francs, yen, and French francs. Maturities tend to be six months or less, although single-year and multiyear contracts are often available. There is no secondary market in forward contracts, since they are for odd maturities and values. The futures market at the Chicago Mercantile Exchange offers fixed contract sizes and maturities for six currencies, and in this case there is an active secondary market.

The forward market is also used for swap contracts. These agreements involve both a spot purchase or sale of foreign currency and a forward sale or purchase of the same currency. By carrying out both operations simultaneously, a bank can obtain forex for a fixed period, guaranteeing what the future price will be for reselling it. Or, on the other side, the bank can sell forex today, with a guarantee of how much it will cost to repurchase it at a fixed date in the future. Swaps are typically used when the bank finds an opportunity to earn a desirable amount of income on a foreign-currency-denominated investment or deposit yet wants to assure reconversion to domestic currency at the end of the investment period. Obviously, the foreign currency investment needs to be compared with domestic alternatives. This type of decision is called interest arbitrage.

[6] Arbitrage in Foreign Exchange Markets

With the forex market functioning in different locations, time zones, and kinds of contracts, all traders still deal in the same currencies. If prices diverge between two segments of the forex market, arbitragers naturally seek to profit from such opportunities until they disappear. Exchange arbitrage may be two-way, between one segment of the market and another; three-way, moving among three currencies; or intertemporal, moving between two currencies at different transaction dates. All of these types of forex arbitrage involve simultaneous contracting in two or more forex market segments to buy and sell foreign currency, profiting from exchange rate differences without incurring exchange risk.

Two-way exchange arbitrage tends to keep spot forex quotations from varying between locations around the world. If at any time a trader can buy U.K. pounds for $1.7092 each in one place and simultaneously sell pounds for $1.7162 each, the trader can earn $0.007 for every pound exchanged. For transactions of $1 million in value, the trader will earn $2,386 each time the two transactions are carried out. This will more than pay the telephone bill, so such arbitrage opportunities tend to disappear quickly when they arise. Arbitrage may just as well occur between the futures market in Chicago and the interbank market in New York or London. If the Chicago market price of three-month deutsche marks diverges from that in the interbank market, a bank can contract in the Chicago market through an exchange broker there and simultaneously contract in the interbank market to complete the arbitrage.

Three-way exchange arbitrage occurs when a trader moves through three currencies rather than just two to take advantage of price differentials between segments of the forex market. This may happen because of restrictions on the market or for any other reason. For example, the trader may start with U.S. dollars, buy French francs in London, then buy deutsche marks in exchange for the francs in Zurich, and finally buy back dollars in New York. If the exchange rates offered by each partner in the transaction are sufficiently favorable, the trader will obtain a profit from the arbitrage. Banks use computer programs to search for profitable two-way and three-way arbitrage opportunities, from which traders quickly try to profit.

Intertemporal, or interest, arbitrage is similar to the previous two forms in that it requires starting and ending with the same currency and incurring no exchange risk. In this case, profits are made by exploiting interest rate differentials as well as exchange rate differentials. Also, the intertemporal exchange arbitrager (or interest arbitrager) must use funds for the period between contract maturities, whereas the two-way and three-way arbitragers need funds only on the delivery date.

EXAMPLE: Consider the following hypothetical information:

- At Bankers Trust in New York, the spot exchange rate is Sfr1.5615 per U.S. dollar.
- At Bankers Trust in New York, the 180-day forward rate is Sfr1.5167 per dollar.
- At Barclays Bank in London, the dollar (Eurodollar) deposit rate is 8.625 percent per year.
- At Barclays Bank in London, the Swiss franc (EuroSwiss franc) deposit rate is 3.125 percent per year.

The interest arbitrager that begins with U.S. dollars has two alternatives for using funds in interest arbitrage. First, the funds may simply be invested in a dollar-denominated instrument, such as a Eurodollar time deposit at Barclays Bank. This investment pays 8.625 percent per year for the six-month investment. Alternatively, the arbitrager may buy Swiss francs, invest in a franc-denominated instrument, and buy dollars in the forward market. These three transactions create a dollar-denominated instrument that pays 3.125 percent per year plus the percentage exchange rate change. The forward premium on Swiss francs (i.e., the implicit exchange rate change in percentage terms) is

$$\frac{XRf - XRs}{XRs} = 2.869\% \text{ for the six-month period}$$

where *XRf* is the forward exchange rate and *XRs* is the spot exchange rate. This means that the dollar value of the francs increases by 5.738 percent per year between the purchase and sale of the francs. Thus, the full return on this arbitrage is approximately 3.125 percent plus 5.738 percent, which equals 8.863 percent per year or 4.432 percent for the six months. This is clearly more than the return on the dollar-denominated instrument, so interest arbitrage should be undertaken.

To avoid this approximation, an exact return can be calculated by using the interest parity relationship. The basic relation between interest arbitrage and domestic investment may be shown as

$$(1 + i \text{ domestic}) = (1 + i \text{ foreign}) \left(\frac{XRs}{XRf}\right)$$

where *i* is the interest rate. This is called the interest parity equation. In equilibrium, both sides are equal. Most of the time, either domestic investment or interest arbitrage is preferable, and arbitrage tends to push interest and exchange rates to eliminate the differential and establish parity. In the example, the U.S. investment yielded 1.043125 times the principal, while the Eurofranc investment yielded 1.045624 times the principal.

Because the interest parity relationship is generally close to equality, the percentage gains available to interest arbitragers are low. Large banks, which can commit funds to foreign currency investments with low transactions costs (usually in the Eurocurrency market), are the main participants in interest arbitrage.

4.06 EUROMARKETS

[1] Scope of the Markets

A Eurodollar is a dollar-denominated bank deposit located outside of the United States; the Eurocurrency market is simply a set of bank deposits located outside of the countries whose currencies are used in the deposits. For example, French francs deposited outside of France are considered Eurofrancs. Since almost three quarters of the deposits in all locations where governments permit Eurocurrency operations are denominated in U.S. dollars, it is reasonably accurate to call this the Eurodollar market. Because loans as well as deposits are made in the Euromarkets, outside of the regulatory grasp used in their domestic markets by the governments involved, Euroloans are part of the total picture.

Although it originated in London and spread to other European cities first, the market is not limited to Europe. Very large Eurodollar markets exist in Hong Kong, Singapore, Bahrain, Panama, and other locations throughout the world. (In fact, through a legal fiction created in 1981, international banking facilities in the United States permit banks to hold Eurodollar deposits on foreign clients within the same country in a separate set of books from their domestic business. Today, New York rivals London for the lead in the value of Eurodollar deposits.) Given the much broader spread of these deposits outside of Europe, the Eurocurrency market is sometimes called the international money market.

[2] Key Role of the Markets

Because the Eurocurrency market rivals domestic financial markets as a funding source for corporate borrowing, it plays a key role in the capital investment decisions of many firms, and, because this market also rivals domestic financial markets as a deposit alternative, it absorbs important amounts of savings from lenders (i.e., depositors) in many countries. In fact, the Eurocurrency market complements the domestic financial markets, giving greater access to borrowing and lending to financial market participants in each of the countries where it is permitted to function. Overall, the Eurocurrency market is now the world's single most important market for international financial intermediation.

This market is completely a creation of the regulatory structures placed by national governments on banking or, more broadly, on financial intermediation. If national governments allowed banks to function without reserve requirements, interest rate restrictions, capital controls, and taxes, the Eurocurrency market would just involve the foreign-currency-denominated foreign-owned deposits and loans made in each country's banking system. Instead, national governments heavily regulate national financial markets in efforts to achieve various monetary policy goals. Thus, the Eurocurrency market provides a very important outlet for funds flows that avoid many of the limitations placed on domestic financial markets. Many national governments have found the impact of the Eurocurrency market on their firms and banks to be favorable, so they have allowed this market to operate.

[3] Bases of the Markets

There are essentially three conditions that must be met for a Eurocurrency market to exist:

1. Some national government must allow foreign currency deposits to be made, so that, for example, depositors in London can hold dollar-denominated time deposits.

2. The country whose currency is being used—in the previous example, the United States—must allow foreign entities to own and exchange deposits in that currency, so that payment of loans and deposits can be cleared in that currency.

3. There must be a reason, such as low cost or ease of use, that prompts people to use this market rather than other financial markets, such as the domestic ones.

The Eurocurrency market has met these conditions for the past three decades, and its phenomenal growth testifies to the fact that the demand for such a market has been very great.

A wide range of countries allow foreign currency deposits to be held in their banking systems. Many of them impose restrictions (interest rate limits, capital controls, and so on) on foreign currency deposits as well as on local currency deposits, so that a free market does not exist. Other countries, including most of the developed countries and many of the newly industrializing countries, allow foreign currency deposits that are not subject to the regulations placed on domestic deposits. In such countries, participants find more favorable interest rates, greater availability of funds, and greater ease of moving funds internationally. These countries tend to be the Euromarket centers.

Only a few currencies have become popular as Eurocurrencies. They are the ones

FIGURE 4-9

Interest Rates on Domestic and Eurodollar Deposits

Source: Federal Reserve Bulletin *(various issues), Year Table 1.35*

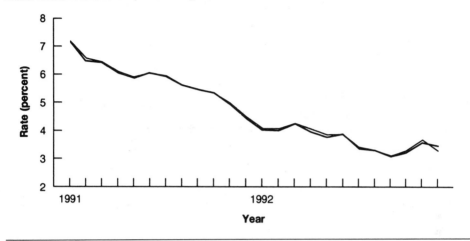

that are used widely in international trade: the U.S. dollar, the U.K. pound, the French franc, the deutsche mark, the yen, and a handful of others. The governments of all of the nations whose currencies are being used have consented (or more accurately, have not objected) to allow foreign banks, corporations, and individuals to hold and use deposits denominated in those currencies. This may appear to be a trivial point, but any limitation on nonresidents' use of dollar (or other Eurocurrency) deposits would quickly eliminate that currency from the Euromarket. The U.S. government's temporary freeze on Iranian assets held in U.S. banks in 1979 caused a crisis in the Eurodollar market, because other participants saw the possibility of losing use of their Eurodollars at the whim of the U.S. government. The potential problem will continue to exist, but on the whole participants in the Euromarket expect that full freedom to use the dollar-denominated deposits will continue indefinitely.

The third condition fundamental to the success of the Euromarket is that the market must possess advantages that will attract participants, such as the ability to carry out dollar-denominated transactions outside of the United States and the availability of favorable interest rates relative to rates in the domestic market. The first advantage clearly exists, because Eurodollar account owners can sell their accounts to pay for other transactions without any need to deal directly in the United States. The second advantage also exists, primarily because lack of regulation of the Euromarket allows banks to reduce their costs and pass on the savings to clients in the form of lower loan rates and higher deposit rates. Figures 4-9 and 4-10 show that the Eurodollar deposit interest rate does have a very small positive spread over the comparable domestic deposit rate. Loan rates are more difficult to compare because of size differences (Euroloans are generally larger) and because large banks tend to quote approximately equal rates in both markets owing to competition. That is, banks have been forced to lower their domestic loan charges for large borrowers to compete with Euroloans, so

FIGURE 4-10

Difference in Three-Month Eurodollar Interest Rates Over Domestic Deposits

Source: Federal Reserve Bulletin *(various issues), Year Table 1.35*

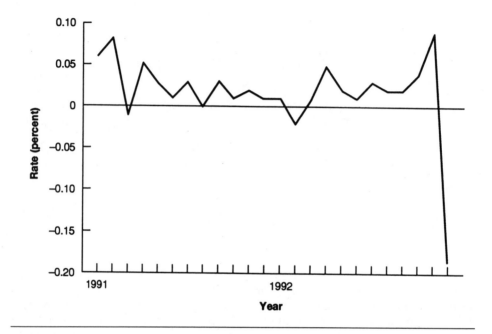

the differential that existed in the early years of the Euromarkets mostly disappeared after the 1980s.

[4] Eurocurrency Interest Rates

The base interest rate paid on deposits between banks in the Eurocurrency market is the London interbank offered rate (LIBOR). In locations other than London, which is the center of the Euromarket in terms of volume, the base rate on deposits is generally slightly higher. Even within London, the rates quoted by the highest-quality banks are lower than those offered by the presumably more risky banks; this "tiering" of the market exists in all Euromarket locations. LIBOR is determined by the supply and demand for funds in the Euromarket for each currency. Because participating banks could (and infrequently do) default on their obligations, the rate paid for Eurodollar deposits is always somewhat above the domestic rate on Treasury bills (or other short-term government securities in other countries). Also, because domestic banks must comply with Federal Reserve requirements in the United States, they offer slightly lower deposit rates than unregulated Eurobanks.

The Euro lending rate has no name comparable to the prime rate; rather, it is determined as LIBOR plus a spread charged to the borrower. Banks generally do not

FIGURE 4-11

Three-Month Eurocurrency Deposit Rates (Year-End)

Source: OECD, International Financial Trends *(various issues)*

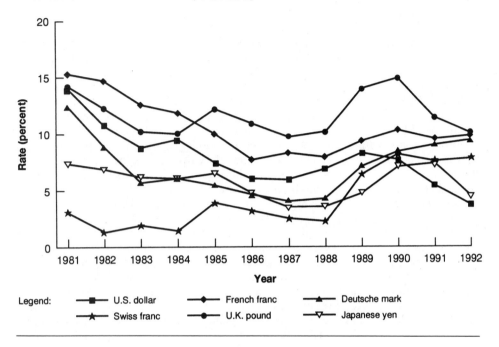

require compensating balances or other implicit charges in addition to the spread over LIBOR in the Euromarket, which helps to reduce the borrower's cost of using the market. The total cost of borrowing in the Euromarket for a prime U.S. corporation historically was marginally below the domestic U.S. prime rate until the 1980s, when domestic and Euro borrowing rates converged.

Interest rates on other Eurocurrencies follow the same pattern, although when capital controls exist in a particular country (e.g., France), borrowing rates may be higher in the Euromarket (which is not restricted) than in the domestic market. Figure 4-11 traces three-month Eurocurrency deposit rates from 1981 to 1992 for several currencies. The countries whose currencies have tended to decline relative to other currencies during this period (such as France and the United Kingdom) show generally higher Eurocurrency deposit rates than the strong currency countries, such as Germany and Japan. This phenomenon results from the interest parity and international Fisher relationship.

Transactions in the Eurodollar market usually involve values of $1 million (U.S.) or more, although in the past several years deposits of $50,000 to $100,000 have been given at LIBOR, and loans of similar amounts have been offered at the analogous lending rates. The market is directly accessible to banks, which carry out about three quarters of the total volume of transactions among themselves. Companies and individuals participate through their banks at interest rates slightly less favorable than those offered between banks. (Smaller investors may also participate in the Euromarket indirectly by purchasing some money market funds in the United States; these funds themselves place large portions of their pooled investments in Eurodollar accounts.)

[5] Instruments of the Euromarkets

On the deposit side, most of the instruments used in the Euromarkets are time deposits of relatively short maturity. Strictly speaking, since the deposits must be cleared through funds transfer in the country of denomination of the deposit (usually the United States), these are not transactional accounts. However, since a significant portion of Eurodeposits mature in one month or less, they are often used on a near-cash basis. The Bank of England found that about 25 percent of all London Eurodeposits had maturities of less than one month at year-end 1986.

Another form of Eurobank liability is the Eurodollar certificate of deposit (or Euro CD). These deposits differ from the Euro time deposits, just as their analogues do in the domestic market: They offer greater liquidity; a secondary market exists; and they pay a slightly lower interest rate because of these benefits.

For longer-term deposits, banks have created variable interest rate depositary instruments such as floating-rate notes (FRNs) and floating-rate CDs. Both of these instruments pay the depositor an interest rate (typically LIBOR) that is adjusted to current market conditions every three or six months during the life of the deposit. By creating these types of deposits, Eurobanks enable themselves to capture funds for longer maturities without locking in long-term interest rate risk. From the client's view, the floating-rate deposit permits funds to be deposited long term without being limited to the initial rate of return if rates rise during the period of deposit. The client may also simply wish to match a variable-rate deposit with a variable-rate asset during the same period, exactly as the bank attempts to do to avoid mismatching maturities of its own assets and liabilities.

On the lending side, Euromarket instruments include fixed-rate notes and floating-rate loans, single and multiple-lender financing, and other arrangements limited primarily by the creativity of the bankers and the kinds of needs of the clients. The most common Euroloan is a fixed-rate, short-term loan from one Eurobank to one client priced on the basis of LIBOR plus a spread reflecting the creditworthiness of the borrower. This is wholly analogous to the domestic commercial loan market. For longer-term borrowing, the most common instrument since the advent of volatile interest rates in the 1970s has been the floating-rate loan or note, with the interest rate adjusted every three or six months based on LIBOR and retaining the same spread for the life of the loan.

When the size of the loan is very large, Eurobanks often prefer to share the funding and risks in a syndicated loan, which is originated by one bank that then sells participations (portions) to other interested banks. Loan syndications were very popular in the 1970s during the petrodollar recycling, when jumbo loans were made to Latin American governments, and the banks preferred to share the risk of credit extension to them. Obviously, that market segment disappeared in the 1980s, and today syndicated loans are fewer in number, although still employed for the same purposes of reducing the amount of funds loaned by each bank and distributing risk among the participating banks. Governments of industrial countries and their agencies, along with multinational firms, are the main recipients of syndicated loans at present.

These listings of both deposit and loan instruments are intended to be instructive rather than exhaustive. Although the major instruments used today in the Euromarkets have been discussed, there are many more instruments that have been developed and surely will be developed to better serve clients' needs in the future.

[6] Criticisms of the Euromarkets

The Eurodollar market has been criticized over the years as contributing to worldwide inflation and creating major new risks in the international banking system. While neither of these claims has been proven (or disproven) conclusively, they are worth considering.

Because the Eurodollar market adds to the worldwide volume of dollar-denominated assets, it has been accused of increasing the global money supply beyond the control of the U.S. authorities. This may be true to some extent, but a number of factors mitigate the total impact of Eurodollars. First, Eurodollars exist only as time deposits and CDs, not as demand deposits or cash. Hence, in the narrow definition of money that includes only cash and demand deposits, Eurodollars do not even appear at all; they are not technically usable to settle transactions, and Eurodollar checks thus could not be written. Second, as already noted, about three fourths of all Eurodollars are interbank deposits rather than new credit to companies or individuals that may use it for capital investment and thus economic growth. The interbank transfers (pyramiding) do not create any new credit, however measured. Finally, the Eurodollar deposits that are used by companies and individuals for investment and consumption probably replace other (e.g., domestic) bank deposits that would have been used for the same purposes anyhow. That is, because Eurodollar deposits pay interest rates higher than domestic deposits, they often substitute for domestic deposits, and thus they serve the same purposes that those deposits would have served.

Analogous reasoning holds for loans. Euroloans compete with domestic loans for the same borrowers, and they add to total lending only by providing slightly less expensive sources of funds. All in all, Eurodollars probably add slightly to the total volume of economic activity worldwide because they provide a form of financial intermediation between depositors (savers) in many countries and borrowers (investors or spenders) in many countries that is more efficient than that of individual domestic financial markets.

On the issue of increased risk, it has been argued that the Eurocurrency market has led to much greater extension of loans to troubled borrowers, such as the governments of LDCs that were facing virtual impossibility of repayment in the 1980s. Unquestionably, the Eurodollar market provided the mechanism through which these governments borrowed most of the money that was loaned to them in the 1970s. It is not clear, however, that any other financial markets would have fared any differently in the absence of Eurodollars. Essentially, participation in the Euromarket has opened one more type of business to international banks, and these banks must manage this business with the same prudence with which they manage the other businesses in which they participate.

[7] European Community

The EC has grown from 6 member states in 1957 to 12 now, embracing more than 320 million people. The ultimate goal of the EC is to make Europe a full common market and perhaps even an economic union without any internal frontiers, which means that

FIGURE 4-12

Composition of the ECU

Source: Services of the European Commission

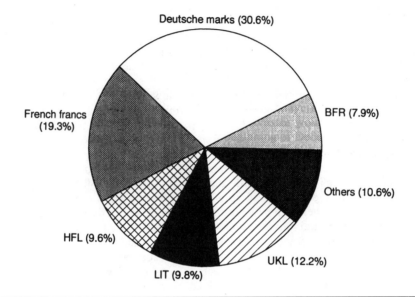

people, products, and money could move within the region without any restriction or observance of any legal formality. For the international banker, the central point of concern is the monetary integration that has gathered momentum since the EC 1992 initiative and the Maastricht proposals. Under these proposed rules, the 12 EC member countries (or those that choose to participate) would harmonize their monetary and fiscal policies, establish a common currency, and ultimately move to a single central bank.

The original timing for these adjustments targeted 1999 as the goal for achieving monetary union. By mid-1993, the countries had found varying levels of success in achieving policy goals, such as maximum government budget deficits relative to GDP and inflation limits, so that the original timetable was unlikely to be met. At the same time, approval of the monetary union proposals was much less rapid than expected, and by mid-1993 several countries had not approved the Maastricht Agreement, while the United Kingdom and Italy had dropped out of the European Monetary System's exchange rate mechanism. In short, full monetary union appears unlikely before the end of the century.

At the same time, a large number of steps have been taken in the direction of monetary union. Capital flows have been mostly liberalized among the 12, such that investors are not limited in moving their funds within the EC. Banking rules have been greatly harmonized, and banks from any member country are permitted full access to any other EC country. Although inflation has not been brought down to the target 4-percent-per-year rate in all of the countries, most of them are close to this goal, and nowhere is inflation greater than 6 percent per year. The European currency unit

(ECU) has become a de facto regional currency, even though it remains an accounting convention rather than an actual physical currency. Hundreds of billions of dollars of bond issues and other financial transactions are now denominated in ECUs, implying a growing acceptance of this instrument. The present composition of the ECU is explained in Figure 4-12.

4.07 TRADE FINANCING

As in domestic banking, the primary activities of international banks are lending and deposit taking. The specific form of lending that has always typified international banking is trade financing. Turbulent economic conditions during the past two decades and concomitant changes in government policies have resulted in a wide range of new trade financing techniques. Other cross-border forms of credit extension include direct corporate lending to foreign clients and lending to foreign governments.

All of the following methods described involve commercial banks or their affiliated companies. Additional methods may be instituted at any time, with the permission of the local legal jurisdiction, whenever such methods can better deal with the main concerns of trade participants: funding of each party's needs, obtaining assurance of payment, and protecting against exchange risk and political risk.

[1] Export-Import Transactions

Financial concerns of companies involved in export and import transactions are quite similar to those of companies that operate purely in a domestic market, with the main exceptions being that (1) many more instruments are available at the international level; (2) more than one currency may be involved at this level; and (3) at least two legal jurisdictions apply their rules to such transactions. Companies at both the international and domestic levels are concerned with commercial risk that the buyer or seller will not fulfill the terms of the sale/purchase contract and with the cost of financing the transaction until revenues are received. The banks typically included as intermediaries in these transactions are also concerned with the same problems, though obviously from their own perspectives. The banks operate mainly as providers of guarantees, documentation, and information in export-import transactions, although they may also extend credit to exporters and importers. (Also, the banks deal in very small profit margins, e.g., 0.125 to 0.25 percent, and they take very little risk, in comparison with exporters and importers.)

Each participant in an export-import transaction will face four main concerns:

1. Protecting against the risk of noncompliance by the other parties

2. Obtaining funds to cover cash needs before payment is received

3. Protecting against exchange rate risk, if the contract is denominated in a foreign currency

4. Protecting against political risks that could prevent the transaction from being completed as contracted.

From the exporter's point of view, the risk of noncompliance is the possibility that the importer will fail to accept the goods or that an intermediary, such as a shipping company, will fail to perform its contracted task. For the importer, the noncompliance risk arises from the possibility that the goods will not arrive as agreed. Each of these participants seeks to obtain guarantees of performance from the other parties involved. The banks that function as intermediaries in the process are concerned with financial compliance by the exporter and importer as well as with the proper documentation of the transaction.

From the exporter's view, the problem of obtaining funds to cover cash needs before being paid for the transaction may be a serious one. If the exporter is a manufacturer, funding must be obtained for production of the goods, as well as for the time between shipment to the importer and ultimate payment. If the exporter acts only as an intermediary between a manufacturer and the importer, funds are needed to cover the period between payment to the manufacturer and ultimate receipt of payment from the importer. During the 1980s, this was not too serious a problem for most U.S. exporters, since about two thirds of shipments were paid in cash. This leaves the burden of financing on the importer, which needs to finance the period between payment to the exporter and final sale of the goods to customers. If the importer is a manufacturer receiving parts or materials, it will probably need financing until its own production is complete and final products sold. The bank functioning as intermediary will face a need for funds if it extends credit to the importer or exporter; otherwise, the bank's main concern are the risks involved.

The third main concern to an exporter is forex risk. U.S. exporters can often avoid this risk simply by billing in dollars; in fact, over half of world trade is denominated in U.S. dollars. However, depending on the relative bargaining positions of importer and exporter and the currency that each finds desirable, the exporter may be induced to accept payment in a foreign currency and thus to accept exchange rate risk. Of course, the amount of risk depends on the exporter's other commitments in the same currency. The importer faces analogous concern with exchange rate risk. Taking the example of a U.S. importer, the risk may not appear, since it is most common to bill in dollars. Also, if the payment occurs in cash, exchange risk is avoided because currency can be exchanged in the spot market before the exchange rate changes. Exchange risk does exist even in this case if the original contract is negotiated before payment and the exchange rate changes unexpectedly between the contracting date and the payment date. Finally, from the bank's point of view, exchange risk often occurs because for one of the two final parties the payment must be denominated in foreign currency, and the bank may be asked to provide it. For this reason, banks with active international departments usually have active forex risk management programs.

The exporter should also be concerned about political risk that may complicate shipment of goods or payment for the transaction. Political risk affects the importer and the intermediaries as well, although their options for protecting against it differ to some extent from those available to exporters. This kind of risk involves the possibility that a national government may change its policy, e.g., by placing new tariffs, quotas, or other barriers on imports, as a result of which the transaction may come undone. Similarly, if the government limits access to forex for payment by the importer, the transaction may be stopped or hindered. Other political events such as wars, changes in government, and the like may result in policy shifts that alter the transaction significantly or even disallow it. Political risk became a central concern in cross-border lending during the 1980s, as dozens of governments in LDCs failed to meet their credit terms in sovereign loans, and international banks had to cope with billions of dollars of problem loans, some of which were trade financing lines (although most problems arose with longer-term loans for other purposes).

Trade finance is broadly classified into traditional and nontraditional forms and can be short, medium, or long term. Traditional forms of trade finance include all types of credit available from banks, and nontraditional forms include credits available from nonbank sources. Presently, certain specialist departments in the banks provide the nontraditional forms of finance. The following is a classification of credits available to exporters:

- Short term (traditional):
  - —Loans and overdrafts
  - —Short-term supplier credits
  - —Documentary credits
- Medium term (traditional):
  - —Currency loans
  - —Medium-term supplier credits
- Long term (traditional):
  - —Bonds
  - —Shares
- Short term (nontraditional):
  - —Factoring
  - —Credits from export houses
- Medium term (nontraditional):
  - —Forfaiting
  - —Government-sponsored agencies

The various methods of import finance can be classified as follows:

- Short term:
  - —Open account
  - —Loans and overdrafts
  - —Documentary credits
  - —Credits from confirming/indent houses
  - —Export finance houses
- Medium and long term:
  - —Installment credit
  - —Leasing
  - —Hire purchase

Figure 4-13 lists the concerns of each of the three main participants in export-import transactions and some of the means of dealing with them.

[2] Traditional Forms of Trade Finance

The traditional form of trade finance in the United States when credit is extended to the importer is direct credit from the exporter. In a detailed study several years ago, it was discovered that financing was carried out through some form of supplier credit for almost half of U.S. exports to industrial countries. Bank financing accounted for only one third of the total, while government programs supported another 14 percent of exports to industrial countries. For LDCs, the distribution was somewhat different, with bank financing accounting for close to half of the total and credit from the exporter only financing 18 percent of the total.

It is likely that these broad characteristics of trade financing have not changed dramatically since that study. In 1991, the Export-Import Bank (EXIMBANK) financed or guaranteed about 3.5 percent of U.S. exports. Supplier credits appear to be continuing as the most common form of financing. Financing by the exporter is usually trade credit, as in domestic business, with payment terms depending on the relation between the exporter and the importer, as well as on industry norms. Since

FIGURE 4-13

Main Concerns of Participants in Export-Import Transactions

Issues and Instruments	Exporter	Importer	Bank
1. Risk of noncompliance	Failure to receive payment as agreed	Failure to receive products as agreed	Failure by any other party to make payments as agreed
Instruments for protection	LOC; prepayment; government guarantee	LOC; open account; insurance policy	LOC; other documents; importer's deposit
2. Financing needs	Funds for production and during period before payment	Funds for downpayment and during period before resale	Funds to cover any credit extended
Instruments for obtaining funds	Working capital loan; prepayment discounted receivables	LOC and time draft; open account; bank loan	Standard sources, e.g., deposits and borrowings
3. Exchange rate risk	If payment is accepted in foreign currency	If payment is made in foreign currency	If foreign currency is obtained for either exporter or importer
Instruments for protection	Prepayment; forward contract; other hedging techniques	Forward contract; prepayment; other hedging techniques	Forex management program
4. Political risk	Failure to receive payment as agreed owing to government intervention	Failure to receive products as agreed owing to government intervention	Inability to carry out transaction or failure of other parties to perform as contracted owing to government intervention
Instruments for protection	OPIC insurance contracts; EXIMBANK insurance contracts; private insurance policies	Private insurance policies	EXIMBANK insurance contracts; private insurance policies

about one third of U.S. exports go to affiliated companies of U.S. firms (for the most part, overseas subsidiaries of multinational enterprises), it is not surprising to see them contract on open account and on consignment. Open-account contracts imply large risk for the exporter unless the importer is a controlled affiliate, because title to the goods passes to the importer. Similarly, sale on consignment, even though legal ownership of goods remains with the exporter, is very risky to the exporter, and such transactions may be justified when the importer is a related firm. Despite the high visibility of countertrade as a nontraditional financing technique, estimates for U.S. exports show that countertrade is used in only about 5 percent of the total.

Financing by banks traditionally has been done through letters of credit, in which

FIGURE 4-14

Comparison of Export Financing Alternatives

Source: The Wall Street Journal *(Jan. 1993); Business International Corporation,* Business Europe

Funding Source	Cost	Risk	Availability
Prepayment	Firm's cost of capital	None	Typical for U.S. exporters in 1980s
Domestic commercial loan	10%	Bank default	Common for reasonable-quality borrowers
Commercial Euroloan	8.5%	Bank default	Common for medium and large firms
EXIMBANK guaranteed loan	7.3%	Document inaccuracy	Available to U.S. exporters on a selective basis
Banker's acceptance	8.08%	Default by accepting bank	Common as long as documents are structured properly
Commercial paper	8.15%	None	Restricted to high-quality borrowers
Factoring	Prime + 1%–2%	Default by factor	Fairly common but not in all countries
Forfaiting	LIBOR + 1%–5%	Default by importers' government	Used mostly for large transactions in Eastern Europe
Countertrade	n.r.	Many types	Must be discovered by the firm

a bank substitutes its promise to pay the exporter for that of the importer. The exporter typically prefers to have the guarantee of payment made by some entity in the same country, so a local bank or affiliate of the importer's bank offers a confirmation of the original letter of credit. The LOC gives the exporter a guarantee of payment and may also offer financing to the importer, if it is payable at a future date. Most U.S. exports are paid in cash, with no financing of the importer. For those that are financed, a time LOC credit provides the importer with a period of financing (usually 180 days or less), as well as the promise to pay the exporter.

LOCs can be broadly classified as revocable credits, irrevocable credits, and confirmed irrevocable credits. In practice, other types of credits such as transferable credits, back-to-back credits, red-clause credits, green-clause credits, revolving credits, standby credits, and transit credits are also prevalent. The type used depends on the purpose and nature of transaction.

The time LOC offers an exporter the opportunity to obtain immediate payment, if desired, by selling the account receivable back to the bank as a banker's acceptance. The acceptance is simply the package of documents including a time LOC that constitutes an account receivable, with payment due from the bank at the time specified in the contract. Active secondary markets for banker's acceptances exist in New York and London, so the bank itself may choose to sell the acceptance to another financial institution. Although the most common form of bank credit for international trade, it is by no means the only form. LOCs and several other kinds of trade finance are compared according to their costs and risks in Figure 4-14.

[3] Government Loans and Loan Guarantees

Most countries today offer government support to their exporters in one form or another. Japan offers low-interest loans to exporting firms; France rebates part of the firm's taxes paid on exported products; Brazil allows exporters to exchange foreign currency at a favorable exchange rate; and most other governments do one or more of the preceding.

The U.S. government offers two types of support to its exporters. First, it allows firms that incorporate an overseas export sales subsidiary under the provisions for a foreign sales corporation (FSC) to reduce taxes paid on their export earnings by as much as 50 percent. Although this is not a loan in the strict sense, it is a means of reducing the cost of export sales, which affects the exporter in a manner similar to a low-interest loan.

A second form of U.S. government support for exporters is the system of loans and guarantees provided by EXIMBANK, an independent agency of the U.S. government, which operates as a lender to exporters and export-financing banks as well as a guarantor to banks for loans used as payment for U.S. exports. While it makes no short-term (up to six-month) loans, EXIMBANK does offer loan guarantees through the Foreign Credit Insurance Association (FCIA). Political risk coverage as well as normal, commercial risk coverage is available in the EXIMBANK policies. EXIMBANK also offers guarantees to U.S. exporters on bank loans with durations of six months to five years. Another policy guarantees that EXIMBANK will purchase eligible medium-term payments obligations of foreign importers that buy U.S. exports, which encourages U.S. banks to discount the obligations, thus making funds available immediately to U.S. exporters. The various forms of assistance rendered by EXIMBANK in 1991 are given in Figure 4-15.

For periods greater than five years, EXIMBANK offers both financing to foreign importers and guarantees to U.S. banks that lend to such importers to purchase U.S. exports. Another facility provides direct credit to foreign banks that make loans to local importers to buy from U.S. exporters. This facility, the Cooperative Financing Facility, establishes lines of credit to participating foreign banks. Yet another program provides joint funding along with banks for U.S. exporters through the Private Export Funding Corporation. This facility is primarily used to finance large projects that are unable to obtain commercial financing from normal, private sources.

In total, in the case of the United States, government lending programs are used to finance about 17 percent of total exports, while private sources fund the rest. The limits on EXIMBANK activities come from both its lending and guaranteeing limits, which are established by Congress and reviewed annually, and the costly problems of paperwork and other bureaucratic hurdles facing banks that seek to participate in the various programs.

[4] Countertrade

A central problem of trade financing is the need of the importer for access to forex to make payment. The previously mentioned techniques do not deal with this problem. Countertrade, in which products or services are exchanged for others, avoids the use of currency and thus the problem of obtaining forex. Such a concern is clearly crucial in many LDCs, the former Communist countries, and even periodically in industrial countries.

FIGURE 4-15

EXIMBANK Authorization Summary (Fiscal Year 1991)

Source: EXIMBANK 1991 Annual Report

Program	Number of Authorizations	Amount Authorized	Export Value
Loans			
Direct loans	17	$ 424.6	$ 523.2
Intermediary loans	106	206.2	228.4
War chest grants	8	145.4	302.6
Total loans	131	$ 776.2	$ 1,054.2
Guarantees			
Long-term guarantees	46	$ 3,845.8	$ 4,068.2
Medium-term guarantees	189	2,121.7	2,295.6
Working capital guarantees	54	66.7	74.1
Total guarantees	289	$ 6,034.2	$ 6,437.9
Export Credit Insurance			
Short-term insurance	1,072	$ 4,045.5	$ 4,045.4
Medium-term insurance	73	508.1	521.2
Total insurance	1,145	$ 4,553.5	$ 4,566.6
Total	1,565	$11,363.9	$12,058.7

Note: U.S. dollars in millions.

The basic idea of countertrade is that of barter. The exporter accepts goods instead of funds to pay for the exports. In this way, the exporter's problem of financing the sale is transformed into the problem of using or selling the goods received in payment. Even the relatively simple concept of barter is complicated by the fact that the timing of payment may be delayed, in which case nonpayment risk still exists and financing may still be needed by the exporter.

Although there is no standard form of countertrade, a few categories of transactions can be distinguished, namely:

- Counterpurchase
- Compensation agreements
- Link purchase
- Barter
- Buy-back agreements
- Offset
- Evidence accounts

When commercial compensation is paid by the importer in the short or medium term, the transaction may be labeled a counterpurchase. This type of transaction involves two separate but parallel contracts, one for delivery and the other for counterdelivery. (For example, the former Soviet Union purchased construction machinery from the Japanese firm Komatsu in return for Komatsu's agreement to buy Siberian timber in the early 1980s.)

In the compensation agreement, the delivery and counterdelivery are covered by the same agreement. These kinds of typically one time deals are most akin to barter as it is usually defined. A link purchase is often a marriage transaction by an international banker to identify two separate companies in two different countries that will sell goods for cash to the other country. This type of transaction does not alter the countries' balance-of-payments position.

While all of these transactions are only barter in essence, balanced barter, unbalanced barter, and triangular barter make each one a distinct point of interest. In a balanced barter, the values on both transactions will be the same; in an unbalanced barter, the difference is settled in cash; and in a triangular barter, an import from one country is matched by an export to a third country.

Another type of transaction involves long-term repayment and often compensation with industrial products. This form of countertrade is labeled a buy-back agreement. The compensation may be raw materials or intermediate goods (i.e., industrial products) or it may be output from the technique or installation that was exported. (For example, in 1980, after the U.S. government forced U.S. suppliers out of the market, U.K., German, Japanese, and Italian companies participated in constructing a $4 billion natural gas pipeline in the former Soviet Union; Russia is paying for this project with natural gas exports today.)

In deals associated with certain advanced technology products, the importer insists that some specified components and/or a certain percentage of raw materials should be procured from the importing country. This offset helps the importing country develop its own capabilities. In this type of deal, the importer may insist that the exporter establish the production process in the importing country.

When there is a continuing business in a certain country, it is not possible for firms to match item for item. Therefore, they establish running accounts (evidence accounts) showing debits and credits. The account is brought to order on a periodic basis, in most cases once in every year. Each of these kinds of transactions involves all goods and no money; hence, the term countertrade or barter conveys the appropriate idea.

Countertrade imposes serious constraints on the exporter relative to other means of trade financing. First, there is the problem of trying to value the products to be received in payment. Second, there is the problem of disposing of these goods. Third, if payment is not simultaneous with the exporter's shipment, another form of financing will still be necessary (even if it is generated internally by the exporter). Fourth, the exporter assumes all of the political risk of dealing with the importer. These difficulties may outweigh the value of the possible export sale. The value of countertrade transactions is 9.5 percent of world trade, and about 90 countries use it. Countertrade has been the forte of big, sophisticated firms with more than $1 billion sales. The practice of countertrade lost its rationale of facilitating trade in the Communist countries of Eastern Europe, but it is likely to continue in the republics of the former Soviet Union, which are generally short on hard currency to pay for imports. Most governments consider countertrade an inefficient way of financing international trade, since it requires a lengthy negotiation process and only about 1 out of 20 negotiations end up in a firm deal.

[5] Factoring

For financing the period between the shipment of its merchandise and payment by the importer, an exporter may turn to a factoring company (factor). This arrangement is a direct alternative to acceptance financing. A factor buys the exporter's receivables at a discount and assumes the risk of nonpayment by the importer, as well as the right to payment of the receivables. Factoring consists of two separate functions for an exporter, namely, risk management and finance. Factors cover political and commercial risk without recourse and also provide finance to the exporter.

Factoring involves a greater commitment from the exporter than does acceptance financing, because a factoring contract generally calls for the exporter to sell all receivables to the factor during the contract period. Because factoring is a contractual arrangement between the exporter and the factor, the terms of the contract may include virtually anything to which the two parties agree. Typically, the factor agrees to buy all export accounts receivable from the exporter at a specified discount and to assume all of the responsibility for collecting from the importer. In return, the factor receives the discounted receivables, on which it gains effective interest when it is paid their full value by the importer. The factor also charges a fee for accepting the nonpayment risk and for performing this service.

The choice for an exporter between use of a factor and use of a bank as intermediary in the export-import transaction depends on four conditions:

1. Availability of each service

2. Cost of using each intermediary

3. Amount of business being committed

4. Flexibility desired

[6] Forfaiting

Forfaiting is a method of trade financing that was developed explicitly to handle large-scale, long-term capital goods exports from Western firms to the former Eastern bloc countries. The financial concept of forfaiting is analogous to factoring and the use of banker's acceptances; that is, it is another means of nonrecourse export finance. Forfaiting is the purchase of debt instruments due to mature in the future and that represent export of goods, without recourse to any previous holder of the instruments. It adds a new dimension to export finance because the exporter can include financing costs in the contract price and quote a price including the cost of insurance and freight (CIF) value and the costs of credit. As with factoring, the exporter sells its receivable at a discount to a forfaiting firm, which accepts the risk of nonpayment by the importer and the right to payment under the exporter's sales contract. However, the forfaiting firm obtains a guarantee (or aval) from the government of the importing country, which takes responsibility for payment if the importer does not pay as contracted.

Forfaiting originally gained acceptability among some Western European banks, especially in Switzerland, during the 1960s. For export sales to the former Communist countries, these banks (through their forfaiting subsidiaries) began to purchase the payment contracts from exporting companies when suitable guarantees of payment by the host government could be arranged. The banks agreed to purchase these contracts "a forfait," that is, without recourse to the exporting firm. Thus, full nonpayment risk was shifted to the forfaiter, which accepted the guarantee of the host government risk as sufficient to justify the transaction. Because the forfaiter operated regularly as an analyst and accepter of host government risk, it was presumably better able than the exporter to assess and manage that risk. Although forfaiting remains primarily oriented toward East-West trade, it is now more broadly available for large transactions involving medium-term and long-term payment by the importer.

The costs to the exporter are multiple and generally are justifiable only if the transaction is too complex to be handled through the banker's acceptance method. Forfaiting is more expensive than other forms of credit because of the high risk. These costs commonly include (1) a charge for political and transfer risks, about 0.5 percent to 5 percent per year; (2) a charge for the use of money and for the covering of interest rate risks, generally the Eurocurrency rate, LIBOR; and (3) a charge for administrative work, about 0.5 percent per year.

There are several advantages in forfaiting:

- A forfait finance is a fixed-rate finance.
- The exporter's operating capital is replenished immediately.
- Documentation is simple and quickly compiled for all parties to the transaction (exporter, importer, forfaiter, and guarantor).
- The title to the goods is easily transferable, and thus trading in the secondary market is possible.

Since forfaiting is the only form of export finance that carries a fixed rate and presents no risk to the exporter, it has all of the advantages of commercial borrowing—leasing, hire purchase, and factoring—without any of the limitations of these methods. Fees paid and received, provision for writing off bad debts, and different laws of taxation in different countries bring an interesting complexity to the whole concept of forfaiting.

[7] Leasing

Leasing is another form of finance frequently used in very large deals, especially in international transactions involving aircraft, ships, oil rigs, and production plants. In this method also, the exporter receives cash without recourse but the lessor experiences difficulties as the deal is subjected to fluctuating interest rates. Multicurrency packages and the presence of international leasing associations facilitate cross-border leasing, which may be of great importance to an international banker. Leveraged or geared leases are another source of complexity when the lessor provides only part of the capital required and the balance is raised in money markets. Currently, financial leases are available even for small deals, such as those involving office equipment and furniture.

4.08 CROSS-BORDER CREDIT EXTENSION

Cross-border extension of bank credit generally follows a pattern similar to that of its most important component, the Euromarkets. Most of the credits are interbank; most are between industrial countries, with a few tax havens thrown in; and most are short-term commitments. The Eurocurrency market itself is the most important source of cross-border lending, followed by the national banking systems of the large industrial nations.

[1] Interbank Lending

Credits to banks in other countries are the largest part of foreign lending by most international banks. From Eurocurrency placements to simple correspondent balances, dealings between banks far outpace any other form of international credit. The primary instruments used in this segment of international lending are deposits: time deposits and CDs. Related to trade financing, there are also various forms of LOCs and confirmations, each of which imply credit from the issuing or confirming bank. Beyond these instruments, many more credit forms are used, such as short-term and long-term direct loans (which, in turn, may be secured or unsecured), standby credit facilities, and others.

To some extent, interbank credits are used as a "borrower of last resort" by lenders, since the spreads tend to be quite small and banks prefer to find more profitable borrowers when possible. Particularly in the Euromarkets, interbank deposits are used both as credit extensions and as information-gathering activities, with money market traders buying and selling short-term deposits largely to keep abreast of the market, to demonstrate their willingness to regularly buy and sell funds, and to see what other banks are doing.

A second major part of the interbank market is the range of credit instruments used in maintaining correspondent bank relationships. To entice other banks to offer credit facilities, guarantees, and other noncredit services, a bank needs to establish some kind of mutually beneficial relationship with those potential partners. The simplest demonstration of goodwill can be made through depositing funds in the other, correspondent bank. Additional credit forms that typically develop in correspondent relationships are confirmations of LOCs issued by the correspondent, willingness to issue LOCs to clients recommended by the correspondent, and the purchase of banker's acceptances from the correspondent. Many of these credits add to the amount of interbank lending, since they are forms of funding directly between the banks. Of course, many noncredit services, such as provision of credit information, foreign exchange, collections, and check clearing, are also important to correspondent relationships, although they are not relevant to the present context.

[2] Commercial Lending to Foreign Clients

The most desirable form of cross-border lending is to private-sector, high-quality corporate clients in industrial countries. This market segment offers the most familiar kind of client to the bank, and it pays much better than the interbank market. While banks try to concentrate their resources on this part of the market, competition is intense for the blue-chip firms, and margins were reduced greatly during the 1970s and 1980s. By now, many medium-size firms in industrial countries have discovered the Euromarkets, and credits have been extended far beyond the Fortune 500-type firms. The segment reached a size in the Euromarkets of about $600 billion in 1987.

[3] Credit to Government Borrowers

Lending to sovereign governments and their agencies traditionally was not a central thrust of international commercial banking. Such funding historically came from other governments, international lending agencies such as the World Bank and IMF, and investors through purchases of government-issued bonds. During the 1970s, sovereign lending blossomed into a major part of total international bank lending, and today it accounts for about one third of total cross-border lending to LDCs and one half of cross-border lending to industrial country borrowers. Most of the sovereign lending takes place through the Euromarkets, and, during the past two decades, sovereign loans accounted for about one half of total lending in the Euromarkets.

Sovereign loans are generally made for three purposes:

1. General government funding needs

2. Project finance

3. Government-guaranteed private-sector finance

The first of these categories includes government requests to fund short-term balance-of-payments problems, as well as longer-term infrastructural development (such as building roads, supplying public utilities, and providing public services). General-purpose loans are the most difficult to evaluate for the lending bank, because the funds are not tied directly to projects that generate forex (dollars) to repay the credit. Despite the lessons of history, it was widely believed during the 1970s that sovereign governments would not default on their foreign debts, presumably because governments have the ability to tax their subjects to obtain funds for repayment and because governments should be afraid to default and cut themselves off from international credit markets. Both of these assumptions were proven false during the 1980s, and sovereign lending has both decreased overall and shifted more to project finance and to finance of private-sector loans with government guarantees.

The second category of sovereign lending is for specific projects, which lead to generation of revenues to repay the loans. During the past decade, funds were sought for projects including construction or modernization of airports, port facilities, and other revenue-creating transportation facilities, as well as for specific funding needs of state-owned companies whose financial conditions lead them to be judged creditworthy. These loans were particularly common in the oil sector during the 1970s, as petroleum prices skyrocketed and government-owned oil companies undertook major projects in exploration, refining, and petrochemical production.

The third category of sovereign lending is private-sector lending when a government guarantee is used to establish creditworthiness of the ultimate borrower. This kind of lending may appear to be reasonably straightforward, with a private firm requesting funds for business needs that can be evaluated by a bank's credit committee. However, the reality sometimes becomes much more complex, as countries encounter economic crises and governments discover insufficient forex reserves to meet their commitments. In these cases, although an ultimate private-sector borrower may possess sufficient available local funds to meet the loan conditions, restrictions on access to forex nonetheless may preclude debt servicing. During the 1980s, many Latin American governments unilaterally revised the terms of private-sector foreign loans to local borrowers, with the government's assuming responsibility for repayment to foreign lenders and requiring local borrowers to make payment to the government instead.

In this way, the governments became guarantors of private-sector debts, and the risk became sovereign risk for the lending banks.

In all of the types of sovereign lending, the problem of evaluating the creditworthiness of the government is crucial. This idea of sovereign risk, or more broadly country risk, became a major aspect of cross-border lending in the 1980s, when it became clear that even private-sector loans could be caught up in the economic problems of governments and foreign bank loans could be very negatively affected.

[4] Instruments in Cross-Border Lending

In addition to the trade financing instruments previously presented, a wide variety of direct bank loans with fixed or floating interest rates, in different currencies, for different maturities, and with varying types of guarantees are used to finance international business. Three types of these instruments are syndicated loans, project financing, and debt-to-equity swaps.

[a] Syndicated Loans. Syndicated lending has become a major part of the international long-term credit market during the past 20 years, today accounting for about half of Eurocurrency lending to nonbanks. This technique is used for large, medium-term (three-to-ten-year) loans in which a lender wants to share the burden of both funding and risk taking. The borrower seeks a group of lenders that are each able to participate in the total loan funding, management, and advising according to their interest in it. The loan itself may be a direct loan, a line of credit, or any other form of medium-term or long-term credit. Until the 1960s, this type of lending was primarily carried out through the issue of bonds by merchant banks, and the main lenders were institutions and wealthy individuals.

Eurocurrency syndicated loans, as a wholesale, medium-term source of corporate and government finance, initially began as a vehicle offered by a handful of the largest multinational banks for funding the needs of blue-chip corporate borrowers and highly creditworthy governments. As the market developed, borrowers spread downward into a wider range of corporations and governments, and lenders likewise diversified into dozens of banks. By the late 1970s, almost all of the commercial bank lending to LDCs was of this form, as was most lending to then-Communist countries. Lenders are attracted to syndications because of the relative ease of dealing with the client and the ability to place responsibility for credit and performance evaluation onto the lead bank or banks. By placing only a part of the total funds into such syndicated loans, banks maintain their flexibility to participate in other direct or syndicated loans, with other partners, and in other countries. Borrowers are also attracted to syndicated loan financing because they must enter the capital market only once and demonstrate their creditworthiness only once and still can obtain (essentially) loans from several banks, which altogether provide very large sums of financing.

Most Eurocurrency syndicated loans are unsecured, so that loan covenants specify many performance requirements that are designed to assure the lenders that the borrower retains its ability to repay. Corporate borrowers are often required to maintain particular financial ratios and to avoid taking on new debt except if it is subordinated to the syndicated loan. Country borrowers may be required to meet fiscal targets and balance-of-payments performance limits, again to ensure that repayment is feasible. Generally, a cross-default clause appears in syndicated loans stating that a default on any loan by the borrower is a default on the syndicated loan as well. Presently, the market is going through a phase of cyclical contraction. Cross-border and foreign currency local claims, according to the Bank for International Settlements, increased by only 2.5 percent in 1991, compared with an annual growth rate of 15 percent in 1988–1990. As of 1992, the volume of syndicated credits was over $120 billion.

[b] Project Financing. Another means of forcing long-term, large-scale overseas lending into a palatable structure for commercial banks is through project finance, which contractually ties the loan to cash flows generated by the project. In more concrete terms, an international project loan is contracted between a lender or group of lenders and a foreign borrower, with repayment to be made through future revenues produced by the project, in a specified currency and at specified dates. Project lending can be a form of sovereign lending when host governments are the sponsors or the guarantors of the projects. Project lending may also be a form of international syndicated lending, since the large size and long term of the projects often leads the lenders to form groups to share the funding and risk involved.

The main users of project finance are operators of large capital projects that require major long-term funds commitments and involve multiple risks in addition to commercial risk. These include raw materials ventures such as oil wells, copper mines, and agricultural projects, as well as construction projects such as building manufacturing plants, electric power plants, and other public utilities. Because raw materials industries and public utilities are often government-owned, governments are often the borrowers in project financing situations.

For the lender, evaluation of the project is the crucial phase of lending. Not only does the lender need to evaluate the borrower's estimates of future cash flows of the project, but numerous risks need to be considered. First is the risk of the project's actually being completed and functioning as planned. There is commercial risk that the project's output may be worth less (or more) in the future than expected now. Also, there is sovereign risk when the borrower is a government and the risk of not having access to forex to make repayments regardless of the type of borrower. Because many cases of project finance occur in LDCs and/or countries with chronic forex shortages, country risk is a central concern.

The many complexities of judging the creditworthiness of the borrower, obtaining guarantees where possible, putting together a syndicate group, assuring future buyers for the project's output, and other considerations make project finance an expensive and time-consuming business for lenders. As a result, most banks participate in relatively few project financings, and they tend to choose large projects that can cover the many costs and risks involved.

Project financing by the European Investment Bank (EIB) is a typical example of this category. As a long-term lending institution, the EIB finances projects that are economically viable. As of 1991, the EIB had financed projects worth ECU13,656 million within the EC and ECU916 million outside the community. Transport, environment, industry, energy, community infrastructure, and small and medium-sized enterprises are the areas of concentration for the EIB. Build-own-operate-transfer (BOOT) projects have taken project financing into a new age. A BOOT project requires that the private sector build a facility, own it, and then transfer it to the government. Such projects have increased the complexity of international banking and also the competition between all banks, especially those owned by Japan, the United States, and the United Kingdom. Because such undertakings will have only assets of an incomplete project if they fail, banks need to exercise more caution than with normal projects.

The construction period tends to be longer than for other projects. BOOT projects are usually single, unconventional projects, and so the banks are exposed to project-specific risks. In addition, such projects are capital intensive and so need a main bank facility, an LOC facility, and a standby facility.

[c] Debt-To-Equity Swaps. Debt-to-equity swaps are among the private-sector re-sponses to the LDC foreign debt crisis. A debt-to-equity swap transforms a problem loan into another form of credit to the borrowing country, namely, an equity invest-ment. Beginning in 1985, commercial banks negotiated the sale of some of their sover-eign loans to Latin American governments in exchange for local currency that was committed to investment in capital projects. Chile and Mexico established the first programs for these swaps, and by 1988 almost $10 billion of foreign debt had been swapped for direct investments in various countries of the region. Swap activity more than tripled this figure during 1989–1992, as major privatizations in Argentina, Mexico, and elsewhere permitted the use of foreign debt as one means of payment for equity shares in the government corporations being privatized.

The debt-to-equity swap often involves at least four parties in the total group of transactions. First, there is a foreign bank that wants to dispose of a loan to the government or a private-sector borrower in the country in question. Second, there is another foreign firm that wants to invest in a capital project in that same country. Third, there is the monetary authority (and perhaps other government agencies) of the given country, which must agree to permit exchange of the loan contract for local currency that will be used in the investment. Finally, there is an investment banking intermediary that looks for buyers and sellers of the loans and negotiates with the monetary authorities for permissions that are required. A simple debt-to-equity swap is depicted in Figure 4-16.

Since the loan is nonperforming or otherwise impaired in its servicing, the originat-ing bank may be willing to sell it at a discount just to dispose of it and get it off the books. The discounts at which foreign commercial banks have been willing to sell their Latin American loans grew to over 50 percent for most countries in the region. The potential loan seller typically is contacted by an intermediary, such as an invest-ment banking firm that is seeking sources of funds for clients that want to invest in Latin American countries. These intermediaries seek out both loan sellers and buyers, trying to put them together and profit from arranging the deals. Once a loan seller and buyer have been found, the intermediary must negotiate with the Latin American government involved to obtain whatever permissions may be necessary to redeem the dollar loan for some value in local currency. The value received by the loan buyer typically is some percentage below the direct face value of the loan translated from dollars into local currency. This is still substantially higher than the dollar value that the buyer paid to obtain the loan. Once permissions have been arranged, the loan buyer takes the local currency (e.g., pesos) and invests it in a capital project that was proposed in the permission request to the government in that country.

The transaction is viewed favorably by each participant, because the original lending bank is able to sell its problem loan (taking the discount as a real loss in value of the original loan as the price of this sale), the new investor is able to obtain local currency at a substantial discount relative to ordinary financing costs, the host government is able to eliminate some of its foreign dollar debt and related servicing problems by issuing new local currency for direct investment, and the investment bank earns fees by bringing the various parties together.

FIGURE 4-16

Swap of Sovereign Debt for Equity in a New Capital Project

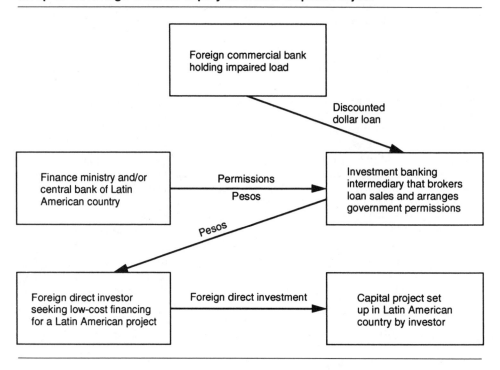

4.09 CROSS-BORDER LIABILITIES

On the liability side, international banks obtain new funds primarily through deposit taking from other banks and from sale of money market instruments such as federal funds (fed funds) (in the United States) and banker's acceptances. In addition, a bank may seek funding through the issue of its own securities, just as an industrial corporation does. The focus here is only on the issue of deposit taking.

The primary source of international deposits is the interbank Euromarket, with its large-scale, low-margin deposit trading. A second source is corporate deposit accounts, which are used for transactions and as investments by international industrial or commercial firms. A third source is official government deposits held by central banks, other monetary authorities, and state-owned companies. The OPEC petrodollar deposits provide an excellent example of the massive size of these accounts. A final source is personal banking, the acquisition of accounts of wealthy overseas individuals and families. The size and distribution of these deposit liabilities for U.S. international banks is shown in Figure 4-17.

Interbank deposits lead the liabilities, with about two thirds of the total value ($543 million). Central bank and other government accounts follow, with about one fifth of the total value. Corporate deposits are made largely in foreign bank offices and thus

FIGURE 4-17

Deposit Liabilities of U.S. International Banks to Nonresidents Reported by U.S. Banks

Source: Federal Reserve Bulletin *(Apr. 1993), Table*

Central banks and official institutions	$159.2
Nonmonetary international and regional organizations	9.1
Commercial banks	543.1
Other foreigners	94.7
Bank total	$806.1
Reported by nonbanking institutions	46.2
	$852.3

Note: U.S. dollars in billions.

appear here only as part of the interbank category. Finally, the "other foreigners" heading includes primarily personal banking clients, whose deposits constitute about 14 percent of the total. Additional personal banking–type liabilities are shown as deposits in nonbank institutions, which bring the category up to almost 20 percent of the total of international deposits in U.S. banks and other financial institutions. (Since petrodollars are held largely outside of the United States, the size of that activity cannot be seen in the figure.)

[1] Petrodollars

The most disruptive forces in international financial markets during the past two decades have been the move to floating exchange rates and the massive shift in wealth from industrial countries to OPEC members. The former phenomenon created the system that operates today. The latter phenomenon resulted in hundreds of billions of dollars of transfers of funds from industrial country oil purchasers to OPEC oil vendors. Initially, these recipients of the petrodollars deposited most of them in the international banking system, causing a reshuffling of accounts between owners. Figure 4-18 gives some idea of the buildup of the current account surpluses since 1973 that resulted from the overwhelmingly positive trade balances of OPEC countries. It also shows the dramatic switch of these countries' fortunes with the lower oil prices in the 1980s, which produced much lower oil revenues and current account deficits into the early 1990s.

In the aftermaths of the oil shocks in both 1973–1974 and 1979–1980, the banks had to find new borrowers for the funds, since industrial countries were hit by recessions, and loan demand diminished. The issue of the LDC debt crisis, which was in large part due to the petrodollar recycling, was discussed previously. Here it is simply noted that the petrodollars provided a flood of excess liquidity in the international banking system during that period.

FIGURE 4-18

OPEC Current Account Surpluses (1973–1991)

Year	Current Account
1973	$ 4.9
1974	70.4
1975	38.4
1976	43.6
1977	27.2
1978	5.7
1979	58.5
1980	101.5
1981	40.4
1982	(11.5)
1983	(19.6)
1984	(4.1)
1985	(10.2)
1986	(189.1)
1987	(100.6)
1988	(155.2)
1989	20.0
1990	55.1
1991	(247.4)

Note: Current U.S. dollars in billions.

[2] International Corporate Deposits

International corporate deposits also constitute an important part of the funding base. Although traditional demand deposits remain a significant part of total international bank liabilities, corporations with major deposits have largely moved to the use of Eurodeposits, which pay interest and can be liquidated quickly. This type of funding source tends to be highly sensitive to interest rates, and international banks must compete aggressively to maintain such deposits. One of the ways banks have developed to keep corporate Euromarket deposits is through provision of corporate cash management services.

[3] Personal Banking

At the risk of oversimplifying the issue, consider personal banking as the generation of fee and interest income through the solicitation of depository accounts and other business from affluent, nonresident individual clients. The emergence in recent years of personal banking as a significant market segment for most of the internationally oriented U.S. banks is closely tied to worldwide political and economic developments that have affected the way banks perceive their interests and where they look for their business. Obviously, the oil shocks of the 1970s, leading to excess liquidity in the international banking system, caused a major increase in international personal banking activity. This occurred when the banks recycled the petrodollars into loans to nontraditional customers such as Latin American governments, which in turn stimulated their economies with new spending. Wealthy individuals saw the risk in that strategy and began to place some of their funds in overseas bank deposits. Subsequently, when the debt crisis arrived, simultaneous with major political change in many countries that replaced military regimes with elected governments, many people chose to move more of their wealth overseas to protect against the country risk of their own environments. These historical conditions led to a surge in clients' interest in international personal banking services.

Once the foreign debt crisis began in 1982, the banks themselves discovered that sovereign loans to third world countries were much riskier than originally expected and rapidly moved to find other international business activities that could replace lending in these countries. In addition to refocusing their lending in industrial countries, the banks began to make a much greater effort to sell noncredit products in the third world. Electronic banking services, provision of business information, and deposit taking all came to the forefront in this environment.

Personal banking is an important market because it permits banks to build their international business in areas other than extension of credit to overseas borrowers. This is not a complete picture, because some of the deposits acquired in personal banking became the collateral for loans back to these individuals or their firms. In this way, lending to risky countries still grows. However, most of the personal banking deposits are funneled into the banks' other activities, such as domestic lending and offshore lending to industrial countries. A paradoxical aspect of this business is the fact that a large percentage of the deposits represented flight capital that was leaving the third world in favor of less risky countries, and this very flight capital exacerbated the debt crisis by extracting more dollars from the debtor nations.

4.10 OTHER INTERNATIONAL BANKING SERVICES

There are many more services and instruments offered by commercial banks in international banking activities than those covered in this chapter. This section describes a handful of additional noncredit services that often constitute an important part of international banks' total activity.

[1] Information Services

Just as merchant banks specialize in offering information services to corporate clients, so do commercial banks. These services today range from the true investment banking concerns of advice on issuing new securities and arranging mergers and acquisitions all the way to more traditional commercial banking concerns such as finding highest-yield deposit instruments and advising corporate clients concerning cash management. In addition to these functions, international banks frequently offer guidance on country risk assessment and macroeconomic forecasting to their corporate clients. As the regulatory environment around the world became more open in the late 1980s, commercial banks increasingly moved directly into investment banking functions. In sum, the information services offered by commercial banks to their corporate clients are now quite inclusive along the full range of financial services required by those clients.

[2] Electronic Banking Services

International banks have discovered many new services that can be presented to clients as a result of the computerized information networks that the banks have installed in their offices in many locations. For the multinational banks, which operate branches or other affiliates in several countries, electronic banking services include activities such as moving funds for clients from one office of the bank in one country to another office of the bank (or to another bank) in another country; providing instantaneous access to deposit and lending opportunities in different countries through money-trading operations; check clearance across national borders; and simple provision of information about the client's account in other offices of the bank in other countries.

The most widespread electronic services to date are the informational ones regarding financial market conditions in different countries and clients' account status in different offices of the bank. The largest of the multinational banks are moving aggressively into additional electronic services such as international check clearance, arranging swaps of assets and liabilities across countries, and managing corporate cash in multinational corporations.

[3] Corporate Cash Management

Moving funds between countries and managing deposits to optimize interest earnings for corporate clients has become an important source of fee income for many multinational banks. Clients with operations in several countries generally need rapid and efficient methods of moving funds among them. A multinational bank can provide funds transfer services through its own branch and affiliate network and/or through dealing with other banks. Obviously, the cost to the customer will be lowest if the bank can offer the service within its own network without resorting to other banks to carry out the transfers.

Beyond the funds transfer function, a multinational bank can offer deposit management services that seek out highest-yield uses of funds according to the client's risk and liquidity preferences. These may be Eurodollar deposits in different locations, foreign exchange deposits in various currencies, or investment in instruments such as government securities. These services are limited, of course, in countries that impose various kinds of restrictions on access to forex and on international movements of funds.

[4] Interest Rate Swaps

One form of corporate financial service that has become quite widely used is the arrangement of swaps, including currency swaps, debt-to-equity swaps, and interest rate swaps.

An interest rate swap permits a client to transform a fixed-rate loan or deposit into a floating-rate instrument, or vice versa. Banks can offer a useful service to corporate clients when the bank has access to funding or investing opportunities different from

FIGURE 4-19

Interest Rate Swap

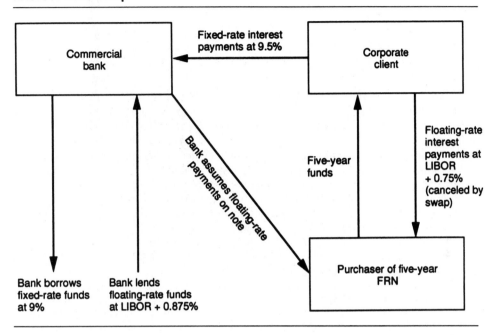

those available to the client and can perform the exchange at a favorable cost to that client. For example, banks have access to very low-cost fed funds, while corporations do not. Similarly, banks trade directly in Eurodollar deposits and banker's acceptances, while corporations must operate through a bank to gain access to such instruments. (Usually, the bank has access to cheaper fixed-rate funds and wishes to hold floating-rate liabilities, while corporate clients often wish to obtain fixed-rate funds.) If the bank can find an attractive alternative funding or lending instrument that changes the client's interest payments and receipts from floating to fixed (or the opposite), a swap may be arranged. Figure 4-19 depicts the basic characteristics of an interest rate swap.

Assume that the client holds a five-year floating-rate note that commits the firm to pay LIBOR (assume that this is 8.5 percent) plus 0.75 percent in interest on a quarterly basis, with the interest rate adjusted each quarter. The client now wishes to convert this borrowing into a fixed-rate commitment (perhaps because the client anticipates an increase in rates or because the client's income stream has become very stable). The bank can offer to trade the existing loan interest payments for fixed-rate ones at prime (assume that this is 9.75 percent) minus 0.25 percent, while the client would have had to pay prime for an equivalent direct request for a fixed-rate loan.

The bank gains because it (presumably) has an opportunity to lend out the floating-rate funds at a rate of LIBOR plus 0.875 percent and it can obtain the fixed-rate funds at prime minus 0.75 percent. The client gains because the loan characteristic has shifted from floating to fixed and the cost of the bank's fixed-rate funds is less than what the client could have obtained separately. Numerically, the client has gained 0.25 percent on the fixed-rate financing, and the bank has obtained a margin of 0.125 percent on its floating-rate position and 0.75 percent on its fixed-rate position.

4.11 MANAGERIAL ISSUES

[1] Risk Management

Success of an international bank depends heavily on success in managing the various risks involved. Exchange risk can be managed through forex-trading activities of the bank and participation in futures and options markets in forex to cover exposures. Interest rate risk can be managed by matching maturities of assets and liabilities and using hedging tools such as interest rate futures contracts and variable-rate assets and liabilities. Country risk can be managed by pricing risky activities to achieve an acceptable risk-return trade-off, seeking government or other reliable guarantees, and diversifying activities across countries to minimize the possible negative impact of problems in any country. Finally, commercial risk can be managed by appropriate pricing, using insurance where available, and diversifying across clients.

[2] Country Risk

[a] **Nature of Country Risk.** "Country risk" refers to the probability of loan losses or other impairments that may result from credits issued to a government borrower or to private borrowers (as a group) in any country. It is a measurement of the possibility that some government policy, political or macroeconomic condition, or other country-related factor may change unexpectedly and affect the servicing of a foreign debt. The impaired debt servicing may occur as a result of the government's failure to make payments as agreed under a loan contract (i.e., sovereign risk), or because of the government's restrictions on loan payments by private borrowers in that country. Such risk is distinguished from the credit risk that exists in loans to individual private borrowers, which may default on payments because of insolvency. Possible impairments include both nonpayment on loans and delayed payment of principal and/or interest, which reduces the present value of the payments that are made.

Second, it may be helpful to distinguish between a government's ability to make payments and its willingness to do so. What, after all, is the ultimate problem that bankers fear when they try to deal with country risk? Certainly it is the nonpayment or delayed payment of interest and principal, typically denominated in forex (from the borrower's point of view). The sovereign borrower may face this problem because of a balance-of-payments deficit that uses up formerly available foreign currency reserves, so that the ability to pay is lacking. Alternatively, the government may argue that debt servicing is too detrimental to national economic growth goals and choose not to make payments as a political decision, so the willingness to pay would be lacking. The only problem for a private borrower that should be considered country risk is the possibility that the government may restrict access to forex and thus preclude the private borrower's ability to repay.

Unavailability of forex may arise from these causes, but it also may occur because of currency devaluation. If a government fixes its currency value relative to some foreign monetary unit (e.g., the U.S. dollar), a government-declared devaluation can create an inadequacy of funds to purchase needed forex for both private borrowers and the government itself. Moreover, during the period before devaluation, borrowers in this country may obtain excessive amounts of foreign debt, because of its relative cheapness. Once the (presumably overvalued) currency is realigned downwards, borrowers are squeezed. The Venezuelan crisis of 1983 after the devaluation is an excellent example of what can happen when private borrowers are overwhelmed with a more than 100 percent devaluation of their currency overnight.

A final point concerning the nature of country risk is the range of six possible outcomes of risk events, which include the following:

1. Payment as agreed

2. Payment arrears

3. Rescheduling of payments

4. Renegotiation of loans

5. Default

6. Interrupted payments due to exchange controls

Outcomes 1 through 5 relate especially to sovereign borrowers, while outcomes 1 and 6 concern private-sector borrowers. Payment as agreed under a loan contract involves no added costs to the lending bank; all other alternatives can be expected to reduce the bank's earnings on a loan. The normal result of LDC debt reschedulings and renegotiations during the 1980s was for the borrower to pay an interest penalty for the period of arrears, sometimes with a higher interest spread for subsequent periods. Thus, banks lost a small amount of income but a large amount of flexibility in their lending, since they remained burdened with the risky loans. Since the 1980s, this situation has changed, with banks placing large loan loss reserves against the impaired LDC debts and realizing major portions of their losses currently. In addition, many banks have sold or traded their LDC debts in the secondary market that has developed, again realizing their losses and escaping the spiral of increasing amounts of this debt.

[b] Measuring Country Risk. The possibilities for modeling country risk are endless, ranging from personal opinions of experts on particular countries to complex econometric techniques that can define an optimal portfolio of loans based on historical country risk evidence. However measured, the risk itself should be an indicator of the probability that an event will occur leading to a reduction in the bank's return on loans in a given country; thus, economists are led into attempts to model the economic process and the political process in ways that illuminate outcomes of (1) foreign exchange unavailability and (2) exchange controls.

[c] Dealing With Country Risk. Four basic strategies exist for lenders to reduce the impact of country risk on their portfolios. The simplest is *risk avoidance*, in which the bank establishes an acceptable trade-off relationship between country risk and expected return for its international loans. If the bank's own risk preference is such that borrowers perceived as risky are unwilling to pay the interest and fees sought, the bank will find itself reducing its portfolio of foreign loans. Since sovereign loan spreads have been so small during the past two decades (from about 0.5 percent to 2 percent above LIBOR), risk avoidance certainly implies a shift to lending that is not subject to country risk.

A second strategy is *risk transfer*, in which an insuring or guaranteeing agency is used to pass on the country risk. Contracts to insure loans against country risk are available in the United States through EXIMBANK, although not all countries or transactions are covered under this agency's programs. Private-sector insurance is often available as well from the FCIA in cooperation with the EXIMBANK and from other insurers such as the American Foreign Insurance Association. Unfortunately, the costs (in money and managerial time) of obtaining either type of protection often discourage banks from using insurance.

By transferring the country risk to an insurance company, the bank incurs a new credit risk, namely, the risk that the insurance company will pay upon presentation of an insurance claim by the bank. This credit risk may be substantial when the bank's insured loan is large and/or when the insurance company or agency has a large exposure in the given country.

The third strategy is *risk adaptation*, in which the bank seeks liabilities from the potential borrower (or in the borrowing country) to offset the loan under consideration. This option is available to very few banks other than those that are multinational, but the idea of dealing with the foreign client in deposits or placements as well as in loans is a sound strategy. "Risk adaptation" in general terms refers to the concept of hedging the asset exposure (to country risk) with another account or agreement that offsets it. While this strategy has been little explored thus far, banks may discover or create new ways to match asset to liability exposures that are subject to country risk.

Finally, *risk diversification* enables the lender to reduce the impact of country risk problems with borrowers in one country by keeping foreign loan exposures spread over several countries. This strategy can be augmented by spreading loans among public-sector and private-sector borrowers and by lending in conjunction with different banks in syndicated loans. Diversification can be combined with the other strategies into a lending position that suits each bank's risk preferences and loan capacity.

[3] Competitive Strategy

The overall objectives of the international part of a bank's activities must be consistent with the entire bank's objectives to earn profits and survive in competition with other providers of financial services. While the specific target levels or growth rates of profitability, market share, customer service, and other goals may differ from one bank to another, the fundamental need to generate profits always exists. Given the growing intensity of competition that characterizes the international parts of banking, individual institutions must look for competitive advantages to distinguish themselves from relevant rivals in various segments of the market.

This task of product and/or institutional differentiation to create competitive advantages is quite difficult in an industry that is said to be characterized by relatively few products and many thousands of competitors. Banks are primarily involved in the provision of money to borrowers and provision of safe, profitable places to store money for lenders (depositors). Nonetheless, this view is highly oversimplified, since money can be provided in the form of bank deposits in different currencies at spot and future dates, drafts, telephone or cable transfers, and even cash, all with varying degrees of assurance of delivery and compliance with other contractual stipulations. On the lending side, banks can provide funds with different maturities, with different fee and interest charges, and again in different currencies. The explosion of new financial services belies the argument that the banking industry deals with a standardized product.

FIGURE 4-20

Key Competitive Advantages in Banking

Service to clients
Proprietary technology (including managerial know-how)
Network of service-providing locations
Human resource management
Government protection
Economies of scale or scope
Access to funds in different money and capital markets

In the present environment, how can a bank differentiate its international services from those of competitors? There appear to be three general avenues of differentiation: new products, new locations, and better service. The first avenue certainly is difficult to maintain as a competitive strength, because other banks normally can copy new instruments or practices once they are known in the market. However, the actual mobilization of a bank's effort to inform both internal staff and the public about new services is not straightforward, and a bank can distinguish itself from the rest by better accomplishing these goals. Also, technology that is used internally within the bank for record keeping, information transfer, and decision making can often be protected against immediate copying by competitors.

The second avenue of differentiation is locational: By offering services in more locations than competitors, a bank may establish a preferred position in the eyes of clients (especially multinational clients). Third, just as in domestic banking, the actual service received by clients does differ from bank to bank, and a competitive edge can be gained by successfully gaining a better understanding of clients' needs and better tailoring the bank's efforts to meet those needs. Figure 4-20 presents a sketch of these and other competitive advantages that exist for banks in their international business. The primary competitive advantages that have distinguished large multinational industrial firms from their rivals, proprietary technology and economies of scale, typically account for far less of an edge in the banking sector. This clear difference in the nature of competition between industrial business and banking is due to the ease of copying technological advances in banking and the structure of bank costs, which normally are very similar in institutions of a wide range of sizes. In any event, in international banking, the leading competitive advantages relate to availability and quality of services to clients in various countries.

In a study during the late 1970s, Davis (1979) found that multinational corporate clients of international banks made their selections of banking relations based on the bank's ability to provide specific services to meet the particular needs of the company, rather than on the bank's total array of services or pricing of those services. This can be interpreted today as well as then to mean that a competitive advantage exists for banks that can define new services (or instruments) tailored to clients' needs, as well as providing them where the clients' needs occur.

[4] Lending Strategy

In many banks, foreign lending is handled exactly or virtually the same as domestic lending, using the same credit committee and decision-making procedures. Since the basic decision is the same at both levels, namely, selecting borrowers whose likelihood of meeting loan conditions is high and committing manageable amounts of funds with various maturities to various borrowers, it makes sense to keep the credit process uniform at both levels. Difficulties nonetheless arise because of the key differences involved in international credits: sovereign risk, exchange risk, and less knowledge of foreign markets and competitive environments of the borrowers.

Exchange rate risk can be somewhat controlled through the use of forward and futures contracts and by participation in foreign exchange markets in the key Eurocurrency centers, where exposures can often be quickly covered. Most banks choose to take some level of foreign exchange exposure, thus permitting their currency traders to pursue profits by anticipating exchange rate changes.

The fact that a bank's managers know more about their own domestic market than markets in other countries also makes international lending more difficult to evaluate for the credit committee. One method of dealing with the daily occurrence of this problem is to decentralize credit decisions to an international division up to some monetary limit. Beyond the limit, credit decisions must be made at the home office level. In this way, the number of such decisions is reduced, and the daily concern with foreign credits is allocated to specialists in such activity. This solution unfortunately does not help with the very large sovereign and project loans that have become a major part of the total international lending environment.

In his study of 40 international banks, Davis found that

> As the typical bank's international portfolio has evolved from virtually riskless short-term loans to medium-term credits involving corporate risks, and eventually to the predominance of long-term loans of a sovereign risk character, there has been a similar evolution of controls over the loan portfolio. One of the principal themes of such controls has been diversification of risk via limits to individual country exposure which will often be broken down further by maturity (short versus medium term), public sector versus private sector, nature of exposure (local currency versus euro-currency) and so forth. In fixing such limits, banks usually establish some relationship with their own net worth or overall loan portfolio. Similar limits may be applied to specific industries or sectors such as real estate or shipping which carry a perceived level of generic credit risk.

All of this discussion focuses on the key differences between international and domestic lending. In the international portfolio, there are also the general asset management problems to consider: maturity structure of loans, commercial lending risk, interest rate risk, and the comparison with the bank's liability structure.

[5] Funding Strategy

On the liability side, international banks are faced with the same problems as their domestic counterparts, although the consumer deposit bases are usually far less significant internationally. Most international funding comes from interbank and other wholesale borrowing activities. These funding sources typically require more competitive pricing than their domestic counterparts, so international banks must manage their margins even more carefully. (The favorable side of the story is that assets also tend to be large, so small spreads still can lead to acceptable levels of profit.)

There are three major objectives of liability management: (1) The bank needs to manage its exposure to volatile interest and exchange rates, which may differ between assets and liabilities; (2) maturities of both assets and liabilities must be managed to avoid excessive mismatching, which could lead to short-term illiquidity or to transaction losses when rates change; and (3) the bank needs to minimize its cost of obtaining funds. All of these concerns also appear in domestic banking, but at the international level there are the added factors of exchange risk and the wealth of additional instruments available.

To counter the problem of volatile interest rates, a standard Euromarket practice has developed: Interest rates on medium-term and long-term loans are variable, with quarterly or semiannual adjustments to LIBOR, prime, or some other base rate. The proliferation of variable-rate instruments has swept the Euromarkets to the point where most international loans of one year or longer are priced at the floating rates. Even though the floating-rate instruments reduce the bank's commitment of fixed interest rates to periods of three or six months, deposits still generally mature in less than three months, and so interest rate risk remains to some extent.

A second method of coping with interest rate volatility is through the use of futures contracts on interest rates. Financial futures exchanges in Chicago and London now offer futures contracts for 3-month, 6-month, 9-month, and 12-month maturities that enable a bank to directly hedge interest rate commitments when the risk is viewed as unacceptable.

Even a bank using both floating-rate loan contracts and interest rate futures contracts cannot completely avoid the risk, because many loan agreements in the Euromarkets provide the borrower with the option of shifting the period of rate fixing (e.g., from 3 months to 6 months or to 30 days) and the interest rate base (e.g., prime or LIBOR). In addition, loan disbursement may be contracted flexibly for the borrower, enabling it to draw funds at unpredictable times for the bank. One conclusion to draw from this complex situation is that the bank should try to extend liability maturities and reduce asset maturities (or at least rate-fixing periods), so that the mismatching of maturities is minimized and the remaining unavoidable interest rate risk is tolerable.

The problem of mismatches in the maturities of assets and liabilities is particularly difficult in international banking. As sovereign loans and corporate medium-term financing have grown as a proportion of Euromarket lending, both types of assets have tended to lengthen the average maturity of the loan portfolio. On the deposit side, however, short-term deposits continue to dominate, with the result that maturity mismatches have grown substantially. This is not to say that the problem is a threat to financial markets; one of the key functions of commercial banks as financial intermediaries has always been to transform short-term sources of funds into long-term investments. Nonetheless, the risk to a given bank increases as its short position grows, and a capital shortage in the market has more likelihood of causing difficulties under these circumstances. Fortunately for the banks, or perhaps necessarily as an underpinning of their portfolios, interest rate futures markets and variable-rate loans have developed, and they offer the bank an opportunity to avoid some of the interest rate risk that remains, even for fixed-rate liabilities.

The issue of liquidity remains a concern, even when interest and exchange rate risks have been dealt with. Typically, liabilities mature more frequently than assets. Refunding efforts may be hindered by credit shortages or if a bank displays some weakness in its performance (e.g., because of large exposure to depressed borrowing sectors such as agriculture, Latin American governments, or maritime shipping). There is no simple solution to this problem; like a domestic bank, the international bank must seek to protect its creditworthiness, i.e., its access to deposits, money market funding, and other sources of funds. For this reason, international banks often choose to operate actively in Eurocurrency and forex trading on both sides of the market, demonstrating their willingness and ability to provide investors with good opportunities and simultaneously establishing access to those investors if the need arises.

The cost of funding international bank activities is often relatively high, since financing is sought in wholesale interbank markets rather than in retail markets. This fact puts overseas branches and subsidiaries of international banks at a disadvantage relative to local banks, which have access to retail, less-costly local deposits. One compensating factor is that international banks, with their knowledge of and participation in financial markets in different countries, can find low-cost funding sources overseas when they arise, where domestic banks are substantially limited to domestic funding. The same dollar funding needs can be financed in New York, London, and Singapore, yet the rates available in each market differ to varying degrees all the time.

Funding costs may also be reduced by obtaining foreign currency funds with or without hedging against exchange rate risk. Interest arbitrage allows an international bank to obtain foreign currency funds for a fixed period, with guaranteed future resale at a predetermined price.

[6] Organizational Structure

Historically, a bank's entry into international business has occurred in response to clients' requests for international services, particularly those involved in financing export-import transactions such as LOCs, collections, and forex. There has also been a great increase in clients' awareness of better interest rates on deposits and loans that can be secured in the Euromarkets rather than in domestic financial markets; therefore, international money market services today are also a typical entry point into international business. In both cases, the bank commonly establishes a small group of people to provide the particular kind of service requested, and international business remains a small portion of total activity.

As banks look for new opportunities to generate profitable business, foreign markets eventually become attractive targets. Once some expertise has been developed in an area such as trade financing or Eurocurrency dealing, the bank may decide to establish an overseas presence to serve new clients and existing clients' foreign affiliates. Ordinarily, this presence is begun through a correspondent relationship with a foreign bank that has offices in place in the target market and can provide services on behalf of the original bank. At some point, the original bank may choose to set up its own branch or other affiliate overseas to provide services directly and to grow in the new market. This is a particularly attractive option for Eurocurrency business, in which the bank needs a foreign presence to book the offshore deposits and loans. Given the relatively low cost of establishing a "brass plate" branch in a Euromarket center such as London or Nassau, hundreds of banks have done so.

Beyond this level of international activity, a bank must really make a major commitment to international business as part of its use of funds and staff. The next logical step in overseas activity is the establishment of local operations in countries where existing (domestic) clients have their own foreign operations; this means, in most cases, in countries such as the members of the EC, North America, and Japan (i.e., the leading industrial nations). At this level, the bank becomes a multinational enterprise, subject to many of the concerns and opportunities of multinational firms in other industries, such as coordination of disparate activities, melding views and styles of personnel of different nationalities, and coping with different national legislation in several countries.

The forms of legal presence available to the bank vary by country, but a few are common in most jurisdictions. A *branch* is the most common form of operation permitted to foreign banks. A branch is generally able to operate as a legal part of the parent bank, lending on the full bank's capital base and providing a full range of banking services. The branch is desirable because of these powers but risky because it requires the full backing of the parent bank in the event of financial difficulties.

A *subsidiary* is another option for foreign banks that seek to offer full services in a host country. The subsidiary is limited to lending based on its own capitalization rather than that of the parent, which is generally a major constraint. On the other hand, a subsidiary may participate in other types of business permitted in the host country, such as securities underwriting and sale, investment in nonbanking business, and whatever other activities are permitted under the law of that country.

An *agency* in the United States permits a foreign bank to offer most financial services except domestic deposit-taking. An *Edge Act Corporation* in the United States permits a domestic or foreign bank to establish an office in one or more states for purposes of international business, including deposit taking from foreign residents, lending for foreign trade or investment, forex services, and Eurocurrency services. Finally, a *representative office* allows the bank to provide information only about services available through other offices of the institution, but it does establish a physical presence in the target country and the ability to guide potential clients to other divisions of the bank that may provide the desired services.

In terms of organizational structure, a bank's international business may be divided along functional, product, or regional lines, or in some combination of these. That is, a bank may choose to place its international services into an international division with responsibility for all overseas, Euro, and forex services. The international division then may be subdivided into a regional authority structure, with each division having responsibility for all aspects of banking in a particular region, such as Europe, North America, Japan, and the LDCs. Alternatively, the bank may place decision making in a functional structure, with worldwide responsibility for lending in one division, responsibility for funding in another, and responsibility for other services in yet another division. Third, a product structure may be created in which products such as money market activities are placed in one division, consumer services in another, government services in another, and information services in another. Because these product divisions are generally based on types of end users, banks often consider them customer divisions that group all relevant services for that category of customers.

Most large international banks are organized in some combination of these structures. For example, most large U.S. banks have international divisions with geographical subdivisions while they have customer divisions with responsibility for specific types of clients. Coordination of the necessarily overlapping concerns of these divisions is a critical concern that can only be solved in an ongoing process, as competitive conditions, clients, and the bank's own officers change over time. There is no optimal organizational structure for all situations, so what is sought is clear lines of authority where possible and flexibility to respond to changes in the market. The structure that is actually chosen tends to result from the historical development of the bank in terms of size and geographical spread of activities, the nature of its activities, and the people involved in top management of the bank.

[7] Marketing International Services

Marketing of international banking services is wholly analogous to that of domestic banking services. In both cases, banks have traditionally paid relatively little attention to this function, since government regulations and stable rates have placed banks in a seller's market. Perhaps this comment should be qualified by noting that banks have traditionally emphasized quality of service as a key feature of their business, and provision of high-quality service undoubtedly is a central part of marketing. Taking a wider view of marketing and including the selection of target market segments, definition of customer needs, and market positioning has only recently come to the fore in international bank management. Because intense competition in the Euromarkets has brought spreads down to minimal levels, international banks must plan their marketing efforts carefully both to choose potentially viable market segments and to attract clients.

Strategic marketing requires that the international bank first define its business or businesses. The definition begins with traditional services such as provision of credit to foreign clients and for the specific purpose of trade finance as well as for the provision of attractive investment and deposit opportunities to clients in different currencies and markets. During the past decade, additional services have mushroomed, from risk protection through forward contracts and interest rate swaps to international corporate cash management to investment advisory services.

Defining the businesses also requires focusing on the specific types of clients that will be served. In international banking (except for personal banking), the clients are generally other banks, large corporations, and governments. Each of these client types has different kinds of needs for funding, risk protection, and information services. Thus, the target markets are defined in terms of types of services and types of customers.

Next, the specific needs of target client groups must be defined, so that the bank can provide not only standard services but also those tailored to the clients' particular concerns. For example, corporate clients may need not just financing but financing that varies by currency at different times and financing that varies in quantity on a seasonal basis. New loan services can be designed to meet such needs and attract desirable clients away from competitors.

When target client groups and their needs have been identified, they can be evaluated according to the significance of each to the bank's total objectives. For example, a low-profit service may be deemed desirable because it contributes to the bank's ability to keep large clients for whom other, more profitable services are also being provided. Also, the 80/20 rule may be applied: Since frequently about 80 percent of the international bank's income is generated by only 20 percent of the clients, those highly profitable clients should be cultivated and some of the other 80 percent of the business should be eliminated. Many other decision rules can be applied to the defined target groups to determine the bank's actual services to be provided. A matrix of such activities may be a useful tool for conceptualizing the problem. Figure 4-21 is a client-service matrix for an international bank.

Finally, the bank must establish a position in the market for each client and service. The decision may be made to pursue leadership in the particular segment, only medium participation, or even just a minimum presence. The market position clearly relates to profitability of the business, so generally the larger the market share, the more desirable the business.

FIGURE 4-21

Client-Service Matrix

Source: Aidan Harlan, "Marketing International Services," The International Banking Handbook, *William Baughn and Donald Mandich, eds. Homewood, Ill.: Dow Jones-Irwin, 1983, p. 628.*

	LOCs	Collection	Forex	Drafts and remittances	Money market	Credit
Correspondent banks						
Nonbank financials						
Capital goods importers						
Private-sector manufacturers						
U.S. client subsidiaries						
Trading companies						
Multinationals						

4.12 OTHER INTERNATIONAL BANKING STRUCTURES

[1] Offshore Banking Centers

An offshore banking center is a country whose banking system is structured to permit external accounts, typically those associated with preferential fiscal treatment, beyond those associated with its normal economic activity. The IMF recognizes the Bahamas, Bahrain, the Cayman Islands, Hong Kong, and Panama as major offshore banking centers. Such banking centers accept deposits and extend credits in currencies other than the local one, as well as offer full Euromarket services. Money center banks are generally also tax havens. By virtue of their locations, they eliminate time zone constraints on their parent banks. Their ability to provide confidentiality to their clients is the prime factor in attracting business. Hong Kong accounts for about 200 offshore centers and the Bahamas about 275 centers, one third of them owned by U.S. banks.

[2] International Banking Facilities

International banking facilities (IBFs) are a legal fiction that permits the operation of the Eurodollar market in the United States, despite the fact that dollars are the domestic currency as well. An IBF is in fact just a separate set of books maintained by any banking institution in the United States, in which these books are used to record Euromarket deposits, loans, and so forth. They operate as if they were physically outside the United States and outside the domestic banking regulations of the Federal Reserve System.

IBFs are only permitted to deal with nonresident entities and with other IBFs. IBF deposits are not subject to reserve requirements, and they do not offer FDIC insurance coverage. These units can undertake business transactions with foreigners as offshore branches, they can help a parent bank to reduce its cost structure, and they can help smaller banks to enter the highly competitive Eurodollar market easily.

4.13 FUTURE OF INTERNATIONAL BANKING

Amidst increased competition, banks have realized that the barriers between them and other sectors of the financial industry are fading away. The squeeze that banks have experienced in interest margins, and enormous loan losses from sectors such as real estate and sovereign lending, have led to effective cost control strategies. In some instances, certain banks, despite sufficient expertise in their own select niches, have been compelled to pull out. Somehow, multinational banking has not attained the success first visualized. All of these difficulties have rendered the banks financially fragile, evoking regulatory responses such as demands for tougher capital adequacy standards, conservative asset evaluation, and adequate loan loss financing.

Many corporations have in-house banking, and the banks' privilege of issuing capital market instruments on behalf of their clients is lost, affecting their role in financial intermediation. Clients also prefer sophisticated investments instead of low-interest bank instruments, and thus banks are caught on all sides. Conglomeration of several financial institutions into one organization has also reduced the number of banks.

A new institutional setup both in the international banking sector and in the role of supervisors is imminent. Both banks and supervisors will have to specialize in all financial sectors. International regulation is undergoing a period of harmonization, and thus banks will be subject to a more consistent and uniform regulatory process. Banks must use a global approach in studying both threats and opportunities, recognizing that being simply international is not being global. The Basel Committee has prescribed new standards of capital adequacy requiring an international bank to have a minimum capital of 8 percent of its risk-weighted assets. All of these developments will lead to free competition in international banking, and thus quality of service will increasingly be a deciding factor to ensure success.

Suggested Reading

Aliber, Robert, ed. *Handbook of International Financial Management.* Homewood, Ill.: Dow Jones-Irwin, 1989.

The Economist. "International Banking" (annual survey) (March 1993).

Grabbe, Orlin. *International Financial Markets*, 2nd ed. New York: Elsevier, 1991.

Heffernan, Shelagh. *Sovereign Risk Analysis*. London: Allen and Unwin, 1986.

Park, Yoon S., and Jack Zwick. *International Banking in Theory and Practice*. Reading, Mass.: Addison-Wesley, 1985.

Smith, Roy C., and Ingo Walter. *Global Financial Services: Strategies for Building Competitive Strengths in International Commercial and Investment Banking*. New York: Harper Business, 1990.

United Nations Center on Transnational Corporations, *Transnational Banks: Operations, Strategies, and Their Effects on Developing Countries*. New York: UNCTC, 1981.

Walter, Ingo. *Global Competition in Financial Services: Market Structure, Protection, and Trade Liberalization*. Cambridge, Mass.: Ballinger, 1988.

Chapter 5

International Accounting

LEE H. RADEBAUGH

5.01 **International Dimensions of Accounting** 154

5.02 **Differences in Accounting Standards and Disclosure Practices** 154

[1] Reasons for Differences 155

[2] Classification of Differences 155

[3] Impact of Culture 157

[4] Broad Influences on Accounting Principles and Practices 158

[5] Consolidation Practices 160

[6] Accounting for Goodwill 161

[7] Segmental Reporting 163

[8] Harmonization of Standards 164

[a] IASC 165

[b] United Nations 165

[c] OECD 165

[d] EC 166

[9] Disclosure of Information 166

5.03 **Accounting for Foreign Currency Transactions and Translation of Foreign Currency Financial Statements** 167

[1] Accounting for Foreign Currency Transactions 167

[a] Accounting for Forward Exchange Contracts 169

[b] Accounting for Options 170

[2] Translation of Foreign Currency Financial Statements 171

[a] Brief History of Translation 171

[b] Selection of the Functional Currency 172

[c] Numerical Example 175

[d] Translation Practices Outside of the United States 180

5.04 **International Tax Issues** 182

[1] Export of Goods and Services 182

[2] Foreign Branch 183

[3] Foreign Corporations 183

[a] Subpart F Income 184

[4] Tax Credit 184

[5] Impact of Tax Treaties 185

5.05 **Performance Evaluation and Control** 185

[1] Transfer Pricing 186

[2] Currency in Performance Evaluation 187

5.06 **Conclusion** 188

Suggested Reading 189

5.01 INTERNATIONAL DIMENSIONS OF ACCOUNTING

The quality of decision making by financial managers is obviously enhanced if those managers have access to quality information. It is the corporate controller's job to provide this information for internal as well as external users. All of the functions with which the controller is concerned have international as well as domestic relevance. It is easy to assume that what is done domestically must be done exactly the same way internationally. However, that assumption ignores the cultural, educational, legal and political, and economic variables that affect U.S. business abroad.

There are a number of factors that influence the quality of information generated for a multinational firm, such as different accounting standards and disclosure practices worldwide, foreign currencies, and other environmental factors that determine the way that subsidiaries and subsidiary managers are evaluated. In addition, the tax function has some interesting international ramifications. These issues are incorporated in the discussion of five key topics:

1. Differences in accounting standards and practices

2. International financial reporting issues, such as combinations and consolidation practices, accounting for goodwill and intangibles, and international segmental reporting

3. Accounting for foreign currency transactions and the translation of foreign currency financial statements (which is also discussed in Chapter 2)

4. International taxation

5. Managerial accounting and control

5.02 DIFFERENCES IN ACCOUNTING STANDARDS AND DISCLOSURE PRACTICES

It is evident from reading annual reports from companies around the world that accounting standards and practices vary, sometimes significantly, from country to country. Variations exist not only in the amount and type of information disclosed but also in the underlying standards on which the financial statements and accompanying footnotes are based. It is important to keep these two types of variations in mind, since there is a big difference between form and substance. Accounting standards and practices determine how economic events are recorded in the books and records of the company, whereas disclosure requirements determine how the information is presented to the various user groups, including investors, creditors, employees, and government.

The multinational company must face the dilemma of balancing its need for uniform information for reporting purposes in the United States with the reporting requirements that exist in the country where the foreign subsidiary is located. Standardized U.S. requirements come from two basic sources: management and investors. Management wants uniform information in order to evaluate and control foreign operations. For this reason, most companies go to great lengths to develop detailed accounting manuals that are used worldwide.

In spite of the need for uniform standards and practices for home office use, the multinational company must also allow its local affiliates to keep financial records according to local standards in order to satisfy the demands of local capital markets, government regulators, taxing authorities, and so forth. These standards could vary significantly in different countries, depending on the local accounting standards. This results in multiple sets of books to satisfy home office and local country requirements.

[1] Reasons for Differences

Accounting objectives, standards, and practices depend ultimately on the users of the financial statements and the extent of user group influence over the setting of standards. It is impossible to identify all of the factors that influence accounting or to rank the factors, since each country is unique, but a number of factors are very important. The major factor leading to greater harmonization in accounting is the development of international capital markets. Investors seem to have an insatiable appetite for information, and firms that want to raise capital on international markets are obliged to disclose information that is consistent with those markets. In general, this means that firms must develop statements based on accounting and disclosure practices that are in harmony with those of the United States and the United Kingdom. Although there are differences in practices between these two countries, they are similar and are based on the informational needs of investors, which are roughly the same worldwide.

Accounting standards and practices are influenced by many factors. Some of the most important are the nature of firms, major enterprise users, the government, and local environmental and business influences in each country. In countries where there is no organized capital market and where family-owned or closely held firms predominate, accounting tends to be creditor- and management-oriented. In some of the European countries, employees are major enterprise users of information, and they have been able to get some interesting employee-related disclosures guaranteed by law. Governments play an important role in the development of accounting standards, especially in countries where the accounting profession is not highly developed. In other countries, such as France, the government essentially sets accounting standards by means of tax legislation. Local environmental influences, such as high rates of inflation in some Latin American countries, have also been influential in the setting of standards. Colonial influences, such as that of the British in the Commonwealth countries and the French in their former colonies can also be important in setting standards and practices.

[2] Classification of Differences

Although there is no systematic classification of accounting practices across all countries, Nobes attempted to group the major industrial countries in the manner shown in Figure 5-1. His approach was to divide countries into those where the influence on accounting is micro (strong business influence) and those where the influence on accounting is macro (strong government influence). Micro-based systems were further disaggregated into those that are relatively pragmatic and business-oriented, such as those found in the United States and United Kingdom, and those that are based more on economic analysis, such as those in the Netherlands. The macro-based systems are divided among those that are tax-based (such as those in France), legal-based (such as those in Germany and Japan), and government policy–based (such as those in Sweden).

FIGURE 5-1

Hypothetical Classification of Financial Reporting Measurement Practices in Developed Western Countries

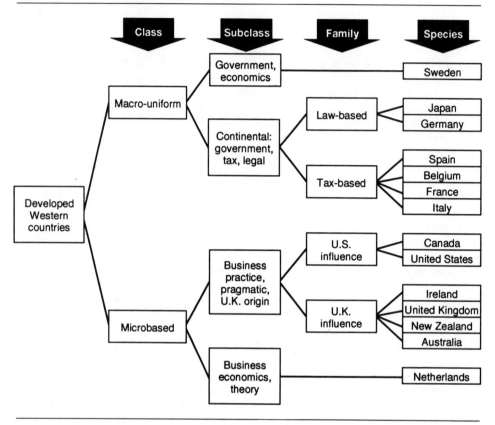

In order to classify countries, Nobes used the following criteria:

- Types of users of the published accounts of the listed companies
- Degree to which law or standards prescribe in detail and exclude judgment
- Importance of tax rules in measurement
- Conservatism or prudence (e.g., valuation of buildings, inventory, and debtors)
- Strictness of application of historical cost (in the historical cost accounts)
- Susceptibility to replacement cost adjustments in main or supplementary accounts
- Consolidation practices
- Ability to be generous with provisions (as opposed to reserves) and to smooth income
- Uniformity between companies in application of rules[1]

---

[1] C.W. Nobes, "A Judgmental International Classification of Financial Reporting Practices," *Journal of Business Finance and Accounting* (Spring 1983), p. 8.

[3] Impact of Culture

Culture is a major determinant of business practice in a country, and it also influences accounting practice. Gray identified four pairs of accounting values that are influenced by a country's business culture:

1. *Professionalism versus statutory control.* A preference for the exercise of individual professional judgment and the maintenance of professional self-regulation, as opposed to compliance with prescriptive legal requirements and statutory control.

2. *Uniformity versus flexibility.* A preference for the enforcement of uniform accounting practices among companies and for the consistent use of such practices over time, as opposed to flexibility in accordance with the perceived circumstances of individual companies.

3. *Conservatism versus optimism.* A preference for a cautious approach to measurement so as to cope with the uncertainty of future events, as opposed to a more optimistic, laissez-faire, risk-taking approach.

4. *Secrecy versus transparency.* A preference for confidentiality and the restriction of disclosure of information about the business only to those that are most closely involved with its management and financing, as opposed to a more transparent, open, and publicly accountable approach.[2]

For example, a major controversy in many Western countries surrounds the issue of the extent to which the accounting profession should either be subject to public regulation and statutory control or be permitted to retain control over accounting standards as a matter of private self-regulation. The accounting profession is well established in Anglo-Saxon countries, such as the United Kingdom and the United States, and there is a tendency in those countries to favor professionalism in accounting. In Germany and France, however, the professional accountant's role has been concerned primarily with the implementation of relatively prescriptive and detailed legal requirements.

In terms of uniformity versus flexibility, countries such as France have adopted uniform accounting plans that force a particular format and content of the financial statements that bring book accounting and tax accounting in line with each other. In contrast, in the United Kingdom and United States, there is more concern with consistent reporting across periods, together with some degree of intercompany comparability, subject to a perceived need for flexibility.

The most significant accounting value is conservatism versus optimism. Conservatism or prudence tends to be strong in Japan and European countries such as France, Germany, and Switzerland, whereas accountants in the United States and the United Kingdom tend to be much less conservative and more risk tolerant.

The final value, secrecy versus transparency, is related closely to the values of conservatism and optimism. The extent of secrecy appears to vary across countries, with lower levels of disclosure, including instances of secret reserves, evident in Japan, France, Germany, and Switzerland than in the United States and the United Kingdom. These differences also seem to be reinforced by the differential development of capital

---

[2] S.J. Gray, "Towards a Theory of Cultural Influence on the Development of Accounting Systems Internationally," *Abacus* (March 1988), p. 8. See also Geeret Hofstede, *Culture's Consequences: International Differences in Work-Related Values* (Beverly Hills, Cal.: Sage Publications, 1980).

FIGURE 5-2

Accounting Systems: Authority and Enforcement

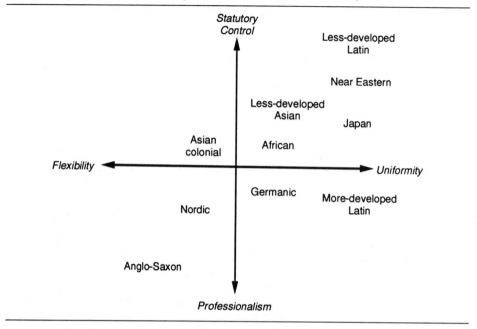

markets and the public ownership of shares, which may provide incentives for the voluntary disclosure of information. Figures 5-2 and 5-3 show how these values are interrelated and how countries might be categorized.

[4] Broad Influences on Accounting Principles and Practices

It is impossible to identify accounting principles and practices for all countries in the world, but it is helpful to look at influences on a narrow set of countries: Anglo-Saxon countries, Nordic countries, Germanic countries, Latin countries, and Asian countries. Because of colonial influence and foreign direct investment, there are a few countries, such as the United Kingdom, the United States, Germany, and France, that have had significant influence worldwide and are continuing to influence the development of accounting in the emerging economies of Central and Eastern Europe and the former Soviet Union.

In the United States, accounting is focused very much on large corporations and the interests of investors, although the needs of creditors and other users are also recognized. The relevance of information to business decisions is paramount and subject to the constraint of reliability. In the United Kingdom, as in the United States, priority is given to the information needs of investors. It is expected, however, that most of the needs of other groups will be similar to those of investors and thus will be satisfied in any event. The special needs of other groups are usually met privately or on a voluntary basis.

FIGURE 5-3

Accounting Systems: Measurement and Disclosure

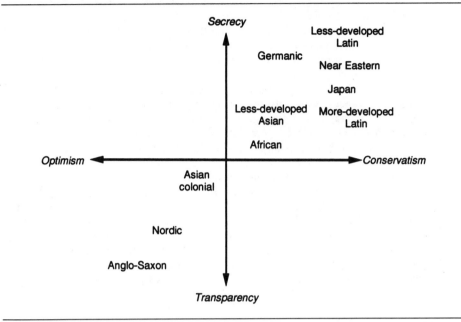

The Nordic countries are similar in geography but not necessarily in accounting practices. The Netherlands is famous for its business economics approach to accounting and the use of replacement values (or current costs). While investors have pride of place as users of accounts, the information needs of other users and especially of employees are recognized on a voluntary basis. The practice of social reporting was established in the 1970s and involves disclosures mainly about employment and personnel policies in both annual reports and special reports.

The accounting tradition in Sweden gives preference to the informational needs of creditors, government, and the tax authorities. However, this situation has been changing owing to the growing involvement of major Swedish companies in international mergers and acquisitions (M&As) and the need to seek financing in international financial markets. The Swedish stock market has also grown in importance and is a potential focus for the Nordic countries. A two-tier approach to corporate reporting exists with the accounts of individual companies prepared on a traditional basis, in contrast to the consolidated accounts of major groups, which tend to be focused more on shareholder informational needs and the standards applicable in an international capital market context.

Although the Germanic countries are usually thought to include Germany, Austria, and Switzerland, the German influence has also been significant in France, Japan, and a number of former German colonies. The accounting tradition in Germany gives preference to the informational needs of creditors and tax authorities. However, large listed corporations and especially multinational enterprises (MNEs) are endeavoring to present more shareholder-oriented corporate reports. Their approach is very conservative with regard to historical cost accounting, and the law also requires firms to establish legal reserves in order to protect creditors. The secrecy of the Swiss is world renowned; Swiss accounting is still among the most conservative and secretive in Europe and the world. Like that of Germany, Swiss accounting practice is dominated by company law and the tax regulations, rather than the accounting profession, which is small and in the early stages of setting accounting standards. In contrast to those in Germany, the legal requirements relating to accounting in Switzerland are minimal and permit the creation of secret reserves.

As in the Germanic countries, company law seems to be the predominant influence on accounting in France, along with the informational needs of creditors and the tax authorities. This emphasis is changing, to some extent, with respect to large listed corporations and especially MNEs. International market pressures seem to be encouraging a much more shareholder-oriented approach, especially with reference to consolidated accounts.

The government has been a major influence on all aspects of accounting in Japan. The Japanese Commercial Code was modeled on the German Commercial Code and was introduced in 1899 with the objective of protecting creditors. The 1948 Securities and Exchange law was modeled on the U.S. securities laws of 1933 and 1934 to protect investors in public corporations listed on stock exchanges or traded on the over-the-counter market. In addition, the tax law is very influential. Despite the significance of the stock market, the accounting tradition in Japan gives preference to the informational needs and priorities of creditors and tax authorities.

[5] Consolidation Practices

While there is a recognized need for information about operations of MNEs on a worldwide basis, it is a matter of some controversy as to how best to report this. Consolidation is currently accepted in practice as the best means of accounting for groups and business combinations internationally. Consolidated reports are relevant not only to external users (e.g., investors) but also to managers as a basis for overall control and evaluation of performance. Consolidation involves aggregating, on a line-by-line basis, information about the assets, liabilities, revenues, and expenses of the many individual legal entities of the MNE in statements of income, financial position, and funds flow relating to the single economic entity. At the same time, the complexity of MNE operations is such that consolidations are likely to be less revealing without some disaggregation of the information accumulated. Hence, there is a corresponding demand for segmental (disaggregated) information by lines of business and geographic markets.

Apart from the United States and the United Kingdom and, more recently, the countries in the European Community (EC), legal and professional requirements relating to group accounts are not comprehensive or widespread, although the number of countries with regulations in this area is growing. In a recent world survey of major companies, 91 percent of the companies surveyed provided worldwide consolidated financial statements.[3]

In practice, the quality and quantity of consolidated information varies considerably both among and within countries. In certain cases, such as the voluntary disclosures by some Italian and Swiss companies, only summarized consolidated information may

---

[3] D.J. Tonkin, ed., *World Survey of Published Accounts* (London: Lafferty Publications, 1989).

be presented in addition to the parent company statements. In the United Kingdom, a parent company balance sheet is always provided in addition to a consolidated balance sheet and income statement. In contrast, U.S. companies provide only consolidated financial statements, while in Germany, it is normal practice to provide both parent company and worldwide consolidated financial statements.

An alternative to full consolidation on a line-by-line basis is proportional consolidation, in which only the ownership share of assets and liabilities is consolidated on a pro rata or proportional basis. This is typically considered appropriate for joint ventures.

With respect to associated or affiliated corporations, where there is a significant influence but not a controlling interest, the majority of MNEs use the equity method, in which a share of profits is consolidated on a one-line basis according to the equity owned by the MNE. The assets and liabilities of the associate are not consolidated. Instead, the investment amount is adjusted to reflect the MNE's share in equity. The more conservative cost method, in which only dividends received and receivable are included in the results for the year, is widely used, however, in countries such as Australia and Sweden.

There are also considerable differences in accounting for mergers and takeovers. The majority of companies use the purchase or acquisition method of consolidating financial statements after a merger or takeover, whereas a minority of companies worldwide use the pooling-of-interests method. In Australia and Japan, the pooling-of-interests method is not permitted, whereas in Canada and the United States, the pooling-of-interests method must be used if certain criteria are met.

[6] Accounting for Goodwill

There has been a dramatic growth in the significance of intangible assets relative to tangible assets of MNEs. A number of major factors are responsible for this, including the continuing wave of international mergers; the pursuit of global market leadership, often through the development or acquisition of famous brand names; the worldwide expansion of the services sector; the speed and extent of technological change, with special reference to the impact of information technology; and the growing sophistication and integration of international financial markets.

The dramatic growth of international M&As together with the major expansion of the service industries, where intangible assets are much more significant, has highlighted the significance of goodwill and the problem of how to account for it. Goodwill, in this context, is the excess of the purchase price for the company as a whole over the fair (current) value of the net assets acquired by the bidding company. This purchased goodwill is, in effect, a premium paid to reflect the future earnings capacity of the acquisition, although goodwill may be negative if the purchase price is less than the fair value of the net assets acquired.

The crux of the problem with goodwill is that it is unlike other assets, that is, it incorporates the value of future earnings and relates to the valuation of the business taken as a whole. Accordingly, it is currently a matter of considerable international controversy whether goodwill should be treated as an asset for accounting purposes and, if so, whether it should be amortized against future earnings.

In practice, there are three major approaches to accounting for goodwill: capitalize goodwill as an asset without amortization, capitalize goodwill as an asset with systematic amortization, and immediately write off goodwill.

The logic behind capitalizing goodwill as an asset without amortization is that future economic benefits are expected for which valuable consideration has been given. However, in a successful business, the value of goodwill does not decline, because it is being continuously maintained. If goodwill were to be amortized, this would result in double counting (i.e., the cost of maintaining the goodwill plus the amortization cost). This approach, though theoretically defensible, is rarely used, and Switzerland is the only major industrial country which allows it.

A more popular approach is to treat purchased goodwill as an asset with systematic amortization. The proponents of this method view purchased goodwill as an asset embodying future economic benefits for which consideration has been given. However, they believe that goodwill is a cost of resources that will be used up and therefore should be systematically amortized against earnings. If goodwill is not amortized, future earnings would be overstated, since there would be a failure to include all costs incurred to generate such earnings.

Others claim that it is very difficult to estimate when the goodwill will be exhausted, if at all, and hence the period of amortization will be arbitrary, with a consequently arbitrary and potentially severe impact on earnings. This approach, however, is the most popular one and is permitted in most industrial countries. The major difference among countries is the period of amortization. In the United States, for example, the maximum period is 40 years. Maximum periods in other countries are 20 years (Australia and Sweden), 10 years (the Netherlands), and 5 years (Japan). In practice, companies adopt a variety of amortization periods to suit their circumstances. In Japan, for example, the majority of companies write off goodwill on consolidation against current earnings immediately, the incentive being that it is deductible for tax purposes. However, there are fewer acquisitions in Japan than in the United States and the United Kingdom.

The most controversial approach is the immediate write-off approach, favored by those that argue that purchased goodwill is not an asset for the purposes of financial statements. Goodwill is not separable or independently realizable but exists only by virtue of a valuation of the company or business as a whole. It is not a resource that is consumed or used up as other productive resources are. Further, the true value of goodwill has no predictive relationship to the costs paid on acquisition, as its value fluctuates over time according to a variety of economic factors and changes in investor opinion.

Comparability between firms is also enhanced by the direct write-off approach in that neither purchased nor internally generated goodwill are recognized as assets. Accordingly, goodwill is written off against equity with no charges made against current earnings. A variation of this approach is to write off goodwill immediately against current earnings but usually as an extraordinary or nonrecurring item.

This approach is permitted in several countries, including France, Germany, Hong Kong, Italy, Mexico, Nigeria, Switzerland, and the United Kingdom. In the United Kingdom, the immediate write-off approach has become the preferred method in practice, mainly because of its favorable effect on reported future earnings. The flexible U.K. approach has permitted provisions for reorganization costs and anticipated future losses to be offset against the value of net assets acquired, thus enhancing the amount of goodwill to be written off with a further beneficial effect on future earnings. The majority of large companies in France, Germany, and the Netherlands have followed the U.K. trend.

However, there is significant opposition to the direct write-off approach from those that argue that purchased goodwill is an asset embodying expected future benefits and should be treated as such either with or without amortization. Further, there are likely to be problems with writing off large amounts of goodwill, especially in the case of service companies (with limited tangible assets) and highly acquisitive companies, to the extent that equity may become depleted or even negative and funding by debt unduly high. In such situations, the stated financial position would be misleading as an indicator of the financial strength of the company.

The direct write-off approach championed by U.K. companies has been criticized by U.S. companies on the grounds that U.K. companies have a competitive advantage in making takeover bids internationally because they escape the burden of goodwill amortization against future earnings required in the United States. An example of this occurred in the 1989 annual report of the U.K. company Blue Arrow, which reported earnings in 1989 of £65 million under U.K. rules but losses of £686 million under U.S. rules. The main reason for the difference in earnings was the amortization of goodwill, as required in the United States.

The problem in the United Kingdom is that with the dramatic growth in merger activity, the amounts written off against equity have become so large that many companies are concerned about the effect on the perceived strength of the balance sheet and the degree of leverage. This problem has motivated some companies, especially in the services sector, where the treatment of goodwill has had the most impact, to treat intangibles as assets for balance sheet purposes.

However, changes are occurring internationally. In the case of the United Kingdom, the Accounting Standards Board has proposed the amortization method, but this has met with significant resistance from the business community. The International Accounting Standards Committee (IASC) had previously maintained a relatively flexible approach, but in Exposure Draft 32, it proposed the elimination of the direct write-off method and the adoption of the amortization method, with a normal amortization of five years and a maximum of 20 years in exceptional circumstances.

[7] Segmental Reporting

Investors are likely to be interested in the future cash flows they may obtain from investing in a company and the risk or uncertainty of these cash flows. Therefore, they are interested in the performance of an MNE as a whole rather than the performance of any specific element of the firm's activities. However, this does not mean that only consolidated information is of value to them. Both the size and the uncertainty of future cash flows are likely to be affected by many factors, including those that are related to the industries and countries in which an MNE operates. Different industries and countries have a variety of profit potentials, degrees and types of risks, and growth opportunities. Different rates of return on investment and different capital needs are also likely to appear across the various segments of a business. This diversification of operations has led to a demand for MNEs to report key items of disaggregated information, especially sales and profits. Such disaggregated or segmental data is typically provided for both geographical areas and lines of business.

Despite the benefits to users of the segmental data, there are also some costs. It has been argued that the cost of compiling, processing, and disseminating such information exceeds the benefits. Another, potentially more serious cost is that of disseminating information that is likely to benefit existing or potential competitors. The major argument against segmental information is that in some cases it may be inappropriate and potentially misleading. The assumption of disclosure is that the segments are relatively independent of each other, so that the information can be disaggregated easily. However, that is not the case.

To date, the United States has the most extensive requirements in the world. Financial Accounting Standards Board (FASB) Statement No. 14 requires the disclosure of revenues from unaffiliated customers, intragroup transfers, operating profit or loss or net income, other profitability measures, and identifiable assets for both line-of-business and geographical segments. In addition, for industry segments, companies must also disclose depreciation, capital expenditure, and equity in the net income and assets of associates.

Unfortunately, these requirements do not provide a clear definition of "identifiable segments." It is left to management's discretion to define the segments. Once the segments have been identified, however, clear guidance is given as to what constitutes a reportable segment. Geographical segments should be reported if segment sales account for at least 10 percent of total sales or if identifiable assets account for at least 10 percent of total identifiable assets. Similarly, line-of-business segments should be separately disclosed if either of these requirements are met or if segment profits or losses account for at least 10 percent of the profits or losses of all segments that incurred a profit or loss, respectively.

In the United Kingdom, the Companies Act requires the disclosure of geographical segmental sales, together with line-of-business disclosure of both sales and pretax profit. Geographical profits disclosures continue to be required, although flexibly, by the London Stock Exchange. Discretion as to whether segments need to be identified and how that identification will take place is left to management. More recently, Statement of Standard Accounting Practice (SSAP) No. 25, *Segmental Reporting,* extended the existing legal and stock exchange requirements by requiring the disclosure of segment net assets for both line-of-business and geographical segments. In addition, the geographical segmentation of sales by both source and destination is required. Geographical segmental profit disclosures are also required unequivocally, in contrast to the London Stock Exchange's more flexible requirement.

Many other countries also require segmental information. In particular, Canada and Australia have requirements similar to those of the United States. In the EC countries, the Fourth and Seventh Directives have set a minimum requirement of disclosure (i.e., sales by line of business and geographical area). While the United Kingdom, as a member of the EC, goes well beyond this disclosure, most countries have adopted a more secretive approach.

In Japan, segmental reporting requirements were introduced in 1990 and are currently limited to sales and profits disclosure by line of business. With respect to geographical analysis, only foreign sales as a whole need to be disclosed. However, profits segmented by geographical area are not currently required to be disclosed, although this is expected to become a requirement by 1995.

[8] Harmonization of Standards

The different accounting standards and practices discussed in the preceding sections illustrate how difficult it is for the MNE to keep books worldwide that are consistent with home country and local country requirements. In fact, the Royal Dutch/Shell Group of companies reflects a synthesis of the accounting principles of the Netherlands, the United Kingdom, and the United States. Its extensive operations in all three countries have forced it to take a multinational approach to accounting rather than adopt the standards of any one country. Obviously, Royal Dutch/Shell would benefit from an international harmonization of standards in order to avoid developing its own standards.

The harmonization process is currently occurring on an international and regional basis. However, wide differences in the nature of accounting standards make harmonization a difficult process to pursue.

[a] IASC. Founded in 1973, the IASC's main objective has been to formulate standards to be observed in the presentation of audited financial statements and to promote their acceptance and adherence to them. The board of the IASC consists of the representatives of professional organizations from Australia, Canada, Denmark (representing the Nordic Federation of Accountants), France, Italy, Japan, Jordan, Korea, South Africa, the Netherlands, the United Kingdom, the United States, and Germany. A number of professional organizations from more than 50 countries have joined the IASC. Thus, the IASC is a group of private accounting bodies rather than a group of governments setting accounting standards. As of January 1, 1993, the IASC has set 31 standards covering a variety of topics. There have not been any major differences between IASC standards and those issued by the United States, so there is good reason to assume that adherence to FASB standards implies adherence to IASC standards as well. However, the American Institute of Certified Public Accountants (AICPA) rather than the FASB is the U.S. representative to the IASC. Thus far, the IASC has attempted to narrow alternative practices rather than standardize principles. Given the political nature of standard setting and the strong national pride in accounting standards, this process of harmonization is probably the wisest one to take.

[b] United Nations. The United Nations has become involved in the process of attempting to set accounting standards through the Commission on Transnational Corporations of UNESCO. The commission is concerned with "securing international arrangements for the operations of transnational corporations and furthering understanding of the nature and effects of their activities."[4] A portion of the commission's activities relates to accounting disclosure, most specifically to nonfinancial disclosure, such as the structure of the multinational company, the main activities of its entities, employment information, accounting policies, and transfer pricing policies. The major financial statement disclosures being discussed are not very different from what is already accepted good practice internationally. The commission has been working on these disclosures for several years, but no final standards have been passed. The major difference between these standards and those of the IASC is the heavy input of the developing countries and their concerns over the influence of the multinational company. If standards are ever issued, individual countries could write these standards into national law. So far, that has not been the case with the IASC. As a result, the operations of this commission bear watching.

[c] OECD. The Organization for Economic Cooperation and Development (OECD), which includes most of the industrial countries of Western Europe, plus Canada, the United States, and Japan, has a code of conduct for MNEs that deals in part with accounting issues. The OECD guidelines are very similar to those already

---

[4] *World Accounting Report* (Sept. 1982), p. 9.

in use in most of the industrial countries, and U.S. companies should have no trouble adhering to those guidelines if they comply with already existing accounting standards and disclosure practices in the United States. The OECD, like IASC, has no enforcement mechanism, so its standards depend on the desires of the individual states.

[d] **EC.** The EC is one of the most interesting of the political attempts at harmonization. One of the original goals of the 12-member EC was the free flow of capital. Obviously, this objective would be difficult in the face of widely different accounting standards. The EC is empowered to set directives, which are orders to the member states to bring their laws into line with EC requirements within a certain period, usually two years. A series of directives has been issued; the Fourth Directive deals specifically with accounting issues. Adopted in 1978, the basic aim of the Fourth Directive was to provide the framework for a common standard of accounting disclosure. The major areas covered by the Fourth Directive are the format of accounts and valuation rules. The directive requires firms to present a balance sheet and income statement (but not a statement of changes in financial position) and accompanying footnotes. It allows a country to choose from among two balance sheet and four income statement formats, with additional options for large firms, as opposed to medium and small firms. The directive is a compromise between the heavily legalistic German and French views of accounting and the relatively flexible true-and-fair view of the financial statements prevalent in the United Kingdom.

U.S.-based multinational companies need to be concerned about the Fourth Directive because their subsidiaries in various countries will be required to adhere to the version of the directive legislated in each country. This means that different subsidiaries will be generating financial statements according to different national laws, creating the need for different sets of books to be kept, which may be problematic.

[9] Disclosure of Information

Of immediate concern to the financial executive is the disclosure of information in different capital markets. The Securities and Exchange Commission has set a high standard of disclosure that will probably be sufficient for most capital markets. However, each market has its own listing requirements. Disclosure requirements may necessitate that information be prepared in different accounting terms from those in the United States and may also require information different from that disclosed in the United States. In any event, the following issues need to be addressed by a U.S.-based MNE for each capital market:

- Can the company's financial statements be in English, or do they have to be translated into the language of every country where the company wants to list?
- Can the company's financial statements be in dollars, or do they have to be translated into the local currency? (It is most common to give the annual report in the currency of the parent company rather than to translate the figures into another currency.)
- Can the company's financial statements be presented according to U.S. generally accepted accounting principles (GAAP), or do they have to be recast in terms of local GAAP?

Most firms rely on their footnote disclosures to explain how the financial statements have been generated. However, some firms provide information in addition to the footnotes when issuing capital stock in the United States.

A major solution to different standards would be the harmonization efforts under-way by the IASC. However, the differences in culture and other factors are so great that this may be impossible. Another approach is mutual recognition, where countries agree to accept each other's standards with the burden on disclosure and on the sophistication of the investor to analyze differences. This also assumes some risks to both issuers and investors. Accounting standard setters from the major capital markets are now meeting to determine the next step.

5.03 ACCOUNTING FOR FOREIGN CURRENCY TRANSACTIONS AND TRANSLATION OF FOREIGN CURRENCY FINANCIAL STATEMENTS

The FASB Statement of Financial Accounting Standards (SFAS) No. 52, *Foreign Currency Translation,* deals with two major issues: accounting for foreign currency transactions and the translation of foreign currency financial statements.

[1] Accounting for Foreign Currency Transactions

Foreign currency transactions involve two major problems: accounting for normal sales and acquisitions with settlement due in a foreign currency and accounting for foreign exchange derivatives such as forward contracts and options. U.S. companies may become involved in international transactions without having foreign operations. These companies do so through import-export activities and the financing of operations by borrowing foreign currency. The most important international transactions are the sale or purchase of merchandise, capital assets, or services; the payment or receipt of dividends, royalties, and management fees; and the borrowing or lending of money. The assumption is that these transactions are to be settled in foreign rather than domestic currency, giving rise to some interesting accounting and reporting problems.

Four issues need to be resolved in accounting for transactions denominated in a foreign currency:

1. The initial recording of the transaction

2. The recording of the foreign currency balances at subsequent balance sheet dates

3. The treatment of any foreign exchange gains and losses

4. The recording of the settlement of foreign currency receivables and payables when they come due

Although there are various ways to deal with each of these problems, SFAS No. 52 gives clear direction. According to SFAS No. 52, it is important that each firm decide on its functional currency. "Functional currency" is defined as "the currency of the primary economic environment in which the entity operates; normally, that is the currency of the environment in which an entity primarily generates and expends cash."[5] For the firm involved in import-export operations, the functional currency is

---

[5] *Foreign Currency Translation,* Financial Accounting Standards Board, Statement of Financial Accounting Standards No. 52 (Stamford, Conn.: 1981).

FIGURE 5-4

Foreign Currency Transaction

Assume the following exchange rates:

$1.8130/U.K. pound spot rate on June 1
$1.7120/U.K. pound spot rate on June 30
$1.6605/U.K. pound spot rate on July 15, the settlement date

On June 1, the XYZ Company purchased capital equipment from a U.K. exporter for 500,000 U.K. pounds, with payment to be made on July 15.

June 1	Equipment	$906,500	
	Accounts payable		$906,500
June 30	Accounts payable	50,500	
	Gain		50,500
July 15	Accounts payable	856,000	
	Cash		830,250
	Gain		25,750

normally the currency of the country in which the firm is based. Thus, a U.S. company buying a piece of capital equipment from Germany would normally consider the U.S. dollar as its functional currency, since most of its transactions take place in the United States.

Once the functional currency has been defined, it is relatively easy to account for foreign currency transactions. SFAS No. 52 requires that assets, liabilities, revenues, and expenses be recorded in the functional currency at the exchange rate in effect on the transaction date. At each subsequent balance sheet date, balances denominated in a currency other than the functional currency should be adjusted to reflect the current exchange rate. In practice, an acquisition of merchandise or capital assets is recorded at the exchange rate in effect on the transaction date, as is the liability. At subsequent balance sheet dates, the merchandise or capital asset remains at the initial recorded value, but the liability, which is still denominated in the foreign currency, is adjusted to reflect its value at the new exchange rate. Any gains or losses on that adjustment are recorded as a gain or loss to be taken to the income statement. Figure 5-4 illustrates typical journal entries.

Four things should be noted in this example. First, the equipment is recorded at the original spot rate and its value does not change even if the exchange rate changes. Second, the accounts payable amount is changed at the balance sheet date to reflect the new exchange rate. Third, each time this balance is computed, a gain or loss is determined, and the amount is recorded as a gain or loss in the income statement. Fourth, the amount of cash actually expended is determined by the spot rate in effect on the day of payment.

The approach followed by U.S. companies is not necessarily followed around the world. The Canadians defer and amortize gains and losses on long-term receivables and payables over the term of the underlying transaction (e.g., the purchase of a fixed asset). The British permit the deferral and write-off of the gains and losses that arise from long-term monetary items, which is similar to the Canadian approach. The Japanese carry long-term assets and liabilities at the exchange rate in effect at the transaction date, which results in deferring gains or losses on the monetary items until the day that they are settled.

The French take a relatively conservative approach. It is common to recognize foreign exchange losses, but gains are deferred until the settlement date. Their companies have more flexibility than do U.S. companies in that they have the option to recognize gains and losses currently or defer and amortize them over the life of the underlying transaction.

The German approach is similar to that of the French in that foreign exchange losses are recognized. If the change in value owing to the new exchange rate results in a gain, the Germans carry the items at the historical exchange rate rather than value them at the new exchange rate, which has the effect of deferring the gains until the receivable or payable is settled.

[a] Accounting for Forward Exchange Contracts. The forward market exists to facilitate future transactions in currencies. The forward rate is an exchange rate quoted by the foreign exchange trader and customer for transactions that take place beyond the two business days covered by normal spot market transactions. This rate is a contractual rate that may or may not equal the spot rate in effect when the contract comes due. The contract allows a firm to lock in an exchange rate in order to plan its purchases and sales more precisely when future spot rates are difficult to determine.

There are four major reasons to enter into a forward contract:

1. To hedge a foreign currency commitment

2. To hedge the receivable or payable attached to a foreign currency transaction, such as the one described in the preceding section

3. To hedge a net investment in a foreign operation

4. To speculate

An example can explain the forward contract's effect on the firm. Using the spot rates from Figure 5-4 assume that the 45-day forward rate is $1.8125. In this situation, the U.K. pound is selling at a discount in the forward market because the forward rate is less than the spot rate. (If the forward rate were $1.9000 per pound, the pound would be selling at a premium in the forward market.) If a firm enters into a contract with the foreign exchange trader to deliver dollars to the trader (the contract payable) in order to receive pounds (the contract receivable), the amount denominated in foreign currency (the contract receivable in this case) is recorded at the spot rate on the date of the contract, and the amount denominated in dollars (the contract payable) is recorded at the forward rate. The difference between the two is the discount or premium, depending on which of the two rates is relatively high or low. In this case, the difference is a discount because the forward note is below the spot rate.

In the case of a foreign currency commitment, assume that a U.S. importer agrees to purchase capital equipment from a U.K. manufacturer as soon as it is completed, with payment to be made in pounds. To protect against a possible adverse movement in exchange rates, the importer enters into a contract to deliver dollars in exchange for pounds, with settlement to take place around the same time that the machinery is to be delivered. The forward contract locks the importer into a fixed dollar equivalent for the machinery regardless of the exchange rate when the transaction is finally recorded. Because the forward contract is designed to hedge a foreign currency commitment, the forward rate actually sets the value of the equipment, as well as the amount of payment. Thus, if the spot rate is $1.8130 at the commitment date and $1.6605 at the date of the transaction and the forward rate is $1.8128, the acquisition of capital equipment costing £500,000 is recorded at $906,400, an amount fixed by the forward contract.

Sometimes a forward contract can be used to hedge the payment of a transaction already recorded, such as the one in Figure 5-4. In that case, the equipment has been purchased, but settlement of the liability will not take place for 45 days. That leaves the firm open to a foreign exchange risk, as shown in the example. In this case, the forward contract can eliminate the risk. The only cost of the contract is the premium or discount plus transaction costs. The premium or discount will be written off over the life of the contract and taken directly to income. The gain or loss on the accounts payable adjustment will be recorded at the spot rate when the transaction is recorded, and the amount of cash needed to settle the liability is set by the forward contract. The difference between the spot rate and the forward rate (the premium or discount) is the amount taken to the income statement.

If a U.S. parent decides to enter into a forward contract or other foreign currency transaction to hedge an investment in a foreign entity, the parent may include any gain or loss on the contract as a separate component of stockholder's equity. If a firm enters into a forward contract to speculate on currency changes rather than to hedge an exposure, any gains or losses on that contract are recognized immediately in income. This gain or loss is determined by comparing the book value of the contract with its new market value and then updating that market value each time a balance sheet is prepared.

[b] Accounting for Options. The difficulty in accounting for options is the lack of standards for guidance. Most of the national approaches to foreign exchange were developed prior to the rapid emergence of foreign currency options, so they do not deal with options. Their discussion of hedges allows hedge accounting for fixed currency commitments or transactions. However, options themselves are not fixed commitments, since the holder of the option may or may not decide to exercise.

In the United States, there is a movement on the part of the Emerging Issues Task Force (EITF) to deal with options through the use of concepts developed in a variety of standards and issues papers, such as SFAS No. 52, SFAS No. 80, and AICPA Issues Paper No. 86-2.[6] However, none of these deal specifically with foreign currency options. Issue No. 90-17, *Hedging Foreign Currency Risks With Purchased Options,* provides the most recent pronouncement by the EITF; it allows hedge accounting when enterprise risk is reduced and for purchased options used to hedge an anticipated transaction if the anticipation is relatively certain.

In other words, the holder of the option may defer the premium paid for the option until the underlying transaction is recognized. Thus, the premium is carried as an asset. The option, which is contingent on a future decision, should be carried as a memorandum entry as an off-balance sheet item. Gains and losses on options that are treated as hedges for hedge accounting purposes can be deferred, whereas gains or losses on options considered speculative are required to be taken on the income statement.

---

[6] Frederick D.S. Choi and J. Matthew Singleton, "Accounting for Derivative Products," *Handbook of International Accounting* (New York: John Wiley & Sons, Inc., 1991); N. Landau, "EITF Wrestles With Conflicting Views on Options Accounting," *Business International Money Report* (Jan. 29, 1991); J.E. Stewart, "Financial Instruments: The Challenges of Hedge Accounting," *Journal of Accountancy,* Vol. 168 (Nov. 1989); M.S. Levitin and L.A. Volkert, "Recent EITF Actions: Hedging Foreign Currency Risks With Purchased Options," *Journal of Accountancy,* Vol. 173 (Feb. 1992).

[2] Translation of Foreign Currency Financial Statements

The previous section deals with amounts receivable or payable in foreign currency where conversion will eventually take place. Conversion implies that one currency is actually exchanged for another, usually through the foreign section of the commercial bank with which the firm deals. Translation implies that one currency is expressed or restated in terms of another currency. In that case, only the unit of measure changes, not the properties of the item being measured.

There are many reasons for a financial statement to be expressed in a currency other than the one in which it is issued. Restatement may assist the reader of the financial statements. Some companies issue financial statements in the parent currency but include appropriate exchange rates so that readers in other countries can translate the statements into their own currency. The management of a multinational company may wish to see the results of a foreign operation stated in the parent currency in order to facilitate cross-national comparisons. If an MNE is to prepare consolidated financial statements, it needs to express the statements of its operations in a common currency before combination or consolidation can occur.

In the process of translation, all local currency balance sheets and income statement accounts are restated in terms of the parent currency by multiplying the local currency amount by the appropriate exchange rate. The process of translation is governed in the United States by SFAS No. 52, which applies two different translation methods, the temporal method and the current-rate method (sometimes referred to in Europe as the closing-rate method).

[a] **Brief History of Translation.** The process of translation has gone through some interesting changes in the United States since the early 1930s. Initially, firms were required to use the current/noncurrent method of translating foreign currency financial statements. Under that method, current assets and current liabilities are translated at the current exchange rate (the exchange rate in effect at the balance sheet date), and noncurrent assets and liabilities are translated at the historical exchange rate (the exchange rate in effect when the transaction actually took place).

During this period, the current-rate method was very popular in Europe and the United Kingdom. Under this method, all assets and liabilities are translated at the current exchange rate. Net worth is the only section of the balance sheet translated at historical exchange rates.

Different variations on the current-noncurrent method were discussed and implemented to a limited degree. In October 1975, however, the FASB issued SFAS No. 8, *Accounting for the Translation of Foreign Currency Transactions and Foreign Currency Financial Statements,* which was to become one of the most controversial ever issued by the board. The translation methodology employed by SFAS No. 8 was the temporal method. Under that method, assets carried at past exchange prices (historical cost) are translated at historical exchange rates, and assets carried at current exchange prices (basically monetary assets and liabilities and assets carried at current cost) are translated at current exchange rates. Any gains or losses arising from financial statement translations are taken to the income statement in the quarterly as well as the annual statements.

Several concerns were voiced over SFAS No. 8. The major concern was that immediate recognition of all gains and losses resulted in a distortion of operating results and in misleading information, which in turn led to poor economic decisions. Most critics felt that gains and losses on foreign currency transactions should be taken directly to the income statement but that gains and losses on translating foreign currency financial statements should somehow be taken out of income.

Another concern was that certain accounts were not being translated properly. Inventory, for example, was translated primarily at historical rates. Thus, a rate change in one period might not affect operating profits until the period in which the inventory was sold. This distortion of operating results was perplexing to managers. Many controllers were also concerned about the complexity involved in keeping track of historical costs and historical exchange rates for inventory, an asset that turns over fairly quickly. The preference was to translate inventory at current rates.

Another account that gave rise to concern was long-term debt, which was translated at current rates and thus exposed to foreign exchange losses. Many respondents felt that it was unfair to translate a fixed asset at historical rates and thus shelter that asset from any foreign exchange gains or losses when the debt used to acquire the asset was exposed to an exchange gain or loss. The consensus was that the asset should be translated at the current rate in order to match the exposure of the debt or that the gain or loss on the debt should somehow be taken out of income.

As a result of the criticism and subsequent debate, SFAS No. 52 was issued in December 1981. The objectives of this standard are to "[p]rovide information that is generally compatible with the expected economic effects of a rate change on an enterprise's cash flows and equity, and . . . reflect in consolidated entities as measured in their functional currencies in conformity with U.S. generally accepted accounting principles."[7]

These objectives allowed firms more flexibility in determining how to translate their foreign currency financial statements; it also allowed firms to choose between two translation methods.

[b] Selection of the Functional Currency. The choice of translation method depends on an understanding of the functional currency and how it relates to the currency in which the parent's financial statements are issued. There are several currencies that need to be defined in order to avoid confusion in the remainder of the discussion. The reporting currency is the currency in which the consolidated company prepares its financial statements. In the case of a U.S.-based multinational company, this would be the U.S. dollar. The local currency is the currency of the particular country in the discussion. For example, the local currency of Brazil would be the cruzeiro. The functional currency is the currency of the primary economic environment in which the entity operates. In most cases, the functional currency of a foreign subsidiary is the local currency, but it can also be the reporting currency. Finally, the foreign currency is a currency other than the functional currency of a firm. For example, a foreign currency of a subsidiary operating in France that uses the French franc as its functional currency might be the deutsche mark. For a firm that uses the U.S. dollar as its functional currency, the franc could also be the foreign currency, even though it might also be the functional currency of the French subsidiary and thus the local currency as defined previously.

The functional currency is the key to the process of translation in SFAS No. 52. The FASB offers some general guidelines on the choice of functional currency, but it is up to management to make that decision and then to defend it. The six factors

---

[7] *Foreign Currency Translation, op. cit.,* p. 3.

to be considered both individually and collectively in determining the functional currency are the following:

1. Cash flow indicators

2. Sales price indicators

3. Sales market indicators

4. Expense indicators

5. Financing indicators

6. Intercompany transactions and arrangements indicators[8]

In addition, inflation is an important determinant of the functional currency. If the cumulative rate of inflation in a country is approximately 100 percent or more over a three-year period, the functional currency must be the U.S. dollar.

In a survey of factors used to determine the functional currency, several important ideas emerged. During the period 1981–1983, the maximum number of functional currencies used by firms was in the low fifties, with the average number around 14. Firms tended to expend minor to moderate effort in determining the functional currency. Only 27.5 percent of the responding firms encountered situations in which different functional currencies were used for different foreign entities within the same country. A few firms used different functional currencies for the same entity in a country (some transactions using one functional currency and others using another functional currency). Only 8.3 percent of the respondents changed the functional currency of a foreign entity for a reason other than changes in inflation rates. The four most important economic factors used to determine the functional currency were the following:

1. The denomination of cash flows

2. Location of primary sales market

3. Location of primary input market

4. The market where (sales) price is determined[9]

In a more precise discussion of the translation process, the FASB refers to the processes of "translation" and "restatement." In order to understand the differences between these terms, refer to the conditions set forth in Figure 5-5. Notice that the books and records of the foreign entity can be kept in either the local currency or the reporting currency of the parent company (here assumed to be U.S. dollars). If the books and records are kept in dollars and the functional currency is defined as the dollar, no translation process is necessary.

If the books and records of the foreign entity are kept in the local currency, the translation process depends on the definition of the functional currency. If the functional currency is the local currency, the financial statements are translated into dollars using the current rate method. As noted earlier, there is one exception to that rule: when the foreign entity is located in a highly inflationary economy. In that case, the temporal method must be used. Rapid inflation would erode the value of fixed assets

---

[8] *Ibid.*, pp. 26–27.

[9] Thomas G. Evans and Timothy S. Doupnik, *Determining the Functional Currency Under Statement 52,* Financial Accounting Standards Board (Stamford, Conn.: 1986), pp. 5–7.

FIGURE 5-5

Translation of Foreign Currency Financial Statements Into U.S. Dollars

Source: Lee H. Radebaugh and Sidney J. Gray, International Accounting and Multinational Enterprises, 3rd ed. (New York: John Wiley & Sons, Inc., 1993).

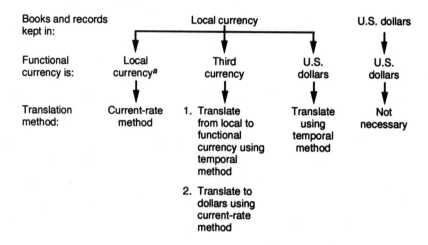

[a] In the case of a highly inflationary economy, the local currency may be the functional currency from an operating standpoint, but the dollar is considered functional currency from a translation standpoint.

very quickly, so the use of the temporal method would permit firms to maintain a fixed dollar value for those assets over time.

Another possibility, although a very rare one, is for the books and records to be kept in the local currency but the functional currency to be a third currency. In this situation, the financial statements need to be translated from the local currency to the functional currency using the temporal method and then translated into dollars with the current-rate method.

The last possibility for translation is for the books and records to be kept in the local currency but for the functional currency to be defined as the U.S. dollar. In this situation, the local currency financial statements are translated into dollars with the temporal method. This is the situation that all firms were required to use under Statement 8.

The important thing to note from this discussion is that SFAS No. 52 uses both the current-rate method and the temporal method of translating financial statements from a foreign currency to dollars. The key is to know the currency in which the books and records are kept and the definition of the functional currency of the foreign entity. Thus, SFAS No. 52 has not necessarily simplified the translation process, and all of the problems that occurred with SFAS No. 8 cannot be ignored. Also, it is incorrect to refer to SFAS No. 52 as the current-rate method, as many people are prone to do, because it encompasses both methods.

[c] **Numerical Example.** In the brief descriptions of the temporal and current-rate methods given previously, the major focus has been on the balance sheet. As noted, under the current-rate method, all assets and liabilities are translated at the exchange rate on the balance sheet date (the current rate); net worth is translated at the historical rate. This means that capital stock is translated at the exchange rate in effect when the stock was issued, and retained earnings and the cumulative translation adjustment are just an accumulation of dollar values from prior balance sheets. Under the temporal method, monetary assets and liabilities are translated at the current exchange rate, and nonmonetary assets carried at historical cost are translated at the historical exchange rate.

However, it is also important to understand how the income statement is to be translated. Under the current-rate method, the income statement is translated at the average exchange rate for the period. The average rate used depends on whether the translation process occurs on a monthly, a quarterly, or an annual basis. The longer the period, the more important the concept of weighting the exchange rate in order to account for the cyclical nature of business. The average rate applies to all income statement accounts, including sales, cost of sales, depreciation expense, and other revenues and expenses. Another point is that translation gains and losses are not included in income, as is the case with the temporal method. However, gains and losses from foreign currency transactions are included in income. Translation gains and losses are included as a separate component of stockholders' equity.

The temporal method of translation involves several differences from the current-rate method. Although revenues and most expenses are translated at the same average rate that would be used under the current-rate method, the cost of sales and depreciation expense are handled differently. The cost of sales is translated at the exchange rate in effect when the inventory was purchased. This is normally an average rate that is older than the one used for revenues and other expenses. Depreciation expense is translated at the rate in effect when the fixed assets were acquired, which is the original historical exchange rate. In addition, translation gains and losses are recognized in the income statement in the period in which the exchange rate changes, rather than included as a separate component of stockholders' equity, as is the case with the current-rate method.

The illustrations in Figures 5-6 and 5-7 show the difference between the current-rate and temporal methods for translating foreign currency financial statements. It should be pointed out that the process of translation and consolidation is a complex one that cannot be adequately covered in a short chapter. Most of the international public accounting firms have developed detailed implementation guides that add considerably more detail than is presented in this simple illustration. However, the illustration is designed to point out some key aspects of the translation process.

To simplify, the foreign exchange gain in the illustration is a balancing figure. In the case of the temporal method, the ending retained earnings balance must be $174,000 in order for assets to equal liabilities plus owners' equity. The determination of the foreign exchange gain is as follows:

Retained earnings (December 31, 1992)	$174,000
Net income	(99,750)
Retained earnings (January 1, 1992)	(57,875)
Foreign exchange gain	$ 16,375

That amount is carried directly to the income statement.

FIGURE 5-6

Balance Sheet (December 31, 1992)

	Local Currency	Temporal Method		Current-Rate Method	
		Exchange Rate[a]	U.S. Dollars	Exchange Rate[a]	U.S. Dollars
Assets					
Cash and receivables	LC[b] 100,000	2.05[c]	$ 205,000	2.05	$ 205,000
Inventory	125,000	2.03[d]	253,750	2.05	256,250
Net fixed assets	300,000	1.95[e]	585,000	2.05	615,000
Total	LC[b] 525,000		$1,043,750		$1,076,250
Liabilities and owners' equity					
Current liabilities	LC[b] 115,000	2.05	$ 235,750	2.05	$ 235,750
Long-term debt	100,000	2.05	205,000	2.05	205,000
Capital stock	220,000	1.95	429,000	1.95	429,000
Retained earnings	90,000	—	174,000	—	172,875
Equity adjustment from translation	—	—	—		33,625
Total	LC[b] 525,000		$1,043,750		$1,076,250

Note: Assume that the beginning retained earnings balance is $57,875.

[a] Foreign currency = U.S. dollars.

[b] Local currency.

[c] Current or year-end balance sheet rate.

[d] Average rate during the period when the ending inventory was purchased.

[e] Rate when fixed assets were purchased and capital stock was issued.

FIGURE 5-7

Income Statement (1992)

	Local Currency	Temporal Method		Current-Rate Method	
		Exchange Rate[a]	U.S. Dollars	Exchange Rate[a]	U.S. Dollars
Sales revenue	LC[b] 700,000	2.00[c]	$1,400,000	2.00	$1,400,000
Cost of sales	(437,500)	2.04[d]	(892,500)	2.00	(875,000)
Depreciation	(45,000)	1.95	(87,750)	2.00	(90,000)
Other expenses	(160,000)	2.00	(320,000)	2.00	(320,000)
Net income before foreign exchange gain (loss)	LC[b] 57,500		$ 99,750		$ 115,000
Foreign exchange gain (loss)	—		16,375		—
Net income	LC[b] 57,500		$ 116,125		$ 115,000
Retained earnings (Jan. 1, 1988)	32,500		57,875		57,875
Retained earnings (Dec. 31, 1988)	LC[b] 90,000		$ 174,000		$ 172,875

[a] Foreign currency = U.S. dollars.

[b] Local currency.

[c] Weighted average rate during the year.

[d] Average rate during the period when the merchandise that was sold was initially purchased.

Under the current-rate method, the total of liabilities and stockholders' equity must be $1,076,250 to equal total assets. Retained earnings is included on the balance sheet, as shown in Figure 5-7. In order for liabilities and stockholders' equity to equal total assets, the firm needs to include $33,625 as an equity adjustment from translation. That includes the translation adjustments of prior years plus the translation adjustment of the current year.

As can be seen in Figures 5-6 and 5-7, the temporal and current-rate methods treat the translation adjustment very differently. Under the temporal method, the translation adjustment appears in stockholders' equity by means of the income statement and retained earnings, whereas under the current-rate method, the translation adjustment appears as a separate component of stockholders' equity.

The FASB requires an analysis of changes in the separate component of equity for the period, including the beginning and ending amounts of the cumulative translation adjustments and the aggregate adjustment for the period resulting from translation adjustments. In a separate financial statement, in notes to the statements, or as part of a statement of changes in equity, the following information must be disclosed:

- Beginning and ending amounts of cumulative translation adjustments
- Aggregate adjustment for the period resulting from translation adjustments and gains and losses from certain hedges and intercompany balances
- Amount of income taxes for the period allocated to translation adjustments
- Amounts transferred from cumulative translation adjustments and included in determining net income for the period as a result of the sale or complete or substantially complete liquidation of an investment in a foreign entity[10]

A good example of how U.S. firms disclose information about foreign exchange gains and losses can be found in the 1992 Coca-Cola financial statements (Figures 5-8 and 5-9) which show a line item for the foreign currency translation adjustment in the shareholders' equity section of the balance sheet. The balance sheet discloses a negative balance of $271,211,000 for 1992, a significant increase in the negative balance over 1991. To find out the nature of the change, it is necessary to examine the detail on the consolidated statements of shareholders' equity found in the annual report. In that report, Coca-Cola provided the beginning balance of the translation adjustment account each year, the adjustment for the year (– $266,302,000 in 1992), and the ending balance.

When firms use the current-rate method of translation, the exposed assets (those translated at the current rate) tend to exceed exposed liabilities. This is because shareholders' equity is translated at historical exchange rates and all other accounts are translated at the current rate. When SFAS No. 52 was instituted, the dollar was strong against most major currencies. Thus, when firms translated their foreign currency net asset positions into dollars, they were showing lower dollar equivalents for their net assets in weak currencies. Thus, the cumulative translation adjustments in the early years were negative, representing a "loss" of purchasing power of the foreign currencies. When the dollar began to weaken during the 1985–1987 period, these losses reversed themselves as the relatively stronger foreign currencies turned the net assets into gains. Movements of the U.S. dollar against foreign currencies since 1987 have resulted in swings in translation gains and losses.

---

[10] *Foreign Currency Translation, op. cit.*, pp. 12–13.

FIGURE 5-8

Consolidated Statements of Share Owners' Equity for the Coca-Cola Company
(Three Years Ended December 31, 1992)

	Preferred Stock	Common Stock	Capital Surplus	Reinvested Earnings	Outstanding Restricted Stock	Foreign Currency Translation	Treasury Stock
Balance December 31, 1989	$300,000	$418,910	$437,324	$5,618,312	$ (45,892)	$ (7,206)	$(3,235,963)
Restatement for change in accounting principle for income taxes	—	—	—	(186,871)	—	—	—
Balance December 31, 1989 as Restated	300,000	418,910	437,324	5,431,441	(45,892)	(7,206)	(3,235,963)
Sales of stock to employees exercising stock options	—	905	28,999	—	—	—	(2,762)
Tax benefit from employees' stock option and restricted stock plans	—	—	13,286	—	—	—	—
Translation adjustments (net of income taxes of $573)	—	—	—	—	—	11,237	—
Stock issued under restricted stock plans, less amortization of $11,655	—	429	33,094	—	(21,868)	—	—
Purchases of common stock for treasury	—	—	—	—	—	—	(303,905)
Redemption of preferred stock	(225,000)	—	—	—	—	—	—
Net income	—	—	—	1,381,904	—	—	—
Dividends							
Preferred	—	—	—	(18,158)	—	—	—
Common (per share—$0.40)	—	—	—	(534,482)	—	—	—
Balance December 31, 1990 as Restated	75,000	420,244	512,703	6,260,705	(67,760)	4,031	(3,542,630)
Sales of stock to employees exercising stock options	—	972	38,422	—	—	—	(2,421)

Tax benefit from employees' stock option and restricted stock plans	—	—	20,015	—	—	—	—
Translation adjustments (net of income taxes of $958)	—	—	—	—	—	(8,940)	—
Stock issued under restricted stock plans, less amortization of $22,323	—	622	68,850	—	(47,149)	—	—
Purchases of common stock for treasury	—	—	—	—	—	—	(396,655)
Redemption of preferred stock	(75,000)	—	—	—	—	—	—
Net income	—	—	—	1,618,002	—	—	—
Dividends							
Preferred	—	—	—	(521)	—	—	—
Common (per share—$0.48)	—	—	—	(639,543)	—	—	—
Balance December 31, 1991 as Restated	—	421,838	639,990	7,238,643	(114,909)	(4,909)	(3,941,706)
Sales of stock to employees exercising stock options	—	2,155	129,109	—	—	—	—
Tax benefit from employees' stock option and restricted stock plans	—	—	92,758	—	—	—	—
Translation adjustments (net of income taxes of $67)	—	—	—	—	—	(266,302)	—
Stock issued under restricted stock plans, less amortization of $24,828	—	58	9,492	—	15,278	—	(34,552)
Purchases of common stock for treasury	—	—	—	—	—	—	(1,224,936)
Net income	—	—	—	1,664,382	—	—	—
Common dividends (per share—$0.56)	—	—	—	(738,001)	—	—	—
Balance December 31, 1992	$ —	$424,051	$871,349	$8,165,024	$(99,631)	$(271,211)	$(5,201,194)

Note: Dollars in thousands except per-share data.

FIGURE 5-9

Liabilities and Share Owners' Equity Portion of Balance Sheet for the Coca-Cola Company (as of December 31, 1992)

December 31,	1992	1991 (Restated)
Liabilities and Share Owners' Equity		
Current		
Accounts payable and accrued expenses	$ 2,252,975	$ 1,914,379
Loans and notes payable	1,967,540	845,823
Finance subsidiary notes payable	104,950	346,767
Current maturities of long-term debt	14,794	109,707
Accrued taxes	962,963	1,038,497
Total Current Liabilities	5,303,222	4,255,173
Long-Term Debt	1,120,064	985,258
Other Liabilities	658,631	493,765
Deferred Income Taxes	81,629	216,072
Share Owners' Equity		
Common stock, $0.25 par value— Authorized: 2,800,000,000 shares; Issued: 1, 696,202,840 shares in 1992; 1,687,351,094 shares in 1991	424,051	421,838
Capital surplus	871,349	639,990
Reinvested earnings	8,165,024	7,238,643
Unearned compensation related to outstanding restricted stock	(99,631)	(114,909)
Foreign currency translation adjustment	(271,211)	(4,909)
	9,089,582	8,180,653
Less treasury stock, at cost (389,431,622 common shares in 1992; 358,390,928 common shares in 1991)	5,201,194	3,941,706
	3,888,388	4,238,947
	$11,051,934	$10,189,215

Note: Dollars in thousands.

[d] **Translation Practices Outside of the United States.** The Fourth Directive, on the format and content of financial statements in the EC, and the Seventh Directive, on consolidated financial statements, do not contain any guidance on accounting for foreign currency transactions and the translation of foreign currency financial statements. Some countries, such as the United Kingdom, Ireland, and the Netherlands, have standards. Others, such as France and Germany, do not have any standards or laws, so there is great variation in practice. Whereas SFAS No. 52 requires that transactions gains and losses be taken to the income statement, there is no such uniform practice in Europe. Although European firms tend to take losses to income, gains are often deferred until payment is settled, which is the practice of the Internal Revenue Service (IRS) in the United States.

Although both the current-rate and temporal methods are allowed in most European countries, most tend to use the current-rate method. The notable exception is Germany, where firms tend to use a form of the temporal method. The Germans do not make a distinction in translation methodology based on the functional currency, as is the case in the United States.

The French use the temporal method for integrated foreign companies (similar to using the reporting currency as the functional currency) and the current-rate method for self-sustaining foreign entities (similar to using the foreign currency as the functional currency). Gains and losses are treated in the same way as in SFAS No. 52. In the case of foreign entities in highly inflationary countries, however, the French allow firms to restate financial statements to reflect the effect of inflation.

The Japanese use the temporal method. Translation adjustments for foreign subsidiaries are reported as either assets or liabilities, whereas adjustments for branches are taken to income. There is no use of the current-rate method and thus no discussion of the functional currency.

In April 1983, the Accounting Standards Committee of the United Kingdom issued SSAP No. 20, *Foreign Currency Translation*. Prior to that time, the method of translation most widely used in the United Kingdom was the current-rate method. However, SSAP No. 20 allows the use of either the current-rate or the temporal method, depending on the operating relationship that exists between the investor and investee. This is similar to the concept of functional currency described in SFAS No. 52.

In spite of the similarities between the standards of the United States and the United Kingdom, some important differences between SFAS No. 52 and SSAP No. 20 also exist:

- SSAP No. 20 does not deal with foreign currency transactions. Comments in the foreword to the standard state that foreign currency transactions must be translated into the reporting currency, but the standard does not deal with many of the issues covered in SFAS No. 52.

- The British use the terms "closing rate" rather than "current rate," although they are interchangeable.

- In the United States, SFAS No. 52 requires that the average exchange rate be used to translate the income statement when the current-rate method is used, but SSAP No. 20 allows U.K. firms a choice between the closing rate and the average rate for the closing-rate method. Until recently, it was more common for U.K. firms to use the closing rate rather than the average rate to translate income under the closing-rate method. The average rate is typically used for the temporal method.

- SFAS No. 52 requires the use of the temporal method to translate the financial statements of operations in highly inflationary economies. SSAP No. 20 recommends that companies, where possible, adjust financial statements to current price levels before translating them into pounds.

- SSAP No. 20 does not require the level of disclosure on translation gains and losses that is required in SFAS No. 52. In addition, U.K. firms do not have to set up a separate section in stockholders' equity to hold translation adjustments, since they already use a reserve account for a variety of adjustments. SSAP No. 20 requires disclosure of the movement on reserves during the year. It also requires that the net amount of exchange gains and losses included in equity and in net income for the period be disclosed somewhere.[11]

---

[11] *Ibid.;* Accounting Standards Committee, "SSAP 20: Foreign Currency Translation," *Accountancy* (May 1983), pp. 120–128.

The Canadian standard on foreign currency translation, adopted in July 1983, deals with both transactions and translation and has elements that are similar to and others that are different from the U.S. and U.K. standards.

In terms of translating foreign currency financial statements, the temporal and current-rate methods can be used, depending on the operating characteristics of the foreign operations. If the reporting enterprise is an integrated foreign operation, the temporal method of translation must be used. This is similar to defining the functional currency as the reporting currency in SFAS No. 52. Translation gains and losses are taken to income unless they relate to long-term debt. Those gains and losses can also be deferred and amortized.

If the reporting enterprise is a self-sustaining foreign operation, the current-rate method must be used. This is similar to defining the functional currency as something other than the reporting currency in SFAS No. 52. Translation gains and losses are taken to a separate section in stockholders' equity rather than to income, which is consistent with SFAS No. 52.

If the foreign operation is in a highly inflationary country, its financial statements should be translated into the reporting currency with the temporal method. This is consistent with SFAS No. 52 but inconsistent with SSAP No. 20, which prefers use of the closing-rate method[12] to adjust price level changes before translation.

5.04 INTERNATIONAL TAX ISSUES

Taxation has a strong impact on the choice of the following:

- Location in the initial investment decision
- Legal form of the new enterprise, such as a branch or subsidiary
- Method of finance, such as internal as opposed to external sourcing and debt as opposed to equity
- Method of arranging prices between related entities

Tax planning is crucial, since it can have a profound effect on profitability and cash flow. In the international situation, the tax accountant not only must be familiar with the laws of his or her own country but must be able to provide management with information about similar laws in the countries where the firm is currently operating or is considering expanding. In addition to laws governing domestic source income, the tax accountant must be familiar with laws governing foreign-source income.

[1] Export of Goods and Services

Many enterprises, such as public accounting firms, advertising agencies, banks, and management consulting firms, deal in services rather than products. Many manufacturing industries also find it easier and more profitable to sell expertise, such as patents or management services, rather than goods. Generally, payment is received in the form of royalties and fees, and this payment is usually taxed by the foreign government. Since the sale of services is made by the parent, the sale also must be included in the parent's taxable income.

---

[12] Canadian Institute of Chartered Accountants, *CICA Handbook,* Vol. 1 (Toronto: Canadian Institute of Chartered Accountants, 1983), sec. 1650.

In order to gain tax advantages from exporting, a U.S. firm can set up a foreign sales corporation (FSC) abroad, according to strict guidelines established by the IRS. If the foreign corporation qualifies as an FSC, a portion of its income is exempt from U.S. corporate income tax. Also, the law provides that any dividends distributed by the FSC to its parent company are exempt from U.S. income taxation as long as that income is foreign trade income.

Certain kinds of economic activity qualify for the FSC legislation, namely, the export of merchandise as well as services, such as engineering services or architectural services. Also, it is important that substantial economic activity take place outside of the United States. The FSC cannot be a mailbox company in Switzerland that simply passes documents from the United States to the importing country. Examples of substantial business activities that the FSC can conduct are (1) developing and conducting advertising and sales promotion campaigns; (2) processing customer orders; (3) arranging for transportation and delivery of products; (4) generating and transmitting final invoices or statements of account; (5) receiving payment; and (6) assuming credit risk.

[2] Foreign Branch

A foreign branch is an extension of the parent rather than an enterprise incorporated in a foreign country, as is a foreign manufacturing subsidiary. Therefore, any income generated by the branch is taxable immediately to the parent, whether or not cash is remitted. One important aspect of taxation of foreign-branch income is that if the branch suffers a loss, the parent is allowed to deduct that loss from its taxable income, thus reducing its overall tax liability. There is no such thing as deferral in the case of a branch, since all income or loss is immediately combined with parent income or loss. Deferral means that foreign-source income generally is not taxed until it is remitted to the parent company. Since the branch also pays corporate income tax to the government of the country in which it is operating, it may take advantage of the tax credit.

[3] Foreign Corporations

From a tax standpoint, it is critical to determine first whether the foreign subsidiary or affiliate is a controlled foreign corporation (CFC). A CFC is any foreign corporation in which 50 percent or more of the voting stock or value of the corporation is held by U.S. shareholders. A U.S. shareholder is a U.S. person or enterprise that holds 10 percent or more of the voting stock of the subsidiary.

Once a CFC has been identified, its income must be divided into two categories: (1) active income and (2) subpart F, or passive, income. "Active income" means income derived from the active conduct of trade or business, whereas passive income usually results from operations in so-called tax-haven countries, often called tax-haven subsidiaries.

The tax-haven subsidiary sometimes has acted as a holding company for its parent of stock in foreign subsidiaries (called grandchild or second-tier subsidiaries), a sales agent or distributor, an agent for the parent in licensing agreements, or an investment company. The tax-haven subsidiary is meant to concentrate cash from the parent's foreign operation into the low-tax country and to use the cash for global expansion. As long as a dividend is not declared to the parent, no U.S. tax must be paid. However, the Revenue Act of 1962 eliminated the deferral concept for tax-haven subsidiaries involved in passive rather than active investments.

[a] Subpart F Income. As noted earlier, subpart F income is passive income, in that the company earning it is not actively seeking income. Subpart F income is basically earned by CFCs in a tax-haven country from activities outside of that country. Subpart F income includes the following:

- Insurance of U.S. risks
- Foreign-based company personal holding company income
- Foreign-based company sales income
- Foreign-based company services income
- Foreign-based company shipping income
- Boycott-related income (from the Arab boycott of Israel)
- Foreign bribes (related to the Foreign Corrupt Practices Act)

Following are three important categories of subpart F income:

1. *Holding company income.* Primarily dividends, interests, rents, royalties, and gains on sale of stocks.

2. *Sales income.* Income from foreign sales subsidiaries that are separately incorporated from their manufacturing operations. The product is either manufactured, produced, grown, or extracted and sold for use outside of the CFC's country of incorporation. Any CFC performing significant operations on the property is excluded, such as when personnel in the CFC are heavily involved in selling the product.

3. *Service income.* Income from the performance of technical, managerial, or similar services for a related person and performed outside of the country in which the CFC is organized.

The importance of distinguishing between a CFC and a non-CFC and subpart F and active income is in the application of the deferral principle. As long as a foreign corporation is not a CFC, its income is not taxable to the parent until a dividend is received by the parent. Thus, the income is deferred from taxation in the United States. If the foreign corporation is a CFC, the deferral principle applies to the active but not to the subpart F income, which is immediately taxable to the parent.

There is one exception, however. If foreign-based company income is the lower of $1 million or 5 percent of gross income, none of it is treated as subpart F income. If foreign-based company income is subject to a tax that is at least 90 percent of the U.S. tax liability, the income is also not subject to U.S. tax.

[4] Tax Credit

Every country has a sovereign right to levy taxes on all income generated within its borders. Problems arise when firms are owned by foreigners, such as foreign corporations, or when they are branches of foreign corporations. This problem has been important for U.S. firms because of the magnitude of foreign direct investment.

As was mentioned earlier, the U.S. parent is able to defer recognition of active income until a dividend is declared to the parent. Then the parent gets credit for a portion of income taxes paid. For example, if 50 percent of the income of the foreign subsidiary is distributed as a dividend to the parent, the parent can claim no more than 50 percent of the tax as a creditable tax. Branches are not allowed the deferral privilege, so their income is taxed immediately to the parent, but all branch foreign income taxes are eligible for inclusion in the tax credit. Credit also is allowed for taxes paid by the parent to the foreign government on dividends paid by the foreign corporation to the parent. These taxes are called withholding taxes.

After the firm adds up its eligible credits, it finds that it is constrained by an upper limit imposed by the IRS. The upper limit is what the firm would have paid in taxes on that income in the United States. If the foreign-source income is $1 million and the applicable U.S. tax rate is 34 percent, the upper limit is $340,000. If the total worldwide tax credits exceeded the $340,000, the firm could carry them forward over five years and try to use them. If the amount is less than the upper limit, the firm would be allowed the full amount.

In reality, the computation of the tax credit is significantly more complex. Foreign-source income must be divided into separate categories, or baskets: overall and passive. The overall category would contain basically active income and probably generate excess credits. The passive category would contain subpart F income and probably use up all of its available credits with room to spare.

[5] Impact of Tax Treaties

A thorough study of international tax issues uncovers a variety of different tax practices worldwide. These differences exist in terms of how to define taxable income and tax-deductible expenses, statutory tax rates, different types of taxes, and whether income is taxed more than once, as is the case in the United States, where corporations are taxed on income earned and shareholders are taxed again when dividends are declared. In addition, countries have different policies on the taxation of income earned abroad and of income earned locally by foreigners. Differences in philosophy on how income should be taxed have given rise to treaties between countries to minimize the effect of double taxation on the taxpayer, protect each country's right to collect taxes, and provide ways to resolve jurisdictional issues. The United States has tax treaties with at least 35 countries. Among other things, tax treaties have an impact on dividend, interest, and royalty payments.

5.05 PERFORMANCE EVALUATION AND CONTROL

Not only are financial executives concerned with the use of accounting information for external reporting purposes, but they also need to use that information for a variety of internal purposes, such as capital budgeting and performance evaluation and control. Five key problems affect the quality of the information used:

1. Accounting requirements in different countries

2. The size and importance of worldwide operations

3. The organizational structure of the firm

4. The purpose of each subsidiary (especially as it concerns profit centers)

5. Different currencies

Because accounting standards are very different in different countries, local people hired by a firm to perform accounting functions may have been trained in the system of that country and may have great difficulty relating to a U.S.-based system. Also, a firm is usually required to keep its books and records in the currency and language and possibly in the GAAP of the country in which it operates.

The size and importance of the foreign operations can be critical, especially in deciding on the complexity of operational reporting. It is common for a multinational company to transfer its internal reporting system worldwide because it is easier and cheaper and management is already familiar with it at the home office. However, that system might be extremely burdensome to a relatively small operation in a country where management is not very sophisticated in the generation and use of accounting data. It might be too much to ask the local operation to use a sophisticated system. Management must thus be sensitive to adjustments that need to be made in the amount, complexity, and timing of information requested from abroad.

The information system has to be suited to the structure and philosophy of the firm. For example, if a firm operates through a highly decentralized structure, its information and control requirements are different from those of a highly centralized firm. Largely autonomous subsidiaries do not require as much control from the parent and therefore need not transmit information as frequently or in as much detail to the parent. Similarly, firms organized along product lines have different lines of data transmission than firms organized along geographical lines. Firms with a matrix structure need to develop reports that take into account product as well as geographic flows of data.

[1] Transfer Pricing

With regard to transfer pricing, the price charged by one related enterprise to another, there appears to be a movement toward vertical integration of the operations of multinational companies as they attempt to shore up sources of supply of key materials and components. In addition, the search for cost advantages has led to greater disaggregation of the production process in order to capitalize on the unique comparative advantages that firms have to offer. Thus, with increasing frequency, semifinished components and finished goods are transferred across national borders from one entity to another controlled by a common parent. A key consideration for each government involved as well as for the firm itself is how the transfer price is set.

Because such transfers do not occur at arm's length, there is room for price manipulation. Governments are concerned because the price attached to a transfer could affect excise taxes (such as border taxes and value-added taxes) as well as corporate income taxes. Companies are concerned because transfer prices affect direct cash flows for payments of goods, taxes, cost structures affecting their competitive position, and evaluation of management performance.

Different conditions in the home country of each subsidiary could lead to different transfer pricing decisions if the firm has the discretion to set arbitrary prices. Tax authorities tend to have the greatest influence in prohibiting companies from setting prices arbitrarily; the preference is to have an arm's-length price instead. Management itself may prefer an arm's-length price for two basic reasons. First, it is often difficult to set priorities for transfer prices. For example, goods being shipped to a politically unstable country where there are low corporate income tax rates are subjected to conflicting possibilities: The unstable environment would imply a high transfer price to get goods out, whereas the low tax rate would imply a low transfer price in order to concentrate on profits.

There has been vigorous debate over how to amend the tax law to eliminate some of the abuses arising from arbitrary transfer pricing. U.S. companies can apply for approval of a transfer pricing policy under an advanced determination ruling (ADR). To get an ADR, an MNE would apply to the IRS for approval of a parent-subsidiary pricing formula by writing a detailed explanation of the transfer pricing system. The MNE also would have to provide otherwise proprietary financial information to the IRS. The IRS would examine the company's books and, if necessary, confer with foreign tax authorities.

While some firms feel that it would be desirable to have the certainty of a ruling on a transfer pricing policy, others are nervous about providing so much information to the government, especially since it could be leaked to competitors. In addition, the cost of complying with the ADR requirements, estimated by Hewlett-Packard to be $1 million for a single application, is onerous.

Although the IRS solidly backs the exact-comparables approach to establishing transfer prices, it may also accept the inexact comparables—pricing based on similar products that are available from similar companies—as a backup. Even though this appears to be a major problem for U.S. firms, the ADR concept is already in place in Germany and the Netherlands, and a similar concept is in place in Japan.

The second reason for wanting an arm's-length price is performance evaluation. Arbitrary transfer prices affect net income as well as the asset base in calculations of return on investment. Thus, management performance is evaluated in areas where management has no control when arbitrary transfer prices are used. As a result, many firms prefer to use cost plus or some other way of setting arm's-length prices on their intracorporate transfers.

[2] Currency in Performance Evaluation

The last area of concern is currency. Management is obviously concerned about the ultimate dollar results of its operations worldwide, since reports to shareholders and home country creditors are made in the reporting currency, the U.S. dollar. However, there is a big gap between the initial transactions that occur in the local or foreign currency and the final results in dollars. In addition, there is the problem of setting budgets, monitoring performance, and evaluating performance of local subsidiaries and their management.

The issue of currency is a critical one. The choice of currency used in evaluations depends a great deal on the evaluation technique being used. Rather than using just the local currency or the parent currency, many firms use both currencies. The choice of currency to set budgets and track performance is more complex and includes top management's attitude toward dollar accountability. Figure 5-10 illustrates the possible combinations of exchange rates that can be used in the control process.

The options that make the most sense are A-1, A-3, P-2, P-3, and E-3. Under options A-1, P-2, and E-3, the same exchange rate is used to set the budget and track performance. In the case of option A-1, the exchange rate in effect when the budget was set is used to translate actual results into dollars. Thus, management sees the information in dollars, but local managers are not responsible for exchange rate changes. Option E-3 is very similar, except that the budget in dollars is updated to reflect the current rate in order to match actual performance translated at the current

FIGURE 5-10

Possible Combinations of Exchange Rates in the Control Process

Source: D.R. Lessard and P. Lorange, "Currency Changes and Management Control: Resolving the Centralization and Decentralization Dilemma," Accounting Review, Vol. L11 (July 1977), p. 630

Rate Used for Determining Budget	Rate Used to Track Performance Relative to Budget		
	Actual at Time of Budget	Projected at Time of Budget	Actual at End of Period
Actual at time of budget	A-1	A-2	A-3
Projected at time of budget	P-1	P-2	P-3
Actual at end of period (through updating)	E-1	E-2	E-3

rate. Option P-2 is slightly different in that while management is not held responsible for exchange rate changes, it is required to project exchange rates. Top management must decide who is responsible for projecting the rate, but there appears to be no attempt to hold anyone responsible for an inaccurate projection.

Options A-3 and P-3 introduce the element of accountability for exchange rate changes. In both cases, a different rate is used to track performance from that used to set the budget. For option A-3, management is accountable for the total fluctuation between the rates in effect when the budget is established and when actual performance is recorded. Top management must decide where to assign responsibility for exchange fluctuations, since A-3 includes operating as well as currency variances. The assumption is that the operating manager is responsible for any currency changes. If that is the case, the corporate or regional finance staff needs to provide assistance to local management on exposure management techniques. Care must also be taken to ensure that local management does not do something to minimize exchange exposure that might adversely affect operating performance.

For option P-3, the same kinds of issues exist as for option A-3. The difference is that with option P-3, management is required to forecast or project the exchange rate. The currency variance that shows up when budget costs are compared with actual costs is the difference between what management forecasts the rate to be and what it actually is. Thus, the corporate finance staff needs to provide assistance to local management in protecting the exchange rate.

As pointed out previously, some companies prefer to use local currency rather than information translated into dollars when setting budgets and monitoring results. This is partly because they believe that the translation process distorts the relationships among accounts that exist in local currency. The introduction of the current rate method in SFAS No. 52 results in dollar statements that maintain the same relationships that exist in local currency. That may add more credibility to dollar financial statements in performance evaluation.

5.06 CONCLUSION

As financial executives make decisions concerning asset management and funds positioning in the highly volatile and complex international environment, they must rely on the accuracy, reliability, and timeliness of the accounting data supplied by the accounting group. Differences in accounting standards worldwide complicate the record-keeping process, since firms must keep one set of books in accordance with local standards and another set to assist in preparing consolidated financial statements according to the parent company's external reporting requirements. In addition, comparability of international results for internal purposes is enhanced when common standards are used for preparing internal reports.

Multinational firms are also faced with a variety of specific accounting problems that are a direct result of their international operations. Foreign currency is a big issue, as firms must account for foreign currency transactions and the translation of foreign currency financial statements. As pointed out earlier, SFAS No. 52 adds a new dimension to the issue, as firms have the option of translating foreign currency financial statements using the current-rate method or the temporal method made popular by SFAS No. 8, depending on the characteristics of the foreign company whose statements are being translated. Under the current-rate method, many of the disadvantages of the temporal method are eliminated, especially since foreign exchange translation gains and losses are put in a separate component of shareholders' equity rather than recognized in income.

Foreign tax principles are important, because the tax practices and incentives that a country has to offer may have an impact on the location of a foreign operation and the timing of various dividend and interest flows to the parent company. Tax treaties should be studied closely to find out how best to protect parent cash flows.

Finally, the performance evaluation of subsidiaries and subsidiary management is complicated by transfer pricing decisions and foreign currencies. A number of international variables encourage the setting of arbitrary rather than arm's-length prices for intracorporate transfers in order to position funds more effectively. However, these arbitrary prices can injure performance evaluation. Management needs to be aware of the effect of intracorporate transfer prices on subsidiary and management performance. Exchange rate changes should also be considered in performance evaluation, since they can distort the picture that corporate management sees. A decision must be made as to who is accountable for dollar results and whether local currency results are relevant for making decisions.

As can be seen, the same issues that accountants face in a domestic context must be dealt with in an international context. However, in the international context, variables such as different accounting standards and foreign exchange can create numerous complexities that affect the accuracy, reliability, and timeliness of the accounting data relied on by the financial group.

Suggested Reading

AlHashim, Dhia D., and Jeffrey S. Arpan. *International Dimensions of Accounting,* 3rd ed. Boston: Kent Publishing Company, 1992.

Arthur Andersen & Co. *Accounting Standards for Business Enterprises Throughout the World.* New York: Arthur Andersen & Co., 1987.

Business International Money Report. Business International Corporation. New York (weekly bulletin).

Choi, Frederick D.S. *Handbook of International Accounting.* New York: John Wiley & Sons, Inc., 1991.

Choi, Frederick D.S., and Gerhard G. Mueller. *International Accounting,* 2nd ed. Englewood Cliffs, N.J.: Prentice-Hall, Inc., 1992.

Cooke, T.E. *An Empirical Study of Financial Disclosure by Swedish Companies.* New York and London: Garland Publishing, Inc., 1989.

Coopers & Lybrand. *International Accounting Summaries.* New York: John Wiley & Sons, Inc., 1991, and 1992 Supplement.

Deans, P. Candace, and Michael J. Kane. *International Dimensions of Information Systems and Technology.* Boston: Kent Publishing Company, 1992.

Mueller, Gerhard G., Helen Gernon, and Gary Meek. *Accounting: An International Perspective,* 2nd ed. Boston: Irwin, 1991.

Nobes, Christopher W., and Robert H. Parker. *Comparative International Accounting,* 3rd ed. Deddington, United Kingdom: Philip Alan Publishers, 1991.

Radebaugh, Lee H., and Sidney J. Gray. *International Accounting and Multinational Enterprises,* 3rd ed. New York: John Wiley & Sons, Inc., 1993.

World Accounting Report. London: *Financial Times* (monthly newsletter).

Chapter 6

Investment and Financing Decisions for Multinational Corporations

MARK R. EAKER

6.01 **Introduction** 192

6.02 **Motives for International Investment** 192
  [1] Possible Competitive Advantages of
      Foreign Firms 192
  [2] Disadvantages Related to Foreign
      Operations 194

6.03 **Assessment of Foreign Cash Flows** . . 194
  [1] Sources of Divergence 195
     [a] Interdependencies 195
     [b] Remittance Restrictions 196
     [c] Taxation 197
     [d] Subsidies 197
  [2] Exchange Risk and Cash Flows 197
  [3] Fisher Effect 198
  [4] Purchasing Power Parity 198
  [5] Alternative Cash Flow Measures . . . 199
  [6] Validity of Economic Assumptions 200
  [7] Impact of Deviations From Parity 201

  [8] Other Relevant Factors 204

6.04 **Capital Budgeting Techniques** 205
  [1] Choosing a Discount Rate 206
  [2] Adjusting for Project Risk 207
  [3] Adjusted Present Value 208

6.05 **Political and Operating Risk** 209
  [1] Monitoring Developments 212
  [2] Anticipating Policy 213
  [3] Adapting to Conditions 214

6.06 **Financing Foreign Subsidiaries** 215
  [1] Option 1: Local Currency Loan 216
  [2] Option 2: Parent Company Loan . . . 216
  [3] Tax Factors 218

6.07 **Managing Foreign Exchange Risks** . . . 219
  [1] Cross-Hedging 220
  [2] Currency Swaps 220

    Suggested Reading 223

6.01 INTRODUCTION

The international dimension of capital budgeting introduces a number of elements that complicate the decision process. Those elements do not invalidate the use of standard capital budgeting techniques, but they do make necessary the explicit recognition of some of the assumptions that are usually invoked in their domestic applications. The procedures and guidelines recommended in this chapter do not come out of a well-developed theoretical model of foreign investment. Instead, the recommendations take into account the problems facing managers who must make investment decisions and the amount of information that is most likely to be available to them at the time those decisions are made.

Capital budgeting involves two broad categories of estimates: First, the analyst must determine the relevant cash flows; second, the analyst must estimate the appropriate discount rate or required rate of return. Both of these estimates are affected by the international elements of a project in a variety of ways. Should the cash flow and cost of capital estimates be for the project or for just those aspects that directly affect the parent? How should inflation and exchange rate fluctuations be taken into account? What is the best way to reflect the added risk of doing business overseas? How do special tax and financing arrangements enter into the capital budgeting calculus? Answers to each of these questions are provided in subsequent sections of this chapter.

6.02 MOTIVES FOR INTERNATIONAL INVESTMENT

Operations in distant and culturally different places are inherently more difficult than domestic operations; domestic companies have a competitive advantage. Consequently, firms must have a variety of positive reasons to invest overseas.

[1] Possible Competitive Advantages of Foreign Firms

There are several possible compensations for incurring the risk and problems of foreign investment. Some industries are characterized by economies of scale; that is, firms with larger market shares globally are able to operate more efficiently, with lower cost structures. A large multinational corporation (MNC) therefore has an advantage over smaller, local firms because of its lower unit costs of production. Moreover, local production might be the only way to capture or maintain market share. Many firms shift from an export orientation to overseas production because trade barriers restrict or threaten their access to current or potential markets. If competitors establish production facilities inside the trade barriers, they might be able to expand their market share, reduce costs, and compete more effectively in all other markets. This is one example of defensive foreign investment, overseas expansion motivated by a desire to protect market position.

Another advantage that firms can exploit is superior knowledge or technical expertise. This might be the result of research and development activities or skills related to the marketing of products. Knowledge-intensive industries, such as the chemical, pharmaceutical, and electronics industries, have been major sources of foreign investment activity. So have consumer products industries where brand identification and promotion skills are important. Both types of knowledge—production and marketing—can be exploited in order to compensate for the additional difficulties of overseas investment. They might provide reduced operating costs or product differentiation that allow the firm to compete even with a higher cost structure.

Although the advantages of superior knowledge explain how firms can successfully compete overseas, they do not necessarily explain why. Those advantages can be utilized to expand export sales, but it is when export sales are threatened by restrictions or competition that overseas production is desirable. Once a foreign firm has established a market for a product or service through exports, domestic competitors enter that market. With protection through quotas or tariffs, the domestic firms are able to compete with and, in some cases, totally displace foreign producers.

In the current economic environment, debt-burdened, less-developed countries are pursuing aggressive trade policies. Those policies frequently include import substitution. Encouraging local production causes imports to be reduced and incentives to be created for foreign investment.

Another primary motive for overseas expansion is directly related to cost reductions. Foreign investment is often necessary in order to secure low-cost raw materials such as petroleum, bauxite, or rubber. Without access to those materials, firms find themselves at a competitive disadvantage in comparison to vertically integrated competitors. Labor can be viewed in this context as a raw material, so establishing foreign operations to take advantage of lower overseas labor costs fits into this category.

Related to cost reductions is the need to establish overseas offices and facilities to serve customers located abroad. Even companies that market primarily through export channels have found that after-purchase relationships with customers require in-country operations. This is true even for nonmanufacturing companies such as banks, which have followed the flag as their domestic customers have expanded overseas.

Another motive for overseas investment is to take advantage of subsidies offered by foreign governments. In order to attract technology, jobs, and foreign exchange, many countries offer foreign firms special tax treatment, tariff protection, or below-market financing. These subsidies frequently represent crucial considerations when a firm is evaluating an overseas location. Without the added inducement, the project would not be justified, but with it, the project is acceptable.

A final motive for direct foreign investment is the desire to diversify one's wealth position. Modern financial theory has shown the advantages of holding a diversified portfolio of assets. Just as there are potential gains from diversification across industries, there are gains from diversification across national borders. Unfortunately, there are a number of factors that make it difficult for individual investors to own securities in other countries.

These factors are the following: (1) Many nations have restrictions on capital flows that disallow portfolio investment; (2) capital markets in most less-developed countries and even many developed nations lack depth and breadth; and (3) there are relatively few traded securities and large concentrations of ownership among them, making it almost impossible for investors to acquire assets in those countries even where formal restrictions are absent.

Investment even in developed countries is hard to accomplish. Tax rules are different from nation to nation, and information about securities is not as available in other countries as in the United States. Consequently, although investors believe that there are benefits to international diversification, they are unable to diversify their own portfolios.

An alternative to individual diversification is to invest in MNCs. With their legal staffs and industry knowledge, these companies are able to engage in direct investment despite the information barriers that thwart individuals. The logical extension of this argument is that shareholders desire management to diversify in order to substitute for individual diversification which is blocked by formal and informal barriers. However, there is no direct evidence that firms are in fact motivated by the diversification issue.

[2] Disadvantages Related to Foreign Operations

As stated previously, firms face added difficulties related to overseas operations. It is worthwhile to keep the following potential difficulties in mind when cash flow forecasts and risk adjustments are discussed in subsequent sections:

- The firm is perceived as being foreign, which causes resentment among consumer groups, domestic competition, and government officials. Often, those interest groups or stakeholders mistrust the foreign parent.

- Foreign operations are physically very far from headquarters. Information is harder to gather and disseminate, making managerial control more difficult.

- Cultural differences exist that need to be considered in determining organizational design and personnel policies.

- A new set of tax and legal rules must be learned and incorporated into financial planning and firm policy.

- Transactions occur in a foreign currency, which adds to the uncertainty of cash flows.

- The firm must operate in a different political environment. A failure to understand that environment and its laws could lead to severe penalties.

In addition, if the political atmosphere is less stable than in the home country, the firm must deal with a rapidly changing environment. Keeping up with events requires resources expended on information gathering.

6.03 ASSESSMENT OF FOREIGN CASH FLOWS

A frequent shortcoming of cash flow forecasts is that they fail to identify all of the potential benefits and problems related to an overseas investment. It is likely that fewer errors will be made if the motivation for the project is kept in mind at the time the cash flows are estimated.

The major difficulty faced by analysts evaluating foreign investment cash flows is the divergence between the cash flows generated by the investment project as a freestanding local project and the cash flows accruing to the parent. Several factors contribute to the differences; some are controlled by the investor and others are determined by the firm's operating environment, including the government. These are elaborated on later, but regardless of the source of the discrepancy, it is important for the investor to recognize that cash flows that affect its position are the relevant ones to include. Estimation of those cash flows involves a three-stage process. The first stage is a forecast of the total or freestanding project; the second stage is the estimation of corporate, system-wide benefits and costs; the third stage takes into account all of the tax and exchange rate effects but leads to an estimation of investor cash flows. This three-stage process requires an identification of the factors that cause the two

FIGURE 6-1

Incremental Cash Flow Analysis

	Current Export Sales	Sales With Expansion		Sales Without Expansion
Units	4,000	1,000	6,000	1,500
Price	$60	$50	$50	$50
Revenue	$240,000	$50,000	$300,000	$75,000

cash flows to diverge and a procedure for converting estimated foreign currency flows into the home currency of the investor.

[1] Sources of Divergence

[a] Interdependencies. As indicated in the preceding section, overseas investment is often prompted by defensive motives: reaction to trade restrictions or competitive pressures. In those cases, some of the sales generated by the project are cannibalized from export sales formerly made by existing divisions of the firm. Sales that are taken away from other units but that would have been maintained without the overseas expansion should not be included among the project's revenues. At the same time, if those sales would have been lost owing to trade restrictions or competition, they are correctly attributed to the project.

An example can help clarify this point. A firm is contemplating an overseas investment that will have sales of 6,000 units per month at a price of $50 per unit. The firm currently services that market with export sales of 4,000 units at a price of $60 per unit. A major competitor is establishing a facility in the same region in order to avoid import quotas that will be in place in the next year. If the firm does not follow suit and make the investment, its estimated export sales will be 1,500 units at $50 per unit. If it does make the investment, export sales will fall to 1,000 units. What is the amount of sales revenue that should be credited to the foreign investment?

The correct answer is the amount that is incremental to the project compared with what would be generated if the project were not undertaken. That amount is $275,000 per month, the difference between the $350,000 total sales with the expansion and the $75,000 that would be realized without it. The $275,000 represents the $300,000 in sales that the investment generates less the $25,000 that is cannibalized from existing sales. The remaining decline in export sales ($165,000) is not deducted from the project because those sales would be lost even if the investment were not made. This example is summarized in Figure 6-1.

Changes in sales revenues are utilized in the example to illustrate interdependencies, but they are only one side of the cash flow equation. In a more complete analysis, costs are also considered. If costs were higher at the foreign operation, the increase would have to be taken into account when cash outflows were estimated. It is the net impact on total cash flows that is relevant.

Interdependencies also show up through transfer pricing. Once foreign operations are established, it is likely that intracompany transactions will cross international borders. Firms establish transfer prices at which those transactions clear between the operating entities. Those transfer prices are not always set at market levels because of tax effects and currency restrictions. Transfer pricing might be used to shift earnings from a high tax jurisdiction to a low tax jurisdiction. An internal effect of that pricing policy is to reduce stated cash flows in the high tax country and increase them in the lower tax country. From a corporate viewpoint, the tax reduction increases total cash flows, but without careful analysis the source of the cash flows might be identified incorrectly. The following problem exemplifies interdependency in transfer pricing.

A firm is considering an overseas assembly plant that will buy components from the parent. The market price of the component is set at $30, at which price the contribution margin for the parent is $8. After assembly, which adds $10 to the cost, the subsidiary will sell the finished product for $50. The effective tax rates in the parent's and subsidiary's countries are 30 percent and 40 percent, respectively. At the existing transfer price, the after-tax cash flows for the corporation are $11.60: $5.60 at the parent level and $6.00 at the subsidiary level. Because of the differences in tax rates, a higher transfer price would lead to higher after-tax cash flows for the corporation as a whole. At a transfer price of $40, the subsidiary's profits are eliminated entirely, whereas the parent's after-tax earnings rise to $12.60. If the $40 transfer price is used in evaluating the overseas project and the subsidiary is not credited with its share of the final cash flows, the investment will be turned down. As an extreme case, suppose all of the sales are dependent on building the assembly plant (because of trade restrictions). The correct cash flows to the project then would be the full $12.60, even though none of these show up on the subsidiary's books. Because of the presence of interdependencies, it is important to identify accurately the amount and source of all relevant cash flows.

[b] Remittance Restrictions. Countries frequently impose limits on the amount of funds that subsidiaries can pay to their overseas parents in the form of dividends. These policies are generally part of a more comprehensive program to reduce a balance-of-payments deficit. Descriptions of restrictions in force and changes in policies can be found in *Exchange Arrangements & Exchange Restriction*, published annually by the International Monetary Fund. At the time that an investment decision is being made, it is important that current restrictions are understood and that some estimate is made of the probability of continuing restrictions or restrictions' being imposed in the future. The latter necessarily involves an evaluation of the host country's balance-of-payments position.

Restrictions come in a variety of forms, usually allowing only a maximum percentage of annual earnings, retained earnings, or sales to be paid. Whatever their form, they have the effect of deferring the receipt of cash flows and thereby reducing the value of those flows. The amount of the loss is determined by the severity of the restriction, the length of time that receipt of the flows is delayed, and the opportunity available for investing the blocked funds before repatriation. For example, assume that an investment with a 10-year life generates annual net cash flows of $1 million. Restrictions on dividends limit payments to $400,000 each year for the first 9 years but allow payment equal to accumulated retained earnings at the end of the tenth year. The appropriate cash flows to consider in this case are then $400,000 per year for the first 9 years and $6,400,000 in the last year. If the funds can be reinvested during the interim, the additional interest income should be included. If the $400,000 can be invested at 10 percent and those earnings are also available for dividends at the end of the tenth year, the final cash flow will be $6,400,000 plus $2,303,600 in interest.

In the example, cash flows and earnings are considered to be the same. That is usually not the case because of the presence of noncash expenses such as depreciation. The disparity between earnings and cash flows creates some ambiguity about which cash flows are available for repatriation. If the dividend restriction establishes a limit on payments that is based on earnings, the positive cash flow related to depreciation will not be available to the firm for repatriation. Unless these funds can be used beneficially elsewhere in the country, it will usually be in the parent corporation's interest to keep depreciation expenses low in order to maximize after-tax income available for foreign dividends. There is no general rule to follow that fits all cases, but it is necessary to understand fully whatever restrictions exist and their implications.

[c] Taxation. Differences in tax rates have already been shown to enter the cash flow calculations. Effective tax rates in different countries vary a great deal. From the standpoint of a U.S. investor, the tax rate that applies is usually the higher of the two effective rates. The United States gives credit for foreign taxes but only up to the maximum U.S. rate. Therefore, any taxes beyond that rate reduce the return to the investor.

[d] Subsidies. Decisions to invest in particular projects are often influenced by inducements offered by the host country. As indicated in the preceding section on motives for foreign investment, these can take a variety of forms. Given sufficient subsidies, projects that otherwise would not be acceptable become viable investments. For potential investors, a key question is whether the subsidies can be taken away if the host country has a change of policy. The current government may offer a tax benefit that is of substantial value if it stays in effect for the life of the project. It serves as the necessary incentive to attract capital or technological knowledge. Once the investment has been made, the government may alter the tax laws or impose a new restriction that offsets the original subsidy.

Potential investors need to evaluate the subsidy and the probability that it will be eliminated. A very conservative approach is to accept only projects that would be viable without the subsidy. A more reasonable method is to adjust the cash flows in order to take account of the risk or probability of losing the subsidy at some future time; being aware of the importance of the subsidy also allows the investor to take steps to reduce the impact of its loss.

[2] Exchange Risk and Cash Flows

In the various examples presented previously, the cash flows are given in dollars even though it is clear that they are generated in some other currency. Conversion from local currency into dollars is consistent with the view that parent or investor cash flows are the relevant cash flows to analyze. A U.S. investor ultimately wants to have dollars to distribute to its shareholders. That much is straightforward. What is not so simple is the process by which estimated foreign currency flows are valued in dollars. That requires forecasts of inflation and exchange rates, as well as the impact of changes in both on the operating cash flows. In addition, the appropriate choice of currency for cash flow measurement is related to the choice of a discount rate. Therefore, the analysis that follows discusses both the numerator and the denominator of the capital budgeting formula. Because the task is so formidable, it is important to start with a very structured approach. Once the basic framework is established, it is possible to build more complicated relationships into the analysis.

To evaluate the investment using the net present value (NPV) criterion, an analyst has several options. Those options are the following:

1. To use real foreign currency cash flows and a real foreign currency discount rate

2. To use nominal foreign currency cash flows and a nominal foreign currency discount rate

3. To use real dollar cash flows and a real dollar discount rate

4. To use nominal dollar cash flows and a nominal dollar discount rate

Real cash flows are nominal flows adjusted for inflation using the inflation rate expected or experienced in that country. The four options are not as different as they might appear at first. Economic theory explicitly links inflation rates, exchange rates, and interest rates to one another. If those theoretical relationships are valid empirically, the choice of one of the four options is immaterial: Each would lead to the same outcome. Because the empirical evidence is in support of the theoretical relationships, some authors have suggested using option 1, since it requires the least information. That option makes both inflation and exchange rate forecasts unnecessary. Unfortunately, the use of real foreign currency cash flows can obscure some important and relevant factors that might influence the desirability of a particular project. As a result, the approach suggested here is to use option 4, the most difficult of the options. It requires forecasting both inflation rates and exchange rates, but the extra effort greatly enhances investment evaluation. In the following sections, the theoretical relationships among exchange rates, inflation, and interest rates are introduced and used to show under what conditions the four NPV calculations are equivalent.

[3] Fisher Effect

The Fisher effect relates interest rates to inflation expectations. Specifically, it hypothesizes that the nominal rate of interest consists of a real or non-inflation-related component and an inflation premium related to price expectations. The following are an algebraic representation and a numerical example:

$$(1 + i) = (1 + r)(1 + \pi) = (1.03)(1.2) = 1.236 \qquad (6.1)$$

  where:
    r = real rate of interest, here 3 percent
    π = expected inflation, here 20 percent

Equation 6.1 is true for both the home and foreign countries. When foreign country variables are used, they are denoted by an asterisk. In the theoretical literature, it is usually assumed that r and r^*, the real rates of return, are equal. Accordingly, the Fisher effect for the foreign country is

$$(1 + i^*) = (1 + r)(1 + \pi^*) = (1.03)(1.08) = 1.1124 \qquad (6.2)$$

[4] Purchasing Power Parity

Purchasing power parity (PPP) relates the exchange rate between two countries to their differential inflation rates. A change in the exchange rate between two periods is determined by the relative inflation rates in the two countries. The nation experiencing the higher rate of inflation has a depreciating currency. The nation with the lower inflation rate sees its currency strengthen. PPP can be expressed as

$$X_t = \frac{X_o(1 + \pi)^t}{(1 + \pi^*)^t} 2 = \frac{1.8(1.2)}{1.08} \tag{6.3}$$

where:

X_o = exchange rate expressed in home currency (dollars) per foreign currency unit at time 0, here 1.8:1

X_t = exchange rate at time t years from 0, here 2:1

[5] Alternative Cash Flow Measures

Once these relationships have been developed, it is straightforward to show that if they are valid, the four alternative cash flow calculations are equivalent. This is first done analytically; it is then demonstrated through an extended example.

Beginning with option 1, the NPV of the real cash flow in the base year C_o, denominated in the foreign currency is

$$\frac{C_o}{(1 + r^*)^t} \tag{6.4}$$

To account for inflation, it is necessary to adjust both the cash flow and the discount rate. Therefore, the nominal flows are

$$\frac{C_o(1 + \pi^*)^t}{(1 + r^*)^t(1 + \pi^*)^t} \tag{6.5}$$

Since the numerator and denominator have been multiplied by the same number, the discounted value of the cash flow has not changed. But the denominator is the right-hand side of the Fisher equation, so in fact Equation 6.5 is equal to

$$\frac{C_o(1 + \pi^*)^t}{(1 + i^*)^t} \tag{6.6}$$

which is the mathematical representation of option 2. Therefore, options 1 and 2 are equivalent.

Option 3 is calculated by converting the foreign currency cash flows into dollars and discounting at the real U.S. rate:

$$\frac{C_o X_o}{(1 + r)^t} \tag{6.7}$$

Making use of PPP, Equation 6.7 becomes

$$\frac{C_o(1 + \pi^*)^t X_t}{(1 + r)^t(1 + \pi)^t} \tag{6.8}$$

which is the nominal foreign currency cash flows converted to dollars and discounted at the nominal dollar rate, i.e., option 4.

To arrive at an NPV figure using option 4, it is necessary to forecast the base year cash flows, C_o; inflation in the foreign country, π^*; and future exchange rates, X_t. Because of the Fisher effect, there is no need to forecast home currency inflation,

FIGURE 6-2

Alternative Cash Flow Estimates When Purchasing Power Parity Holds

Year	Option 1: Real Francs	Option 2: Nominal Francs	Option 3: Real Dollars	Option 4: Nominal Dollars
0	fr(5,000,000)	fr(5,000,000)	$(1,000,000)	$(1,000,000)
1	1,800,000	2,016,000	360,000	378,000
2	1,800,000	2,257,900	360,000	396,900
3	1,800,000	2,528,870	360,000	416,745
4	1,800,000	2,832,335	360,000	437,582
5	1,800,000	3,172,215	360,000	459,461
Discount rate	3%	15.36%	3%	8.15%
NPV	fr3,244,000	fr3,244,000	$648,800	$648,800

since the denominator in Equation 6.8 is equal to $1 + i$, and i, the home nominal rate, is available. For all intents and purposes, however, forecasting X_t requires some measure of π to compare with π^*, so a home inflation forecast is in fact necessary.

These relationships and the advantages of using nominal dollar flows can be clarified with an example. Assume that an investment in a French project requires a cash outlay of $1 million or 5 million francs at the current spot rate. Sales revenues from the project, which has a 5-year life, are estimated to be 3 million francs per year at today's prices, while costs are 1.2 million francs. Both revenues and costs are expected to change by 12 percent per year in line with French inflation. Inflation in the United States is 5 percent. For a project of this type, the required real rate of return is determined to be 3 percent.

With the preceding information, it is possible to evaluate the project according to each of the options. The only additional values necessary to do the various calculations can be arrived at by assuming that the Fisher effect and PPP hold. The cash flows, discount rates, and NPVs are summarized in Figure 6-2.

Examination of the numbers reveals that all four options give the same result. That being the case, it is easy to understand why some people advocate using real cash flows and real returns. That method requires the least amount of information and the least amount of forecasting. It is important to understand, however, that the equivalent results were derived because the economic relations, PPP, and the Fisher effect were assumed to hold perfectly and because the cash flows were of a simple form.

[6] Validity of Economic Assumptions

There is a vast body of evidence concerning the validity of PPP and the Fisher effect. Although much of the evidence is contradictory and subject to varied interpretations, the general view is that over the long run, the relationships are valid. This means, for example, that PPP does not hold month to month or even year to year but that over a 10- or 20-year period, exchange rates do reflect inflation differentials. In addition, there is evidence that the deviations from PPP are not systematic but random. This implies that it is difficult if not impossible to accurately forecast the deviations, making the effort not worthwhile. Thus analysts use PPP as a working assumption about future rates. Since that is the case, there seems to be no reason to use an option other than option 1.

In fact, there are several reasons to do so. First, PPP and the Fisher effect are macroeconomic relationships; for an economy as a whole, they tend to be valid. At a more microeconomic level, they are not as relevant, especially PPP.

PPP is based on some aggregate price performance measure such as the consumer price index, wholesale price index, or gross national product deflator. Within that aggregate, there is a great deal of variation. As a result, even if PPP holds for the economy as a whole, it is not going to be valid for every individual product or industry line. Moreover, it is unlikely that both revenues and costs will follow the same trend, as was assumed in the example. If that is not the case, differences will arise between the values generated by all of the options.

A variety of factors can generate deviations in the growth paths of revenues and costs. The most general reason is that wages, which are a major component of costs, and prices are not perfectly correlated. More specifically, firms often contract long term for sales or labor. Those contracts generally are written in nominal terms with an expected inflation component built in. Deviations from the inflation expectations lead to windfall profits or losses depending on the direction of the forecast error. Along the same lines, other costs are generally not indexed for inflation. The most important of these is depreciation, which in most countries is based on historical costs. Inflation therefore dilutes the value of the tax shield that depreciation generates for the firm.

[7] Impact of Deviations From Parity

To demonstrate the impact of these factors, they can be introduced into the simple example given previously. Assume that the costs of 1.2 million current francs consist of 900,000 francs for labor and 300,000 francs for depreciation expense. The depreciation cash flow is available for remittance to the U.S. parent but is not adjusted for inflation. Labor costs are determined by a contract that has two years remaining and calls for increases of 12 percent each year. After that time, there will be a renegotiation, and management anticipates a 15 percent annual increase. Taxes are levied at a rate of 25 percent. PPP and the Fisher effect are assumed to hold, so the exchange rates for each period will be the same as those implicit in Figure 6-2. The NPV for each of the options is given in Figure 6-3.

A direct comparison between the results in the two tables is not appropriate because of the introduction of taxes in the calculations for Figure 6-3. The appropriate contrast to make is in the relationship of the various options to one another within each table. In Figure 6-2, all four options give essentially the same results. There is no difference introduced by the choice of nominal or real variables, nor is there a change in outcomes when the calculations are done in dollars as opposed to francs. The dollar values are exactly the franc values converted at the current spot rate of exchange. In Figure 6-3, the nominal and real calculations differ. This result was brought about by the use of different inflation rates for revenues and costs, as well as the deviation of those rates from the expected rates implicit in the nominal discount rate. Across currencies, the two nominal NPVs and the two real NPVs are still equivalent. The first set is equal because PPP was assumed to be valid and the second set is equal because the required real return in each currency was the same. Altering those assumptions would lead to greater differences among the results under the four options.

Why then is option 4 the best choice? Because it does not rely on the empirical

FIGURE 6-3
Divergent Cash Flow Estimates

OPTION 1: Real Francs

	Year 0	Years 1–5
Investment	fr(5,000,000)	—
Revenue		fr3,000,000
Labor		(900,000)
Depreciation		(300,000)
Operating profits		fr1,800,000
Taxes		(450,000)
After-tax profits		fr1,350,000
Depreciation		300,000
Cash flow	fr(5,000,000)	fr1,650,000

Net present value (at 3%) = fr2,556,505

OPTION 2: Nominal Francs

	Year 0	Year 1	Year 2	Year 3	Year 4	Year 5
Investment	fr(5,000,000)	—	—	—	—	—
Revenue		fr3,336,000	fr3,763,200	fr4,214,784	fr4,720,558	fr5,287,025
Labor		(1,008,000)	(1,128,960)	(1,298,304)	(1,493,049)	(1,717,007)
Depreciation		(300,000)	(300,000)	(300,000)	(300,000)	(300,000)
Operating profits		fr2,028,000	fr2,334,240	fr2,616,480	fr2,927,509	fr3,270,018
Taxes		(507,000)	(583,560)	(654,120)	(731,877)	(817,504)
After-tax profits		fr1,521,000	fr1,750,680	fr1,962,360	fr2,195,632	fr2,452,514
Depreciation		300,000	300,000	300,000	300,000	300,000
Cash flow	fr(5,000,000)	fr1,821,000	fr2,050,680	fr2,262,360	fr2,495,632	fr2,752,514

Net present value (at 15.36%) = fr2,349,562

OPTION 3: Real Dollars

Investment	$(1,000,000)
Annual cash inflow	330,000
Net present value (at 3%) = $511,301	

OPTION 4: Nominal Dollars

	Year 0	Year 1	Year 2	Year 3	Year 4	Year 5
Investment	$(1,000,000)					
Annual cash inflows		$341,437	$360,474	$372,826	$385,563	$398,672

Net present value (at 8.15%) = $469,914

validity of the PPP and the Fisher effect propositions. If they hold, the results provided by option 4 are still accurate, although more tedious to derive; if they do not hold, option 4 takes the deviations into account. Deviations at the macroeconomic level might be hard to predict, but at the firm level many deviations are in fact very predictable. In the example, depreciation expense was known to have a zero inflation rate. Moreover, financial analysts within the firm have access to information that others do not have, including the firm's intentions, cost structures, and sales patterns. By using nominal rates, they make use of that information. Moreover, the detailed development of pro forma financial statements forces the analyst to consider possible problem areas and to be aware of their potential impact on the profitability of a project.

Numerous examples could be given, but one should be enough to demonstrate the point. For a particular project, labor costs represent 60 percent of variable costs at current year's prices. During the last decade, wages have not kept up with the general rate of inflation, so current real wages represent only 70 percent of the real wage rate of 10 years ago. This has been caused in part by wage controls deliberately set by the government to lag price increases. One result has been stepped-up investment by labor-intensive firms, but another has been labor unrest and union agitation. Consequently, the analyst believes that future wages will rise at a faster rate than prices, thus squeezing the profitability of the project. Had the analyst relied on current real costs or past wage patterns, the problem of rapidly rising future costs would have gone unnoticed.

The final point related to the choice of cash flows is that the use of real variables assumes that there will be no changes in competitive position brought about by exchange rate fluctuations. The traditional view is that a depreciation of a country's currency makes the country's goods more desirable owing to price considerations and that an appreciation makes those goods less desirable. According to this view, when a nation's currency devalues, its exports become cheaper and its imports more expensive. Consequently, foreigners buy more of the nation's goods, as do locals, who reduce their volume of imports. A similar story with opposite results applies to the case of an appreciation.

The problem with the traditional story is that it ignores PPP and the individual firms' competitive positions, both of which have an impact on whether revenues will change owing to exchange rate fluctuations. Recall that if PPP holds perfectly, exchange rate changes are determined by and exactly reflect inflation differentials in the two countries. Since the relative cross-border price of a good is determined by the local currency price and the exchange rate, there is no change in the relative price if PPP holds. Any depreciation that lowers the value of the currency is precisely offset by the inflation effect that raises its local currency price. Therefore, currency fluctuations are neutral with respect to sales volumes and base currency revenues.

[8] Other Relevant Factors

Once the PPP assumption is relaxed there is room for relative price changes and competitive adjustments. The net impact will be determined by the elasticities of supply and demand. They are affected in turn by a variety of factors that should be taken into account when cash flows are estimated even if the analyst cannot measure them exactly. Among the more important considerations are the following:

- The absolute and relative sizes of the domestic and export business of the firm
- The extent of competition in domestic and foreign markets
- Available capacity for expanding sales
- The relative importance of local versus foreign content in manufacturing costs
- Price restrictions and tariffs
- Whether the product is priced for export in local currency or a single major currency

Each of the factors influences the elasticity of supply or demand either directly or indirectly. For example, if a firm competes solely in a domestic market against other local firms, a devaluation will have little impact on sales. There will likely be some reduction in demand as consumers find themselves with lower purchasing power owing to the devaluation, but the firm will not gain any price advantage from the change in exchange rates. If the firm is dependent on foreign sources of new materials or components, the devaluation will increase its costs. Those increases might not be allowed to be passed on to consumers if local price controls are in effect, a fairly common situation in devaluing countries. The scenario described here would apply to many nations that are trying to encourage local manufacturing with protection from exports provided by prohibitive tariffs.

Obviously, there are many factors to consider and a great many uncertainties. These make the whole process more difficult but also highlight the importance of looking closely at the nominal foreign currency cash flows and the impact of deviations from parity relationships. They also suggest that sensitivity analysis should play an important role in the evaluation process. Literally, the question needs to be raised as to how sensitive investor's cash flows are to various perturbations that might take place. Not only does sensitivity analysis reveal interaction effects that might otherwise go unnoticed, but it also provides insights into the riskiness of the investment. More will be said about risk in the next section.

In summary, a three-step process for the evaluation of foreign investment cash flows is advocated:

1. Look at the project cash flows as an independent, freestanding, local-country investment. Those cash flows should be estimated in nominal foreign currency values.

2. Isolate cash flows that would actually accrue to the investor. This involves looking closely at available funds for dividend remittances, transfer payments, and other interdependencies.

3. Convert the investor's foreign currency flows to home currency values in order to produce a set of nominal dollar cash flows to be discounted with a nominal dollar rate of interest.

6.04 CAPITAL BUDGETING TECHNIQUES

Financial theory indicates clearly that a capital budgeting technique or decision rule should meet specific criteria. These criteria include the following:

- The technique should be consistent with the notion of wealth maximization of the current shareholders.
- It should reflect the time value of money.

- It should provide a means of systematically dealing with risk.
- It should yield consistent rankings of mutually exclusive alternatives.
- It should use information available to the manager or decision maker.

It is generally agreed that a discounted cash flow approach is necessary for making capital budgeting decisions. The discount rate or required return hurdle is chosen in order to meet the first three criteria. To accomplish that, the discount rate must reflect the opportunity cost of funds to the shareholders and the riskiness of the investment. There are both theoretical and practical problems related to the choice of the discount rate; those problems are discussed in detail in earlier chapters dealing with capital budgeting for domestic projects. None of those problems disappears when the project involves cross-border investments, and several are compounded. The academic research tends to focus on the choice of the appropriate discount rate with the emphasis on its ability to measure risk. In general, the methods developed for choosing the appropriate rate require information that is unavailable to managers. That problem is manifested in the number of firms that either do not use a discounted cash flow approach at all or make no attempt to adjust for risk using one of the recommended theoretical techniques.

Because the purpose of this chapter is to provide guidance to practicing managers, the emphasis is on an approach that can be implemented with the information available to those individuals. This approach sometimes entails theoretical shortcuts, but it is better than the methods that surveys indicate are prevalent among firms.

This discussion focuses on two aspects of the capital budgeting problem: the choice of a discount rate and the method of risk adjustment. In theory, the two issues are the same, because the theoretical models call for a discount rate that reflects the riskiness of an investment project as it relates to some measure of market risk. Here, they are separated in order to make implementation more tractable for the practicing manager.

[1] Choosing a Discount Rate

The appropriate required rate of return is one that reflects the viewpoint of the parent and not that of the project. The cash flows that are generated by the project differ from those that accrue to the parent. Since the parent is concerned with cash flows that it receives, those cash flows should be discounted at a rate that reflects the cost of capital to the parent.

The correct cost of capital to use is the weighted average cost of capital (WACC) for the firm, assuming that the business risk of the foreign investment is identical to that of the extant corporation. The WACC is calculated by looking at all of the sources of funding for the corporation as a whole and weighing their costs according to their relative market values. The use of the WACC raises several questions in the international context, relating to how the foreign investment is financed and whether the investment alters the financial structure of the corporation.

Frequently, foreign investments are funded by an equity portion provided by the parent and long-term debt raised by the subsidiary. Some analysts mistakenly use only the equity as the parent's cash outflow in the calculations of present value. Their reasoning is that the parent has made an equity investment in exchange for future dividends, so the amount of the equity position and the dividend stream are the relevant cash flows. That argument overlooks two important points. First, the dividend stream is supported by all of the assets of the foreign project regardless of how those assets are funded. Therefore, the total investment or cash outflow is the value of the assets, which is equal to both the debt and equity funding.

Second, it is unlikely that financial intermediaries and markets ignore the debt of the foreign subsidiary when evaluating the debt capacity of the parent. As a result, whether the debt is a direct obligation of the parent or an indirect one by means of the subsidiary, it represents a portion of the total pool of funds available to the corporation. If the debt of the subsidiary is viewed as increasing the financial risk of the firm, or if its operations are seen as increasing the operating risk of the parent, some adjustment might be made in the cost of capital. The adjustment is no different from that suggested in the case of domestic projects involving financial leverage or systematic risk that differs from the corporation as a whole. The problem is that there is no easy way to measure the correct adjustment. One suggestion is to find independent companies with characteristics similar to those of the project whose cost of capital can be evaluated using market data. At best, this alternative is available for a small number of projects.

Another point raised in support of adjusting the cost of capital is the use of subsidized financing for a project. Countries eager to attract investment capital in order to create jobs often provide below-market interest rate financing. Since these funds would not be available to the firm if the project were not undertaken, they are not part of the corporate pool. The argument is sound, although adjusting the discount rate is not the only way to account for the benefit of the subsidy. Another approach, the one recommended here, is to include the value of the subsidy in the cash flows for the project and then discount the cash flows at the WACC. The major reason for doing this is that the NPV calculation assumes that cash flows will be reinvested at the discount rate. If the cash flows are returned to the present, it is unlikely that they will be reinvested at the low subsidized rate; rather, they will be reinvested at a rate consistent with the firm's overall cost of capital.

To calculate the value of the subsidy, it is necessary to compare the after-tax cost of the alternative borrowing. Assume that the host country provides $3 million at 7 percent interest when the market rate is 12 percent and the firm's tax rate is 40 percent. The loan will be repaid in equal installments over three years. The net after-tax value of the subsidy is equal to 3 percent of the outstanding balance in each year. This is derived from the difference in the interest rates $(0.12 - 0.07)$ multiplied by a factor that accounts for the tax deductibility of interest $(1 - 0.4)$. The positive amount added to the cash flows in each of the three years of the loan should be $90,000, $60,000, and $30,000.

[2] Adjusting for Project Risk

The discount rate might be adjusted if the project is in a different risk class from the firm as a whole. That adjustment is not related to the fact that the investment is foreign. However, should there be an adjustment just because the project is located overseas? And if there is an adjustment, does it necessarily increase the riskiness of the investment?

Portfolio theory indicates that shareholders are rewarded only for bearing systematic risk, the portion of variability that cannot be diversified away. In the earlier discussion of the motives for direct foreign investment, it is suggested that foreign investment might serve as a substitute for individual diversification. If that is the case, investment in foreign projects could lead to a reduction in the systematic riskiness of the firm. This result comes about because the firm's operations are now affected by market conditions in more than one country. As long as the economic performances of those countries are not perfectly correlated, foreign diversification leads to the reduction of systematic risk for the U.S. shareholder. Systematic risk is related to market movements. Because market movements in different countries are influenced by economic events in the individual countries, they are not perfectly correlated. Through international diversification, the systematic risk borne by the investor can be reduced as compared to a purely domestic portfolio. Thus, a strong theoretical argument can be made for lowering the required rate of return for foreign projects that have the effect of creating diversified positions.

Few managers would accept this conclusion. Instead, they would cite a list of added risks related to foreign investments and assert the need to raise discount rates rather than lower them. There are enough intuitive reasons to support the pragmatic view as opposed to the theoretical one. The need to adjust for added risk is not disputed here. What is argued here is that having a higher hurdle rate for foreign projects is not the best way to proceed. The reasons are technical but not conceptually difficult.

Projects generally have uneven streams of cash flows. When the discount rate is raised to reflect additional risk, the effect is to lower the value of projects with long lives relatively more than those with short lives. In other words, near-term cash flows are not as greatly reduced as long-term ones. This might but does not necessarily reflect the timing of the added risk elements.

Another difficulty with using a discount rate adjustment is that different components of the cash stream might be subject to different risks. Some uncertainty is related to the operating cash flows and some to a tax break bestowed by the government. Adjusting the discount rate affects all of the elements in the same way.

The alternative to adjusting the discount rate is to adjust the cash flows. Cash flows used in capital budgeting are estimates. These estimates can be adjusted by altering the probabilities of various events that will affect the cash flows. Sensitivity analysis can then reveal how dependent success is on either the mean or the most likely outcome being realized. Using sensitivity analysis is ad hoc; it does not provide a precise measure of a project's riskiness, but it does give management a feel for the range of outcomes that are possible. Sensitivity analysis is also easy to perform and requires no additional information beyond that necessary for the basic cash flow analysis.

[3] Adjusted Present Value

Several researchers have advocated a different approach to risk adjustment. It involves adjusting the discount rates, but it is done in a way that avoids the pitfalls associated with the blanket adjustment. This approach is called the adjusted present value (APV) method and has been applied to both domestic and international project evaluation.

The APV method begins with the premise that the project's cash flows can be decomposed into their constituent parts. Each is discounted at a different rate, reflecting the risk associated with it. With regard to an international project, the cash flow streams might consist of dividend remittances from operating income, royalties or other transfer payments, depreciation-related tax savings, and benefits from a subsidized loan. An argument can be made that these cash flows, beginning with operating income, are subject to decreasing risk or uncertainty. Therefore, progressively lower discount rates would be used on each set.

FIGURE 6-4

Capital Budgeting Using APV

Investment	$4,000,000
After-tax operating cash flows	$800,000 per year
Depreciation tax shield	$350,000 per year
Subsidized borrowing benefit	$50,000 per year
Time horizon	5 years

Using a WACC of 12%:

NPV $= -\$4,000,000 + \$1,200,000(3.605)$
$= \$326,000$

Using an all-equity rate of 14 percent for the operating cash flows and a risk-free rate of 8 percent for the other cash flows:

APV $= \$4,000,000 + \$800,000(3.433) + \$400,000(3.993)$
$= \$343,600$

It has been suggested that the operating flows be discounted using an all-equity rate that reflects the riskiness of a similar project if it were funded without financial leverage. The subsidy benefits should be discounted at the risk-free rate because they are not subject to operating uncertainty. The remaining flows would be discounted at rates somewhere between the two, reflecting their relative riskiness. Figure 6-4 summarizes a very simple example of capital budgeting using APV and compares the outcome to that obtained using a WACC.

Although APV has considerable theoretical and intuitive appeal, it is much easier to describe than to implement. Choosing the various discount rates is not easy. Since most managers are uncomfortable with WACC calculations, it is unlikely that they will be willing to make the distinctions necessary to use APV.

6.05 POLITICAL AND OPERATING RISK

Definitions of political risk vary, but some general characteristics and examples may be readily identified. First, however, it is important to distinguish between the closely related concepts of country risk, economic risk, and political risk, and to note their relationship to each other.

"Country risk" refers to elements of risk inherent in doing business in the economic, social, and political environment of another country. In international lending decisions, for example, bankers typically examine the economic conditions of the country in question, the balance of payments and its management, central bank policies and effectiveness, principal economic sectors (imports and exports, trends and prospects, flow of funds, and financial intermediation), social conditions, international relations, and the impact of world events on the domestic economy.

Generally speaking, economic risks are not politically generated and include those resulting from technological changes, the actions of competitors, or shifts in consumer preferences. In many cases, however, there is a close link between political events in a country and economic risk. For example, the disintegration of the market structure in Lebanon during its civil war, the banning of certain Western products by the Khomeini regime after the success of the Iranian revolution, and the uncertainties posed by the breakup of the Soviet Union are clear instances where economic risks were exacerbated by political events.

Similarly, while most labor strikes are limited in scope and economic in origin (e.g., disputes over wages, benefits, or other work-related issues), many general strikes, such as those in Nicaragua in 1978 and Poland in 1980, are clearly political in nature and have wide-ranging economic repercussions. Even events with clear economic purposes, such as price controls designed to control inflation, often carry political overtones. Thus, it is sometimes very difficult to distinguish between economic risk and political risk, and there are few events that are purely one or the other.

While definitions of political risk vary, for the purposes of this discussion, political risk should be regarded as a subset of country risk, and it may generally be defined as the exposure to a change in the value of an investment or cash position because of government actions or other nonmarket events that are political in nature. Whereas country risk focuses generally on the overall investment environment of a country, political risk arises from the political environment. The following are examples of political risk events that may negatively affect the magnitude and distribution of cash flows from an overseas investment:

- Changes in tax regulations and exchange controls, especially those that are discriminatory or arbitrary
- Host country stipulations about local production, sourcing, or hiring practices
- Commercial discrimination against foreign-owned businesses
- Restrictions on access to local borrowings
- Governmental interference with privately negotiated contracts
- Expropriation without adequate compensation
- Damage or destruction of facilities or harm to personnel, resulting from political riots or civil war

Because the effects of political risk events may be varied, managers should be aware of the full range or types of political risk events that may affect the host country as well as their particular industries, companies, or projects.

Among the most dramatic losses stemming from political risk events are those resulting from revolutionary upheaval and terrorism. For example, in December 1977, GTE signed a telecommunications contract worth more than $500 million with the Iranian government. In accordance with the contract, GTE advanced Iran $94 million in open letters of credit, commonly used in the Middle East in lieu of performance bonds. Given its long-time experience and confidence in Iran, the company did not specify the grounds on which Iran could call the letters of credit, and no insurance was taken to cover the risks. After the revolution, work on the project proved impossible, and the company stood to lose over $50 million, not including the letters of credit. If those are included, GTE's potential after-tax losses could have exceeded $60 million, making the firm the biggest potential loser in Iran.

In addition to revolutions, coups, and violent acts of terrorism, political risk can also take the form of legislative or regulatory changes. In Iran, for example, B.F. Goodrich had built the largest tire plant between Europe and the Far East, with assurances of trade and investment protection from the government. Such protection was prematurely lifted, however, in favor of two competitors in the mid-1970s, forcing the U.S. firm to go from three shifts to a single eight-hour production schedule. Changes in the law or in regulations can also be directed at companies collectively, as when the Shah decided to mandate public stock offerings on the part of Iranian-based corporations so as to increase worker ownership and participation. The action was expensive and very disruptive to foreign businesses.

Changes in government, whether the result of an election or a coup or revolution, may be partly determined by economic events and may thus bring about changes in policy toward foreign investors. For example, shifts in political-economic ideology may lead to the expropriation of most, if not all, foreign-owned firms.

While dramatic events such as revolutions or expropriations attract a great deal of attention and might cause a company to shy away from more turbulent parts of the world, a political event in itself does not necessarily constitute a risk to business. In fact, political instability can present opportunities as well as risks. For example, Gulf Oil Corporation in 1975 was able to negotiate a very favorable relationship with the Marxist governing party during the Angolan civil war, and Dow Chemical was able to reenter Chile after the overthrow of Salvador Allende in 1973.

Such dramatic events are the exception rather than the rule, however. Although the Cuban and Iranian revolutions undeniably created major problems for U.S. firms, most politically generated contingencies present macro rather than micro risk, and, increasingly, affect operations rather than ownership. Rather than full or partial expropriation, such changes in government or ideology more typically entail price controls, restrictions on expatriate employment, local content regulation, or other regulatory constraints. For example, when Venezuela ran short of foreign exchange in 1983, it ordered domestic companies to extend payments on their foreign debts for several years. Recognizing that money has time value, many creditors negotiated immediate settlements at steep discounts and suffered heavy losses.

Indeed, political instability and conflict are not necessary or even frequent prerequisites to constraints on foreign firms as a result of changes in the political environment. Price controls and other regulatory constraints may result from the regular functioning of the political process owing to losses or gains in the regime's power or to changes in the character and power of the opposition or of interest groups. The privatization program in the United Kingdom under Prime Minister Thatcher in the 1980s and, in contrast, the nationalization policy pursued by President Mitterand in France during the same years are examples of how different political philosophies are manifested in economic terms, with important financial consequences for managers and investors.

Another example of how the normally functioning political process affects international investment is the European Community (EC) 1992 single market movement, which carries with it enormous political risks as well as opportunities for global companies. As Europe proceeds with its economic and political unification, companies may find themselves shut out of certain markets owing to regulatory changes. For example, countries such as Spain and Portugal, which are currently enjoying a great deal of foreign investment because of their cheap labor relative to the rest of Europe, may not be so attractive in the future as those countries increase wages to comply with the EC 1992 single market program. Companies that have made significant investments in Western Europe based on pre-1992 economics may thus find their investments turning sour in the post-1992 world. The importance of keeping up to date with political and regulatory changes can hardly be overstated.

Turning to Eastern Europe, the relatively stable economic and political climate that accompanied the Cold War has become turbulent and unsettled as the former

Communist countries attempt the transition to a market economy. A glance at the former Eastern bloc reveals the full panoply of political risk. In Yugoslavia, once-prosperous towns and productive factories have been devastated by ethnic fighting and civil war. In Czechoslovakia, the split between the Czechs and Slovaks over the pace of economic reform has led to the breakup of the country, which could have adverse effects for the foreign companies that have invested in the Slovak republic. General Electric's much vaunted $150 million investment in the Tungsram lighting plant in Hungary has lost money because the government has not devalued the forint in line with Hungary's soaring inflation. Chevron, which entered into a joint venture agreement with the former Soviet government, now finds itself in the position of having to negotiate with several independent republics. Moreover, Russia is chronically short of hard currency, and its vacillating monetary policy and price reforms cast a long shadow of uncertainty over any prospective investments.

As these examples indicate, the global marketplace is by its very nature uncertain and turbulent. The question whether particular aspects of this turbulence and uncertainty constitute a risk to business is problematic, and its answer depends on industry, firm, or project characteristics and managerial actions. Thus, the elements of political risk will vary widely among different countries and different companies. Even within a country, political risk is usually industry-specific and, in many cases, project-specific as well. Rural insurgency, for example, may pose serious problems to a commercial farming operation, but its impact on a company specializing in financial services or insurance might be minimal. Assessing the political risks of direct foreign investment, therefore, involves the analysis both of elements of aggregate or countrywide risk and of elements of political risk specific to the company or to its project.

[1] Monitoring Developments

Monitoring involves establishing an intelligence network that provides political, social, and economic information with which to understand events in the host country. For large firms with extensive worldwide investments, such as the major petroleum companies, the intelligence-gathering process can be almost entirely in-house. The same is true for multinational banks with extensive branch systems. Area or divisional personnel can be assigned the primary responsibility for collecting information and forwarding it to headquarters for evaluation.

Many large companies now have staff economists and political scientists who provide country risk assessments. Although these staff people play an important role in the monitoring process, their analyses should be used in conjunction with evaluations of line personnel who are stationed in the country. Relying solely on either staff or line personnel can provide biased analysis. Staff evaluations tend to be more objective, but because they are done at a distance from a country, they often ignore insights that can be gained only by extensive experience living in an area. Line personnel have that experience but are often unwilling to recognize or admit negative aspects of their own nation or the country for which they have managerial responsibility, in part because negative information might adversely affect their own activities. For example, bank calling officers or branch managers would be the appropriate line personnel to provide country information, but their personal interest is in expanding loans or the sale of other bank services. This basic conflict often introduces a bias into the information-gathering process.

Smaller firms generally do not have the resources to develop their own information networks. Instead, they rely on information purchased from firms organized for that purpose. Even if the company's primary information sources are external, it should still establish an internal monitoring system as a secondary source. Area personnel should file informal country evaluations, and the headquarters' staff should visit the country on a regular basis. Their assessments should be matched against those of the external source to check for consistency and accuracy. A firm should not become too dependent on a single source nor too complacent to change to another advisory service if its current one is missing too many trends or changes.

[2] Anticipating Policy

All information should be evaluated with the objective of anticipating policy changes of the government or in the attitudes of other stakeholders in the host country. Some changes affect the general operating environment of the firm, whereas others have a direct impact on the operating or ownership structure of the firm.

Environment changes can be both general and specific. Among the former are macroeconomic policies that attempt to stimulate or restrict economic activity. Countries with accelerating inflation or difficulty servicing external obligations are likely to pursue contractionary monetary or fiscal policies. For a firm with largely domestic sales, this would reduce revenues. Other changes related to macroeconomic policy are the imposition of price and wage controls and currency restrictions. From the earlier discussion of cash flow forecasts, it should be clear how these changes would affect the firm and the value of the investment. The point is that if management can anticipate the policies, it can take steps to reduce their impact; prices might be raised prior to controls' being enacted, foreign currency payments might be made before the local currency becomes inconvertible, or arrangements for parallel loans might be made to reduce the amount of local currency blocked in the country.

There are other longer-term policies that a firm might pursue to reduce risk. Labor unrest in the form of strikes varies in severity from country to country. In nations where strikes are frequent, the firm might choose less labor-intensive technology or adopt employment policies that reduce the threat of strikes.

A large U.S. electronics firm with major manufacturing facilities in the United Kingdom has a totally nonunion labor force in a highly unionized country. It has been able to maintain that status by having generous benefits and an open employee-management relationship. These policies entail some added costs but reduce the risk of labor strife. The company has not lost manufacturing time owing to strikes and has added flexibility in establishing its seniority and compensation system.

More specific policies that arise from concerns about the economic environment can directly affect the operating structure of the firm. Requirements concerning local content in manufacturing and domestic nationals in management positions, pricing to subsidize local consumption, or requirements that firms provide investment in infrastructure are examples. In general, so are regulations that affect transfer pricing or establish restrictions on licensing arrangements and royalty payments.

The final type of political risk comes in the form of government interference with the ownership of the assets or investment. There are many ways in which governments can garner the wealth of foreign investors ranging from punitive taxes and fees to outright expropriation. In between are requirements for local participation in ownership and nationalization with some form of compensation. Regardless of the form it takes, it is unlikely that any involuntary change in ownership structure will benefit the original investors. If it would, then they would have brought it about without coercion. Generally, increased interference or changes in attitudes toward foreign investment are preceded by significant economic or political events. That is what makes the monitoring and anticipation activities worthwhile: They allow a firm to reduce its exposure while there is still room to maneuver.

[3] Adapting to Conditions

Adjustments and alterations in policies that firms make in response to changes are signs of their adaptability. Doing business overseas requires a willingness and ability to respond to different legal, political, social, and economic environments. Sometimes those adjustments are undesirable on other grounds but necessary in order to reduce risk related to investing overseas. Entering into a joint venture is an important example.

Joint ventures represent shared ownership and control of operating entities by two or more independent firms or groups of investors. A requirement of local joint owner-ship is often mandatory for foreign investors. It arises from a sense of nationalism and a desire that some of the returns on capital investment be retained in the host country. At other times, firms voluntarily seek out joint venture relationships because of synergy. For example, one firm may have capital or an established distribution network and its partner may have special technological skills or a brand name.

Despite some major exceptions, survey research has indicated that the majority of U.S. firms are a priori opposed to joint ventures, especially those involving local partners. There seems to be a variety of grounds for the opposition, most focusing on the control aspects. The partner acquires access to technology and pricing information that might make him a formidable competitor at some future date. Differences in objectives might lead to disputes over dividend policies, transfer pricing, financial structure decisions, licensing agreements, and efforts by the foreign partner to rational-ize production among its worldwide subsidiaries.

The trade-offs in favor of joint ventures include access to markets that might other-wise be unavailable and a reduction in the probability of government interference directed toward foreign investors. By having local nationals involved in ownership and management, the subsidiary loses some of its foreign character. That helps deflect criticisms related to exploitation, capital flight, and external control. The local partners have a stake in the company, which leads them to lobby on its behalf. Any restrictions imposed by the government might adversely affect local interests.

It is important to be careful in choosing a local partner. Under the best of circum-stances, the local partner brings to the enterprise skills or attributes other than a convenient nationality. If nationality is in fact the only contribution, the foreign inves-tor should try to find a partner that is reliable and in the mainstream of local politics. Having a local partner that is in the opposition party might lead to harsher treatment than would otherwise be the case.

A final course that might be followed to reduce risk exposure is the purchase of insurance. A number of developed nations, including the United States, have govern-mental or quasi-governmental programs for insuring foreign investment against the risk of war, expropriation, or currency inconvertibility. There is also a private insur-ance market organized through the auspices of Lloyd's. In the United States, the Overseas Private Investment Corporation (OPIC) provides insurance for U.S. private investments in less-developed countries as well as project financing. Its fees vary depending on the type of coverage and, to some extent, on the risk related to the investment. OPIC has been very successful at marketing its programs, and the majority of nonpetroleum investments in less-developed countries have some form of OPIC coverage.

The decision to buy OPIC insurance must be made along the lines of risk management decisions in general. Firms need to weigh the costs against expected losses and their willingness and ability to bear those losses. Buying OPIC coverage might create a moral hazard situation for firms. Having protection could lead firms to ignore other risk reduction policies and contribute to a higher incidence of loss. Ultimately, this would show up in higher premiums or a lessened availability of insurance. Since settlements under OPIC are usually the result of a long negotiating process, firms should avoid the attitude of "why worry, we're insured."

As a final caveat, investors should not associate political risk only with investments in less-developed countries. Each of the types of risk discussed in this section are or have been present in almost every nation. Certainly, the environmental factors are omnipresent, but even in Western democracies, nationalization and changing attitudes toward foreign investment are prevalent. The investor might have better recourse under the law in those nations, but the interference in business operations and the loss of wealth are real possibilities that must be considered in making investment decisions.

6.06 FINANCING FOREIGN SUBSIDIARIES

Establishing an overseas subsidiary entails making a variety of operating decisions, including selection of the best financing. Financial decisions for an MNC are influenced by the same considerations as those for a purely domestic firm, with some added dimensions related to its international element. This section focuses solely on the international aspect. Therefore, the discussion begins with the assumption that the desired financial structure—debt-to-equity mix and maturity profile on debt—have been determined. What remains to be determined is the currency of denomination for the debt. Making that decision correctly requires an analytical framework that measures the expected cost and risk of the various alternatives. Once the framework is developed, the following factors influence the financing decision:

- Willingness of the investor to bear risk
- Validity of interest parity and the international Fisher effect
- Availability of forward contracts
- Tax policies and tax rates in the relevant countries
- Political risk in the host country

To understand the approach developed here, the simplest case is explored first. In this situation, taxes and forward rates are ignored. The parent must choose between using a local currency loan or a dollar loan provided by the parent in order to finance the subsidiary's working capital requirement for one year. The parent is interested in arranging for the lowest expected dollar cost.

[1] Option 1: Local Currency Loan

The subsidiary requires one dollar of local currency (LC). A local currency loan is available at interest rate i_L. The amount that the subsidiary needs to borrow is 1/SPT, where SPT is the current exchange rate or spot rate of dollars per local currency unit. At the end of a year, the subsidiary will repay

$$\frac{1}{SPT}(1 + i_L) \tag{6.9}$$

worth of local currency. That local currency will have a dollar value of

$$\frac{1}{SPT}(1 + i_L)\text{FU}\hat{\text{T}}\text{SPT} \tag{6.10}$$

where FU̅TSPT is the currently unknown exchange rate that will exist at the time of repayment (the future spot rate). The dollar cost in Equation 6.10 can be converted to an effective dollar interest rate by subtracting 1 from it.

$$\frac{\text{FU}\hat{\text{T}}\text{SPT}}{SPT}(1 + i_L) - 1 \tag{6.11}$$

A numerical example helps to clarify the formulation. Assume the following:

SPT = 0.02 or LC50 = \$1

i_L = 30%

The expected dollar interest cost is

$$\frac{\text{FU}\hat{\text{T}}\text{SPT}(1.3)}{0.02} - 1 = 0.65\text{FU}\hat{\text{T}}\text{SPT} - 1$$

The higher the future spot rate is at the time of repayment, the higher the dollar cost; the lower the future spot rate, the lower the expected dollar cost. That follows because the firm has an obligation to pay local currency. The exchange rate will determine the dollar cost of obtaining the currency to clear the obligation. If the future spot rate is 0.03, the effective interest rate will be 115 percent; if it is 0.01, the cost will be -35 percent; and if it is 0.02, the cost will be 30 percent. Equation 6.11 can be written in a slightly different form:

$$i_L(1 - d) - d \tag{6.12}$$

where d is the expected percentage change in the exchange rate. When d is known, Equation 6.12 can be used to calculate the actual cost of foreign currency borrowing.

[2] Option 2: Parent Company Loan

When the parent provides funds, it incurs a cost i_S, which is its effective borrowing rate. There is also an interest rate transaction between the parent and the subsidiary in which the parent has income and the subsidiary an interest expense. Although in this example the latter two are offsetting, once taxes are introduced that might no longer be the case. Therefore, income and interest expense are included in order to arrive at the dollar cost of providing a parent loan, which is

Interest cost	interest income	interest cost	
to parent	of parent	to subsidiary	(6.13)
i_s	$-$ i_p	$+$ i_p	

where the interest rate charged by the parent is i_p.

The dollar cost of the parent loan is a certain value, since it is not affected by exchange rate considerations.

To determine which funding alternative is desirable, the firm solves for a break-even value of d, the expected percentage change in the exchange rate. Continuing the example, assume that i_s equals 10 percent.

$$i_s = 0.10 = 0.3(1 - d) - d$$

$$d = 0.154 \text{ or } 15.4\%$$

If the firm expects d to be less than 15.4 percent, it should borrow dollars and use a parent loan. On the other hand, if the devaluation is expected to be greater than 15.4 percent, the firm should allow the subsidiary to arrange a local currency loan.

The relationship between the expected change in exchange rates and relative interest rates is the international Fisher effect. It states that interest rates should reflect expected exchange rate changes in such a way as to make borrowers and lenders indifferent between denominating loans in one currency or another.

$$i_s = i_L(1 - d) - d$$

$$d = \frac{i_L - i_s}{1 + i_L} \tag{6.14}$$

What happens to the analysis if forward rates are introduced? Nothing changes with regard to the dollar cost of the parent loan, but the uncertainty related to the local currency loan can be eliminated. Recall from Equation 6.10 that the dollar cost of the local currency option was determined by the future spot rate. If a forward market exists, the rate at which the local currency will be acquired, FWD, can be locked in at the time of the loan by buying a forward contract. The effective dollar cost is then

$$\frac{FWD}{SPT} (1 + i_L) - 1 \tag{6.15}$$

Comparing the known dollar costs of the two alternatives, the firm is indifferent if

$$i_s = \frac{FWD}{SPT} (1 + i_L) - 1 \tag{6.16}$$

Equation 6.16 can be shown to be the interest rate parity relationship. If parity holds, there is no cost advantage for a covered local currency loan versus a parent company loan. Only if there are deviations will one option be better than the other. Using the numerical example started earlier, if the forward discount is less than 15.4 percent, the parent loan is cheaper. At a forward discount greater than 15.4 percent, the local loan is cheaper. At 15.4 percent, the interest parity rate, the two options have the same cost.

It is important to be aware that the interest parity calculation determines the best way of taking a covered position. It does not provide a guide as to whether to cover. That decision must be based on the expected future spot rate and the risk preferences of the decision maker.

A second important point is that the political risk element might lead a firm to choose a higher-cost financing option. By borrowing in the local market, the firm reduces its net country exposure. If the subsidiary is nationalized or expropriated, the local liability acts as a partial offset for the loss assets. Some firms follow a rule of financing all subsidiaries with local debt, regardless of the cost, for just that reason. Such a rule is probably not desirable. It would be better to calculate the cost differential and then determine whether the risk reduction justifies the additional expense.

[3] Tax Factors

The introduction of taxes into the analysis makes the formulations more complicated. It becomes necessary to distinguish between the impact of an exchange gain or loss itself and its tax implications. Of the two options under consideration here, the local currency loan carries exchange risk but no related tax effect. The parent loan involves no exchange risk but has a tax element related to exchange rate fluctuations.

The general formulation for the expected cost of the local currency loan is

Interest cost $-$ exchange adjustment

$$i_L(1 - d)(1 - T_L) - d \tag{6.17}$$

where T_L is the effective tax rate paid by the subsidiary in the host country. The tax term enters into the formulation if interest expenses are tax deductible. If T_L is assumed to be 30 percent, the expected dollar cost is

$$0.3(1 - d)(0.7) - d = 0.21 - 1.2d$$

The cost of the parent loan is affected by the tax rate that the parent pays on domestic income, T_D; the rate it pays on foreign-source income, T_F; and the host country rate. The correct formula to use is

Interest cost	$-$	interest income from subsidiary	$+$	subsidiary's income expense	$-$	tax gain or loss
$i_S(1 - T_D)$	$-$	$i_P(1 - T_F)$	$+$	$i_P(1 - T_L)$	$-$	$T_L d$

The last term arises because the local subsidiary has a dollar exposure. If exchange gains or losses are tax deductible, the subsidiary will realize a tax reduction or increase based on the exchange rate change that takes place. From the standpoint of the corporation as a whole, there is no actual exchange gain or loss because the loan is intracorporate. The company holds both the asset and liability sides of the transaction. If it is assumed that T_D is 50 percent and T_F is 40 percent, the expected cost of the parent loan is

$$0.1(1 - 0.5) - 0.1(1 - 0.4) + 0.1(1 - 0.3) - 0.3d = 0.06 - 0.3d$$

Note that the inclusion of the tax factor makes the cost of the parent loan uncertain. It now also depends on the percentage change in exchange rates. The same break-even analysis as was applied before is used to select the best alternative:

$$0.06 - 0.3d = 0.21 - 1.21d$$
$$0.91d = 0.15$$
$$d = 0.165$$

FIGURE 6-5

Effective Dollar Cost of Financing

Percentage Change in Exchange Rate	Local Currency Loan	Percent Loan
10%	8.9%	3%
16.5	1.4	1.4
23	(6.8)	3

The firm should choose the parent company loan if the expected percentage change in exchange rates is less than 16.5 percent and the local currency loan if it is greater.

Two additional points should be made in relation to the financing decision. First, there are clearly many more options than the two presented here. A firm needs to evaluate those options within the framework developed in this section. The second point is more technical but more important and less obvious: The analysis in this section looks strictly at expected financing costs. In addition, the degree of uncertainty or variance should be considered. In other words, the manager should ask how sensitive these estimates are to error. For the two options analyzed here, the local currency loan is more sensitive. Therefore, it generates a wider range of outcomes than does the parent company loan. Figure 6-5 gives an indication of that range by calculating the effective cost under different exchange rate scenarios. Choosing the best alternative now depends on estimates of the future spot rate, variances about that estimate, and the firm's willingness to bear risk.

6.07 MANAGING FOREIGN EXCHANGE RISKS

Foreign investment creates ongoing foreign exchange exposure. The exchange risks created by foreign operations are more varied than those that arise from a specific trade transaction or even a series of transactions. The investment represents a substantial commitment, and firms frequently are constrained by regulations of the host country or limitations in domestic capital markets. The decision can be made not to enter into a specific trade transaction if the currency situation creates unacceptable risk. However, once an investment is made, it is a larger and more dramatic decision to walk away from it. Managers of multinationals need to be aware of less traditional approaches to risk management.

This section examines two nontraditional hedging techniques: cross-hedging and hedging long-term exposures with currency swaps. These techniques are important to the financial manager, who is frequently called on to manage risks for which standard hedging techniques are unavailable. Cross-hedging allows for the use of forward or futures positions to hedge exposures in currencies that do not have traded-forward contracts. Swaps make it possible to hedge exposures with maturities that exceed those of available forward contracts.

[1] Cross-Hedging

Cross-hedging entails the use of a futures contract in an asset to reduce the risk related to a cash position in another asset that differs materially in location, type, grade, or maturity date. In the context of this discussion, an example of cross-hedging is the use of a deutsche mark futures contract to hedge an Italian lira cash position.

When the futures contract and the spot position are in the same asset, a high proportion of the risk of the spot position can be eliminated. A single cross-hedge, in contrast, typically eliminates a smaller portion of the risk of a cash position. With reference to the lira, for example, a combination of futures positions in the mark and U.K. pound might be used to replicate and hedge lira risk.

Currencies are the most obvious but not the only available hedging instrument. A single-currency cross-hedge exploits the correlation between a pair of currencies to create a portfolio of a cash and a futures position with lower risk than that of the cash position alone. The same type of hedging opportunity may be found in commodity futures markets.

Cross-hedging is important because it greatly expands the opportunity set of hedging alternatives. There are only a limited number of currencies that are traded actively in futures markets or for which bank forward contracts are typically available. In general, currencies for which no organized futures or forward market exists are also currencies of countries with poorly developed capital markets. Consequently, alternative hedging techniques, such as borrowing or lending in those currencies, are also more limited. If effective cross-hedging strategies can be identified, the risk related to taking cash positions in those currencies can be reduced. This research provides some insights into the selection of cross-hedges and measures their effectiveness.

Three factors determine the measured effectiveness of cross-hedges: (1) the true correlation between assets; (2) the accuracy of estimates of the risk-minimizing hedge ratio; and (3) the stability of the true hedge ratio over time. Good hedges are constructed using assets whose prices vary in a predictable relationship to one another. If the variation of the franc exchange is not related to that of the deutsche mark, positions in one cannot be used to hedge exposures in the other. The greater the correlation and the more predictable the relationship, the better the hedge.

[2] Currency Swaps

Swaps represent generically the broad array of transactions in which institutions acting either directly or through third parties exchange payment streams related to underlying debt obligations. Through the use of swaps, firms can exchange debt-service payments denominated in one currency for payments in another currency, fixed-interest-rate obligations for floating obligations, or floating obligations for fixed-interest-rate obligations. Swaps can also be used to alter the amortization schedule of existing debt and to change the benchmark for floating-rate issues (e.g., substituting the London interbank offered rate (known as LIBOR) for prime-based pricing). In fact, there is basically no limit to what can be accomplished with swaps in terms of restructuring liabilities. The only constraint is the institutions' ability to find counterparties willing to swap at mutually acceptable rates.

Swap transactions have grown dramatically since formal currency swaps were introduced in 1979. Although there is no official measure of activity, market participants estimate that $3 trillion of swaps existed by the end of 1992. The increase in the use

FIGURE 6-6

Sample Currency Swap Cash Flows

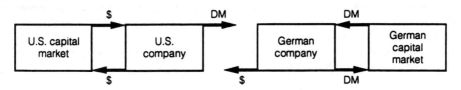

Assumptions:
1. German counterparty borrows DM50,000,000 at an annual interest rate of 6%.
2. U.S. counterparty borrows $20,000,000 at an annual interest rate of 8%.
3. Spot exchange rate is DM1.60/$1.
4. Maturity is 7 years, with bullet principal repayment.

Steps:
1. Counterparties borrow funds in their respective domestic markets.
2. Borrowed funds are swapped at existing spot rate (possibly individually in foreign exchange markets).
3. In years 1 through 6, the U.S. company pays DM3,000,000 to the German company in exchange for $1,600,000.
4. In year 7, the U.S. company pays DM53,000,000 to the German company in exchange for $21,600,000.

of swaps is related to the same factors that have led to the proliferation of financial futures and option contracts and the growth of volume in those markets. Swaps, in the jargon of economic theorists, contribute to more complete markets by making available risk management techniques that are not available in the existing futures markets. Swaps represent both substitutes for and supplements to instruments traded on the futures and option exchanges. The environmental factors leading to the development of swaps and financial futures have been deregulation of financial markets and increased volatility of exchange rates and interest rates. Volatility has led treasurers and funds managers to look for new techniques to manage risk, and deregulation has increased the number of institutions able to compete to provide risk management services. The end result has been significant financial innovation of which swaps are a prime example.

A straightforward, "plain vanilla" currency swap is described in Figure 6-6. (The transaction is simplified by positing that interest payments occur only in the first six years and that no role is played by a financial intermediary; the latter assumption, while eliminating any fees, does not change the structure of the arrangement.) Under the swap arrangement illustrated, the two companies borrow in their domestic capital markets and then exchange debt service obligations. Each of the counterparties retains its own obligations to creditors. The U.S. company must pay the dollar debt service, and the German company pays the deutsche mark debt service.

The cash flows between these counterparties are equivalent to the debt service obligations. Under a more complex swap, the cash flows might reflect differences in the credit standing of the parties or their relative negotiating positions. For example, if the U.S. company were more urgently in need of a deutsche mark position than the

German company, then it might be willing to pay a premium to acquire the swap arrangement.

The end result of the swap is that the U.S. company has effectively borrowed deutsche marks and the German company dollars. The deutsche mark cash flows that the U.S. company has obligated itself to pay represent a sequence of implicit forward contracts with maturities of one to seven years. The forward exchange rate is reflected in the interest rates that are paid on the two debts. The implicit forward rates can be calculated by using the following formula:

$$F_n^I = \frac{S(1 + i_{Dm})^n}{(1 + i_S)^n}$$

where:

F_n^I = implicit forward rate for year n
S = spot rate
i_S = interest rate on the U.S. loan
i_{Dm} = interest rate on the German loan

The formula is derived from the uncovered interest parity theory, which relates interest rates and foreign exchange rates between two countries. The implicit forward rates for the swap transaction described here are as follows:

Year	Deutsche mark/ U.S. dollar
1	1.57
2	1.54
3	1.51
4	1.48
5	1.46
6	1.43
7	1.40

A company considering a swap for hedging purposes must compare the implicit forward rate with the rates available from banks and with the company's forecast of future spot rates. The company may decide that hedging is not desirable or that engaging in an outright forward contract offers a better rate. The problem (and a major reason for the growth of the swap market) is, of course, that long-maturity forward contracts are unavailable. Consequently, the swap rate may represent the only game in town.

There has been some confusion about the risk related to swapping. Funds are exchanged, but no exchange of debt obligations occurs. Thus, the counterparties maintain their obligations to the creditors and have an agreement to exchange payment streams in the future. A default on the part of one counterparty does not alter the other's obligations to its creditors. However, if the firm enters the swap in order to hedge a currency exposure, it is no longer protected from exchange rate fluctuations (that is, the swap creates a foreign currency cash flow, and, without the swap, that cash flow ceases to exist and any position it was intended to hedge is now exposed). Any movement in the exchange rate leaves the firm exposed to gains or losses. The best measure of the gain or loss is the alternative cost of reacquiring a hedge for the remainder of the maturity of the swap. Assessing in advance the risk of a swap entails estimating changes in the future forward rates and the probability of the counterparty's defaulting.

A number of institutions have restricted their swap arrangements to institutions with AAA credit ratings. The World Bank, which is a major participant in the swap market, follows that policy.

Currency swaps are seldom of the "plain vanilla" variety described here. They are usually part of more complicated transactions that combine currency and interest rate adjustments. In order to analyze the desirability of the swap and its pricing, it is necessary to disaggregate the transaction into its components, one of which will be an implicit forward transaction.

Suggested Reading

Eiteman, David K., and Arthur I. Stonehill. *Multinational Business Finance*, 4th ed. Reading, Mass.: Addison-Wesley, 1986.

Lessard, Donald R. *International Financial Management*, 2d ed. New York: John Wiley & Sons, 1985.

Levi, Maurice. *International Finance*. New York: McGraw-Hill, 1983.

Shapiro, Alan C. *Multinational Financial Management*. Boston: Allyn and Bacon, 1982.

Solnick, Bruno. *International Investment*. Reading, Mass.: Addison-Wesley, 1988.

Stern, Joel M., and Donald H. Chew, eds. *New Developments in International Finance*. New York: Basil Blackwell, 1988.

Index

A

Adjusted present value (APV), 208–209
APV. *See* Adjusted present value
Arbitrage, foreign exchange markets,
    109–111

B

Banking. *See* International banking
Banks for International Settlements (BIS),
    64
Basel standards, 85
Beggar-thy-neighbor policies, 10
Bills of exchange, 4
Bimetallic standard, 3
BIS. *See* Banks for International
    Settlements
Bonds. *See* International bonds
BOOT. *See* Build-own-operate-transfer
    projects
Bretton Woods system, 10–11
    breakdown of, 13–15
    post-Bretton Woods, 15–16
    Second Amendment, 17–18
Broker's market, 108
Build-own-operate-transfer (BOOT)
    projects, 132–133

C

Cable transfers, 5–6
Capital budgeting, foreign investment,
    205–209
    adjusted present value, 208–209
    discount rate, choosing, 206–207
    project risk, adjusting for, 207–208

Capital investment. *See* Capital budgeting
Cash flow, foreign, 194–205
CFC. *See* Controlled foreign corporation
Controlled foreign corporation (CFC),
    183–184
    subpart F income, 184
Corporate cash management, 138
Corporate deposits, international banking,
    136
Country risk, 140–142, 209
    dealing with, 141–142
    measuring, 141
    nature of, 140–141
Cross-hedging, 220
Currency forwards, 73–74
Currency swaps, 81–82, 220–223

D

Debt-to-equity swaps, international
    banking, 133
Derivative securities, 72–82
Dual-currency bonds, 68

E

EC. *See* European community
ECP. *See* Euro commercial paper
Edge Act Corporation, 147
EIB. *See* European investment bank
Electronic banking services, international,
    138
EMTNs. *See* Euro medium-term notes
Eurobonds, 68–69
Euro commercial paper, 70
Eurodollar. *See* Eurodollar markets

Eurodollar bonds, 66–67
  See also Bonds, international
  equity-linked, 68–69
  fixed-rate, 67
Eurodollar CDs, 116–117
Eurodollar markets
  See also Foreign exchange markets
  bases of, 112–113
  criticisms of, 117
  EC, 117–119
  instruments of, 116–117
  interest rates, 114–116
  role of, 112
  scope of, 111
Euroequity, 71
Euro medium-term notes (EMTNs), 70
European Community (EC), 95, 117, 119
European currency units, 70
European investment bank (EIB), 132–133
Euro commercial paper (ECP), 70
Euro syndicated credits, 70–71
Exchange rates, forecasting, 36–37
  quotations, 108
  risk, 38–40
EXIMBANK. *See* Export-Import Bank of
  the United States
Export-Import Bank of the United States
  (EXIMBANK), 121, 124, 142
External debt crisis, 93
  Latin American debts, 93–95

F

Factoring, 127
Financial markets. *See* International
  financial markets
Financing
  foreign subsidiaries, 215–219
  international trade, 119–128
Fisher effect, 57, 198
Floating exchange rates, 15
Floating-rate notes (FRNs), 67–68
Floors, 78–79
Foreign bonds, 69
Foreign cash flow, 194–205
  alternative measures, 199–200
  divergence, 95–197
  economic assumptions, 200–201
  exchange risk, 197–198

Fisher effect, 198, 200–201
  interdependence, 195–196
  parity, deviation from, 201–204
  PPP, 198–199, 201
  restrictions, 196–197
  subsidies, 197
  taxation, 197
Foreign exchange markets, 104–111
  See also Foreign exchange risk
  arbitrage, 109–111
  black markets, 29–30
  characteristics, 104–106
  of brokers, 108
  forwards, 108–109
  forward rates, 24
  function of, 22–23
  multiple exchange rates, 29–30
  rates, 30–36
    quotations, 27–29, 108
  risk, 24–27
    exchange, 38–40
    political, 37–38
  spot transactions, 24
  trading, 106
    practices, 27–29
Foreign exchange risk
  See also Foreign exchange markets
  accounting exposure, 40–41
  cash flow exposure, 44
  contractual vs. noncontractual returns,
    45–46
  cross-hedging, 220
  currency swaps, 220–223
  economic exposure, 44, 47
  financial vs. operating strategies, 51
  hedging, 49–55, 56–58
  risk control, forecasting for, 50–51
Foreign sales corporation (FCS), 124
Foreign subsidiary financing, 215–219
  local currency loans, 216
  parent company loans, 216–218
  tax factors, 218–219
Forex funds, 23, 27, 29–30
Forfaiting, 127–128
Forward exchange contracts, accounting
  for, 169–170
Forward market, foreign exchange,
  108–109
Forward rate, 24
  agreements, 79–80
FRNs. *See* Floating rate notes
FSC. *See* Foreign sales corporation
Functional currency, 167–168

Futures
    currency, 74–76
    interest rates, 77–78

G

GATT. *See* General Agreement on Tariffs
    and Trade
General Agreement on Tariffs and Trade
    (GATT), 10
Gold standard, 3–4

H

Hedging, foreign exchange market, 49–55,
    56–58

I

IASC. *See* International Accounting
    Standards Committee
IBFs. *See* International banking facilities
IMF. *See* International Monetary Fund
Interest rate futures, 77–78
Interest rate options, 78
Interest rate swaps, 80–81
    international banking, 138–140
International accounting
    accounting standards and disclosure
        practices, 154–167
    disclosure of information, 166–167
    financial statements, translation of,
        171–182
    foreign currency transactions, 167–170
    forward exchange contracts, accounting
        for, 169–170
    harmonization of standards, 164–166
    performance evaluation, 185–188
    tax issues, 182–185
    tax treaties, impact of, 185
    transfer pricing, 186–187
International Accounting Standards
    Committee (IASC), 163, 165
International banking
    activity in selected countries, 95–98
        Brazil, 104
        Canada, 98–99
        Germany, 99–100
        Hong Kong, 100

        Japan, 100
        Switzerland, 101
        United Kingdom, 102
        United States, 102–104
    arbitrage, 109–111
    banking facilities, 150
    commercial lending, 129
    corporate cash management, 138
    corporate deposits, 136
    countertrade, 124–129
    country risk, 140–142
    credit extension, 128–134
    current perspectives, 93–95
    debt-to-equity swaps, 133
    electronic banking services, 138
    Euromarkets, 111–119
    factoring, 127
    foreign exchange markets, 104–111
        of brokers, 108
        forwards, 108–109
        trading, 106–108
    forfaiting, 127–128
    forms of legal presence, 147
        branch, 147
        representation office, 147
        subsidiary, 147
    funding strategy, 144–146
    future of, 150
    government borrowers, 130–131
    government loans, 124
    historical perspectives, 92
    import/export transactions, 119–121
    information services, 137–138
    instruments, 116–117
    interbank lending, 129
    interest rates, 114–116
    interest rate swaps, 138–140
    leasing, 128
    lending strategy, 143–144
    liabilities, 134–137
    loan guarantees, 124
    marketing services, 148
    offshore banking centers, 149
    organizational structure, 146–147
    personal banking, 136
    petrodollars, 135
    project financing, 132–133
    rate quotations, 108
    risk management, 140
    sovereign loans, 130–131
    syndicated loans, 131–132
    trade financing, 119–128
International banking facilities (IBFs), 150
International bonds
    dual-currency, 68

International bonds (*cont'd*)
Eurobonds, 66–67
equity-linked, 68–69
fixed-rate, 67
Euro commercial paper, 70
Euroequity, 71
Euro medium-term notes, 70
Euro syndicated credits, 70–71
floating-rate notes, 67–68
foreign bonds, 69
markets, 65–66
zero-coupon, 68
International financial markets
bonds, 64–66
derivative securities, 72–82
potential regulation, 83–85
International investment
advantages of, 192–194
disadvantages of, 194
International Monetary Fund (IMF), 2–3, 92
International monetary system
beggar-thy-neighbor policies, 10
bills of exchange, 4
Bretton Woods system, 10–12, 92
breakdown of, 13–15
floating exchange rates, 15–16
future of, 19
inconvertibility, 4–5
nationalization of U.S. gold holdings, 9
nongold international reserve assets, 16–17
postwar period, 7–9
U.S. gold standards, 3–4
U.S. payment deficits, 12–13
World War I gold embargo, 6–7
Investment. *See* International investment

L

LDSs, 98, 121, 130, 132, 133, 135
Leases, international trade financing, 128
Leasing. *See* Leases
Letters of credit (LOCs), 123, 129
LIBOR. *See* London interbank offered rate
LOCs. *See* Letters of credit
London interbank offered rate (LIBOR), 67, 114–116, 139, 141

M

Maastricht Agreement, 19, 118
MNEs. *See* Multinational enterprises
Multinational enterprises (MNEs), 159–160, 161, 163, 164
OECD guidelines for, 165–166
U.S.-based, 166

O

OECD. *See* Organization for Economic Corporation and Development
Offshore banking centers, 149
OPEC, 92, 93, 134, 135
OPIC. *See* Overseas Private Investment Corporation
Options, currency, 76–77
Organization for Economic Corporation and Development (OECD), 165–166

P

Petrodollars, international banking, 135
PPP. *See* Purchasing power parity
Purchasing power parity (PPP), 39, 57, 198–199
theorem, 33–36

R

Rate quotations, foreign exchange markets, 108
Remittance restrictions, 196–197
Risk
See also Foreign exchange risk
adaption, 142
country, 140–142, 209
exchange, 38–40
foreign exchange, 40–49
political, 37–38
transfer, 141–142

S

SDRs. *See* Special drawing rights
Segmented reporting, 163–164
SFAS No. 8, 42, 171
SFAS No. 52, 42–44
  compared to SSAP No. 20, 187
  current rate method, 188
  functional currency, 167–168
  options, 170
  translation, 171–172
Sovereign loans, 130–131
Special drawing rights (SDRs), 13
Swaps
  currency, 81
  debt-to-equity, international banking,
    133
Swaptions, 82
Syndicated loans, international banking,
    131–132

T

Taxation, 197
Tax credit, 184–185
Tax treaties, 185
Trade financing, 119–128
  countertrade, 124–126
  factoring, 127
  forfaiting, 127–128
  government loans, 124
  import-export transactions, 119–121
  leasing, 128
  loan guarantees, 124
  traditional forms of, 121–123
Transfer pricing, 186–187

Z

Zero-coupon bonds, 68